Assessing
GREAT EXPECTATIONS

Assessing
GREAT EXPECTATIONS

MATERIALS FOR ANALYSIS

Selected and Edited by

Richard Lettis

C. W. POST COLLEGE

and

William E. Morris

UNIVERSITY OF SOUTH FLORIDA

CHANDLER PUBLISHING COMPANY

San Francisco

DOCUMENTING YOUR RESEARCH PAPER COPYRIGHT © 1960 BY
HOWARD CHANDLER, PUBLISHER
DESIGNED BY JAMES MENNICK
LIBRARY OF CONGRESS CATALOG CARD NO. 63–9889
PRINTED IN THE UNITED STATES OF AMERICA
COMPOSITORS: SANTYPE, SALISBURY, WILTSHIRE, ENGLAND

Contents

Foreword

THE PURPOSE of this text is to provide the reader with materials which will help him in his appreciation and understanding of *Great Expectations*. It is assumed that in most cases the reading of the assessments will lead to the composition of a research paper, though the materials will be useful for anyone who wishes to pursue his study of what is increasingly often described as Dickens's greatest novel. In any case, the reader will wish to proceed through certain definite steps in order to realize the full benefits of his work. The editors urge the following procedure:

First, read the novel. This step is obvious, but worthy of emphasis, for it is the most important step, and makes or mars all that comes after. The novel must be read before the criticism. The reader must come to the book innocent of preconceptions and prejudices. He should not, in this first reading, be looking for particular qualities or characteristics; he should not have a research topic in mind—if possible, he should forget completely that he is reading *Great Expectations* for any reason other than his own pleasure. Only when such a reading is finished— and with this novel it should not be difficult—may the reader turn scholar, and begin to approach Pip and his world as objects of study.

The scholar's role is not as essential as the appreciator's; most educated people should read *Great Expectations*, but not all need become authorities on it. Once the role is assumed, however, the reader-turned-appreciator must become aware of its nature. He can still pursue his appreciation of the story, of course, but now he finds himself with the responsibility of determining why he likes it, how it works upon him, where it does its work best, and when it leaves something to be desired. Perhaps one can say that the reader changes from spectator to participator, for instead of experiencing a somewhat passive reception of the novel, he is now committed to working in it. To realize what Dickens has done, the reader has to do something too: he has to analyze, explore, and evaluate, until he feels that, insofar as is possible, he is a master of his subject, able to speak intelligently and perceptively about it, and able, if called upon to do so, to write a sound and sensible paper upon it.

A few gifted individuals are able to do all this on their own, but most of us find that, when faced with such a challenge, we can do with some help. The majority of the writers whom you encounter in these pages did not reach their conclusions unaided, as you will note by their references to other critics. You too will want to enrich your response to *Great Expectations* by listening to the opinions of others. Remember, though, that you need not abandon your ideas in favor of theirs—the fact that critics disagree among themselves indicates that there are not necessarily any "right" answers which you must find. Some of the opinions you encounter will be so convincing that they will persuade you to reverse your original impression; others will seem weak, and you will set your own ideas against them, probably finding considerable help from other critics to support your views; still other opinions you will accept as partial modifications of your own thoughts. In any case, reading these essays will strengthen your command of *Great Expectations* so that you will be prepared to talk and write about it to the fullest extent of your intelligence and application.

This text has been prepared to help you to do complete and independent research, whether for investigative writing or otherwise. To this end the following essays have been reprinted in a form as close to their original appearance in journals and books as is practicable. No editing or correcting has been done. Titles appearing in brackets have been supplied by the editors. The essays are not all excellent, nor even necessarily accurate. In short, the responsibility for sound critical reading and careful recording of bibliographical information is yours, just as it is when you conduct your research in a library. Page numbers of the articles as they appeared in their original sources are given in brackets which mark the end of the material on the original page [121/122]. Numbers in brackets following page numbers referring to *Great Expectations* are for students using the Chandler edition of the novel (a companion volume to this text). On the first page of each essay appears all information (though not necessarily in correct form or order for your paper) for footnotes and bibliography.

Following each essay are suggestions which will help you to evaluate the criticism, and which may lead to a research topic. Further suggestions will be found at the end of the text, including some which require outside reading. Those exercises will be useful for upper-class courses, and also for library exercises which are an important supplement in composition courses. Suggestions of topics are not meant to restrict your choice, but are designed to provide beginnings for class discussion, and to start you on a course of reflection and study which will lead to a topic that combines the approval of the instructor with your own interests and abilities.

R.L.
W.E.M.

The Original Ending of
Great Expectations

THE FOLLOWING is the original ending to which the critics in this text refer. It was replaced by Dickens with the ending which is now found in all editions, including the Chandler edition which is a companion to this text. The original ending followed Pip's last words to Biddy (page 410 in the Chandler Edition): 'But that poor dream, as I once used to call it, has all gone by, Biddy, all gone by!'

It was two more years before I saw herself. I had heard of her as leading a most unhappy life, and as being separated from her husband, who had used her with great cruelty, and who had become quite renowned as a compound of pride, brutality, and meanness. I had heard of the death of her husband from an accident consequent on ill-treating a horse, and of her being married again to a Shropshire doctor who, against his interest, had once very manfully interposed on an occasion when he was in professional attendance upon Mr. Drummle, and had witnessed some outrageous treatment of her. I had heard that the Shropshire doctor was not rich, and that they lived on her own personal fortune. I was in England again—in London, and walking along Piccadilly with little Pip—when a servant came running after me to ask would I step back to a lady in a carriage who wished to speak to me. It was a little pony carriage which the lady was driving, and the lady and I looked sadly enough on one another.

'I am greatly changed, I know; but I thought you would like to shake hands with Estella too, Pip. Lift up that pretty child and let me kiss it!' (She supposed the child, I think, to be my child.) I was very glad afterwards to have had the interview; for, in her face and in her voice, and in her touch, she gave me the assurance that suffering had been stronger than Miss Havisham's teaching, and had given her a heart to understand what my heart used to be.

Great Expectations*

THE VERY title of this book indicates the confidence of conscious genius. In a new aspirant for public favor, such a title might have been a good device to attract attention; but the most famous novelist of the [380/381] day, watched by jealous rivals and critics, could hardly have selected it, had he not inwardly felt the capacity to meet all the expectations he raised. We have read it, as we have read all Mr. Dickens's previous works, as it appeared in instalments, and can testify to the felicity with which expectation was excited and prolonged, and to the series of surprises which accompanied the unfolding of the plot of the story. In no other of his romances has the author succeeded so perfectly in at once stimulating and baffling the curiosity of his readers. He stirred the dullest minds to guess the secret of his mystery; but, so far as we have learned, the guesses of his most intelligent readers have been almost as wide of the mark as those of the least apprehensive. It has been all the more provoking to the former class, that each surprise was the result of art, and not of trick; for a rapid review of previous chapters has shown that the materials of a strictly logical development of the story were freely given. Even after the first, second, third, and even fourth of these surprises gave their pleasing electric shocks to intelligent curiosity, the *dénouement* was still hidden, though confidentially foretold. The plot of the romance is therefore universally admitted to be the best that Dickens has ever invented. Its leading events are, as we read the story consecutively, artistically necessary, yet, at the same time, the processes are artistically concealed. We follow the movement of a logic of passion and character, the real premises of which we detect only when we are startled by the conclusions.

The plot of "Great Expectations" is also noticeable as indicating, better than any of his previous stories, the individuality of Dickens's

* Unsigned review in *The Atlantic Monthly*, VIII (September, 1861), pp. 380–382.

genius. Everybody must have discerned in the action of his mind two diverging tendencies, which, in this novel, are harmonized. He possesses a singularly wide, clear, and minute power of accurate observation, both of things and of persons; but his observation, keen and true to actualities as it independently is, is not a dominant faculty, and is opposed or controlled by the strong tendency of his disposition to pathetic or humorous idealization. Perhaps in "The Old Curiosity Shop" these qualities are best seen in their struggle and divergence, and the result is a magnificent juxtaposition of romantic tenderness, melo-dramatic improbabilities, and broad farce. The humorous characteriza-tion is joyously exaggerated into caricature,—the serious characterization into romantic unreality. Richard Swiveller and Little Nell refuse to combine. There is abundant evidence of genius both in the humorous and the pathetic parts, but the artistic impression is one of anarchy rather than unity.

In "Great Expectations," on the contrary, Dickens seems to have attained the mastery of powers which formerly more or less mastered him. He has fairly discovered that he cannot, like Thackeray, narrate a story as if he were a mere looker-on, a mere "knowing" observer of what he describes and represents; and he has therefore taken observation simply as the basis of his plot and his characterization. As we read "Vanity Fair" and "The Newcomes," we are impressed with the actuality of the persons and incidents. There is an absence both of directing ideas and disturbing idealizations. Everything drifts to its end, as in real life. In "Great Expectations" there is shown a power of external observation finer and deeper even than Thackeray's; and yet, owing to the presence of other qualities, the general impression is not one of objective reality. The author palpably uses his observations as materials for his creative faculties to work upon; he does not record, but invents; and he produces something which is natural only under conditions prescribed by his own mind. He shapes, disposes, pene-trates, colors, and contrives everything, and the whole action is a series of events which could have occurred only in his own brain, and which it is difficult to conceive of as actually "happening." And yet in none of his other works does he evince a shrewder insight into real life, and a clearer perception and knowledge of what is called "the world." The book is, indeed, an artistic creation, and not a mere succession of humorous and pathetic scenes, and demonstrates that Dickens is now in the prime, and not in the decline of his great powers.

The characters of the novel also show how deeply it has been meditated; for, though none of them may excite the personal interest which clings to Sam Weller [381/382] or little Dombey, they are better fitted to each other and to the story in which they appear than is usual with Dickens. They all combine to produce that unity of impression which the work leaves on the mind. Individually they will rank among the most original of the author's creations. Magwitch and Joe Gargery, Jaggers and Wemmick, Pip and Herbert, Wopsle, Pumblechook, and "the Aged," Miss Havisham, Estella, and Biddy, are personages which the most assiduous readers of Dickens must pronounce positive additions to the characters his rich and various genius has already created.

Pip, the hero, from whose mind the whole representation takes its form and color, is admirably delineated throughout. Weak, dreamy, amiable, apprehensive, aspiring, inefficient, the subject and the victim of "Great Expectations," his individuality is, as it were, diffused through the whole narrative. Joe is a noble character, with a heart too great for his powers of expression to utter in words, but whose patience, fortitude, tenderness, and beneficence shine lucidly through his confused and mangled English. Magwitch, the "warmint" who "grew up took up," whose memory extended only to that period of his childhood when he was "a-thieving turnips for his living" down in Essex, but in whom a life of crime had only intensified the feeling of gratitude for the one kind action of which he was the object, is hardly equalled in grotesque grandeur by anything which Dickens has previously done. The character is not only powerful in itself, but it furnishes pregnant and original hints to all philosophical investigators into the phenomena of crime. In this wonderful creation Dickens follows the maxim of the great master of characterization, and seeks "the soul of goodness in things evil."

The style of the romance is rigorously close to things. The author is so engrossed with the objects before his mind, is so thoroughly in earnest, that he has fewer of those humorous caprices of expression in which formerly he was wont to wanton. Some of the old hilarity and play of fancy is gone, but we hardly miss it in our admiration of the effects produced by his almost stern devotion to the main idea of his work. There are passages of description and narrative in which we are hardly conscious of the words, in our clear apprehension of the objects and incidents they convey. The quotable epithets and phrases are less numerous than in "Dombey & Son" and "David Copperfield"; but the scenes and events impressed on the imagination are perhaps greater in number and more vivid in representation. The poetical element of the writer's genius, his modification of the forms, hues, and sounds of Nature by viewing them through the medium of an imagined mind, is especially prominent throughout the descriptions with which the work abounds. Nature is not only described, but individualized and humanized.

Altogether we take great joy in recording our conviction that "Great Expectations" is a masterpiece. We have never sympathized in the mean delight which some critics seem to experience in detecting the signs which subtly indicate the decay of power in creative intellects. We sympathize still less in the stupid and ungenerous judgments of those who find a still meaner delight in wilfully asserting that the last book of a popular writer is unworthy of the genius which produced his first. In our opinion, "Great Expectations" is a work which proves that we may expect from Dickens a series of romances far exceeding in power and artistic skill the productions which have already given him such a preëminence among the novelists of the age.   [end on 382]

PROBLEMS: *Atlantic Monthly* Review

1. Are later critics of *Great Expectations* in general agreement with this critic on the quality of Dickens's plot structure? Which critics?
2. Do later critics agree that the novel is logically developed? Which critics?
3. The reviewer mentions that *Great Expectations* was published in installments. Does this help you to understand the nature of its structure in any way?

4. The reviewer indicates that the ending is not guessed by readers of his acquaintance. Does this conflict with his assertion that the novel is well-structured? How could this information be used by critics of our day in judging which ending of *Great Expectations* is better?

5. Are the terms "pathetic or humorous idealization" [p. 381] applied by modern critics of *Great Expectations*? If so, do critics today mean the same things by them? If not, do today's critics say the same things about the novel in different words?

6. Dickens, says this reviewer, "does not record, but invents" [p. 381]. Explain in detail what he means. Is this a criticism of Dickens that is still agreed on?

7. The reviewer says that the events of *Great Expectations* are "difficult to conceive of as actually 'happening.'" [p. 381] What is there about these events that makes him say this? To what extent do you agree? What is the consensus of the critics?

8. The above quotation is followed by, "And yet in none of his other works does he evince a shrewder insight into real life . . ." Is this a contradiction? Explain your opinion.

9. Throughout the article, the reviewer calls *Great Expectations* a romance. Do some research on the meaning of this word as applied to a novel, and consider *Great Expectations* as a romance.

Great Expectations*

by John Forster

THE *Tale of Two Cities* was published in 1859; the series of papers collected as the *Uncommercial Traveller* were occupying Dickens in 1860; and it was while engaged in these, and throwing off in the course of them [360/361] capital "samples" of fun and enjoyment, he thus replied to a suggestion that he should let himself loose upon some single humorous conception, in the vein of his youthful achievements in that way. "For a little piece I have been writing—or am writing; for I hope to finish it to-day—such a very fine, new, and grotesque idea has opened upon me, that I begin to doubt whether I had not better cancel the little paper, and reserve the notion for a new book. You shall judge as soon as I get it printed. But it so opens out before *me* that I can see the whole of a serial revolving on it, in a most singular and comic manner." This was the germ of Pip and Magwitch, which at first he intended to make the groundwork of a tale in the old twenty-number form, but for reasons perhaps fortunate brought afterwards within the limits of a less elaborate novel. "Last week," he wrote on the 4th of October 1860, "I got to work on the new story. I had previously very carefully considered the state and prospects of *All the Year Round*, and, the more I considered them, the less hope I saw of being able to get back, *now*, to the profit of a separate publication in the old 20 numbers." (A tale, which at the time was appearing in his serial, had disappointed expectation.) "However I worked on, knowing that what I was doing would run into another groove; and I called a council of war at the office on Tuesday. It was perfectly clear that the one thing to be done was, for me to strike in. I have therefore decided

* From John Forster, *The Life of Charles Dickens* (London, Chapman and Hall, 1874), vol. III, pp. 360–369.

to begin the story as of the length of the *Tale of Two Cities* on the first of December—begin publishing, that is. I must make the most I can out of the book. You shall have the first two or three weekly [361/362] parts to-morrow. The name is GREAT EXPECTATIONS. I think a good name?" Two days later he wrote: "The sacrifice of *Great Expectations* is really and truly made for myself. The property of *All the Year Round* is far too valuable, in every way, to be much endangered. Our fall is not large, but we have a considerable advance in hand of the story we are now publishing, and there is no vitality in it, and no chance whatever of stopping the fall; which on the contrary would be certain to increase. Now, if I went into a twenty-number serial, I should cut off my power of doing anything serial here for two good years—and that would be a most perilous thing. On the other hand, by dashing in now, I come in when most wanted; and if Reade and Wilkie follow me, our course will be shaped out handsomely and hopefully for between two and three years. A thousand pounds are to be paid for early proofs of the story to America." A few more days brought the first instalment of the tale, and explanatory mention of it. "The book will be written in the first person throughout, and during these first three weekly numbers you will find the hero to be a boy-child, like David. Then he will be an apprentice. You will not have to complain of the want of humour as in the *Tale of Two Cities*. I have made the opening, I hope, in its general effect exceedingly droll. I have put a child and a good-natured foolish man, in relations that seem to me very funny. Of course I have got in the pivot on which the story will turn too—and which indeed, as you remember, was the grotesque tragi-comic conception that first encouraged me. To be quite sure I had fallen into no unconscious repe-[362/363]titions, I read *David Copperfield* again the other day, and was affected by it to a degree you would hardly believe."

It may be doubted if Dickens could better have established his right to the front rank among novelists claimed for him, than by the ease and mastery with which, in these two books of *Copperfield* and *Great Expectations*, he kept perfectly distinct the two stories of a boy's childhood, both told in the form of autobiography. A subtle penetration into character marks the unlikeness in the likeness; there is enough at once of resemblance and of difference in the position and surroundings of each to account for the divergences of character that arise; both children are good-hearted, and both have the advantage of association with models of tender simplicity and oddity, perfect in their truth and quite distinct from each other; but a sudden tumble into distress steadies Peggotty's little friend, and as unexpected a stroke of good fortune turns the head of the small protégé of Joe Gargery. What a deal of spoiling nevertheless, a nature that is really good at the bottom of it will stand without permanent damage, is nicely shown in Pip; and the way he reconciles his determination to act very shabbily to his early friends, with a conceited notion that he is setting them a moral example, is part of the shading of a character drawn with extraordinary skill. His greatest trial comes out of his good luck; and the foundations of both are laid at the opening of the tale, in a churchyard down by the Thames, as it winds past desolate marshes twenty miles to the sea, of which a masterly picture in half a dozen lines will give only average example of the de-[363/364]scriptive writing that is everywhere one of the charms of the book. It is strange, as I transcribe the words, with what wonderful vividness they bring back the very spot on which we stood when he said he meant to make it the scene of the opening of his story—Cooling Castle ruins and the desolate Church, lying out among the marshes seven miles from Gadshill! "My first most vivid and broad impression . . on a memorable raw afternoon towards evening . . was . . that this bleak place, overgrown with nettles, was the church-yard, and that the dark flat wilderness beyond the churchyard, inter-sected with dykes and mounds and gates, with scattered cattle feeding on it, was the marshes; and that the low leaden line beyond, was the river; and that the distant savage lair from which the wind was rushing, was the sea . . . On the edge of the river . . only two black things in all the prospect seemed to be standing upright . . one, the beacon by which the sailors steered, like an unhooped cask upon a pole, an ugly thing when you were near it; the other, a gibbet with some chains hanging to it which had once held a pirate." Here Magwitch, an escaped convict from Chatham, terrifies the child Pip into stealing for him food and a file; and though recaptured and transported, he carries with him to Australia such a grateful heart for the small creature's service, that on making a fortune there he resolves to make his little friend a gentleman. This requires circumspection; and is so done, through the Old-Bailey attorney who has defended Magwitch at his trial (a character of surprising novelty and truth), that Pip imagines his present gifts and "great expectations" to have come from the supposed [364/365] rich lady of the story (whose eccentricities are the unattractive part of it, and have yet a weird character that somehow fits in with the kind of wrong she has suffered). When therefore the closing scenes bring back Magwitch himself, who risks his life to gratify his longing to see the gentleman he has made, it is an unspeakable horror to the youth to discover his benefactor in the convicted felon. If any one doubts Dickens's power of so drawing a character as to get to the heart of it, seeing beyond surface peculiarities into the moving springs of the human being himself, let him narrowly examine those scenes. There is not a grain of substitution of mere sentiment, or circumstance, for the inner and absolute reality of the position in which these two creatures find themselves. Pip's loathing of what had built up his fortune, and his horror of the uncouth architect, are apparent in even his most generous efforts to protect him from exposure and sentence. Magwitch's convict habits strangely blend themselves with his wild pride in, and love for, the youth whom his money has turned into a gentleman. He has a craving for his good opinion; dreads to offend him by his "heavy grubbing," or by the oaths he lets fall now and then; and pathetically hopes his Pip, his dear boy, won't think him "low": but, upon a chum of Pip's appearing unexpectedly while they are together, he pulls out a jack-knife by way of hint he can defend himself, and produces afterwards a greasy little clasped black Testament on which the startled new-comer, being found to have no hostile intention, is sworn to secrecy. At the opening of the story there had been an exciting scene of [365/366] the wretched man's chase and recapture among the marshes, and this has its parallel at the close in his chase and recapture on the river while poor Pip is helping to get him off. To make himself sure of the actual course of a boat in such circumstances, and what possible incidents the adventure might have, Dickens hired a steamer for the day from Blackwall to Southend. Eight or nine friends and three or four members of his family were on board, and he seemed to have no care, the whole of that summer day (22nd of May 1861), except to enjoy their enjoyment and entertain them with his own in shape of a thousand whims and fancies; but his sleepless observation was at work all the time, and nothing had escaped his keen vision on either side of the river. The fifteenth chapter of the third volume is a masterpiece.

The characters generally afford the same evidence as those two that Dickens's humour, not less than his creative power, was at its best in this book. The Old-Bailey attorney Jaggers, and his clerk Wemmick (both excellent, and the last one of the oddities that live in everybody's liking for the goodheartedness of its humorous surprises), are as good as his earliest efforts in that line; the Pumblechooks and Wopsles are perfect as bits of *Nickleby* fresh from the mint; and the scene in which Pip, and Pip's chum Herbert, make up their accounts and schedule their debts and obligations, is original and delightful as Micawber himself. It is the art of living upon nothing and making the best of it, in the most pleasing form. Herbert's intentions to trade east and west, and get himself into business transactions of a magnificent extent and variety, are [366/367] as perfectly warranted to us, in his way of putting them, by merely "being in a counting-house and looking about you," as Pip's means of paying his debts are lightened and made easy by his method of simply adding them up with a margin. "The time comes," says Herbert, "when you see your opening. And you go in, and you swoop upon it, and you make your capital, and then there you are! When you have once made your capital you have nothing to do but employ it." In like manner Pip tells us "Suppose your debts to be one hundred and sixty four pounds four and twopence, I would say, leave a margin and put them down at two hundred; or suppose them to be four times as much, leave a margin and put them down at seven hundred." He is sufficiently candid to add, that, while he has the highest opinion of the wisdom and prudence of the margin, its dangers are that in the sense of freedom and solvency it imparts there is a tendency to run into new debt. But the satire that thus enforces the old warning against living upon vague hopes, and paying ancient debts by contracting new ones, never presented itself in more amusing or kindly shape. A word should be added of the father of the girl that Herbert marries, Bill Barley, ex-ship's purser, a gouty, bed-ridden, drunken old rascal, who lies on his back in an upper floor on Mill Pond Bank by Chinks's Basin, where he keeps, weighs, and serves out the family stores or provisions, according to old professional practice, with one eye at a telescope which is fitted on his bed for the convenience of sweeping the river. This is one of those sketches, slight in itself but made rich with a wealth of comic observation, in [367/368] which Dickens's humour took especial delight; and to all this part of the story, there is a quaint riverside flavour that gives it amusing reality and relish.

Sending the chapters that contain it, which open the third division of the tale, he wrote thus: "It is a pity that the third portion cannot be read all at once, because its purpose would be much more apparent; and the pity is the greater, because the general turn and tone of the working out and winding up, will be away from all such things as they conventionally go. But what must be, must be. As to the planning out from week to week, nobody can imagine what the difficulty is, without trying. But, as in all such cases, when it is overcome the pleasure is proportionate. Two months more will see me through it, I trust. All the iron is in the fire, and I have 'only' to beat it out." One other letter throws light upon an objection taken not unfairly to the too great speed with which the heroine, after being married, reclaimed, and widowed, is in a page or two again made love to, and remarried by the hero. This summary proceeding was not originally intended. But, over and above its popular acceptance, the book had interested some whose opinions Dickens specially valued (Carlyle among them, I remember);* and upon Bulwer Lytton objecting to a close that should leave Pip a solitary man, Dickens substituted what now stands. "You will be surprised" [368/369] he wrote "to hear that I have changed the end of *Great Expectations* from and after Pip's return to Joe's, and

* A dear friend now gone, used laughingly to relate what outcry there used to be, on the night of the week when a number was due, for "that Pip nonsense!" and what roars of laughter followed, though at first it was entirely put aside as not on any account to have time wasted over it.

finding his little likeness there. Bulwer, who has been, as I think you know, extraordinarily taken by the book, so strongly urged it upon me, after reading the proofs, and supported his view with such good reasons, that I resolved to make the change. You shall have it when you come back to town. I have put in as pretty a little piece of writing as I could, and I have no doubt the story will be more acceptable through the alteration." This turned out to be the case; but the first ending nevertheless seems to be more consistent with the drift, as well as natural working out, of the tale, . . .   [mid 369]

PROBLEMS: John Forster

1. Do critics agree with Dickens that the opening of *Great Expectations* is exceedingly droll? Which critics?
2. Support or attack this statement: "What a deal of spoiling nevertheless, a nature that is really good at the bottom of it will stand without permanent damage, is nicely shown in Pip;" [p. 363].
3. What is the "surprising novelty and truth" [p. 364] of Jaggers?
4. Why does Forster praise the characterization in this novel? How well does he analyze it?
5. Forster notes the parallel between the chase and recapture of Magwitch at the beginning of the novel and near the end of the novel. Develop this parallel as fully as you can, and decide what significance it has.
6. Do other critics agree that Dickens's humor is at its best in *Great Expectations*? Which critics?
7. What hints about Dickens's intentions in writing the novel can you discover from the Forster selection?

Dickens's *Great Expectations*[*]

by Edwin P. Whipple

ON THE first of December, 1860, Dickens began the publication, in
All the Year Round, of his novel of Great Expectations, and closed it
in the number of that weekly which appeared on the 3d of August,
1861. His first intention, as in the case of The Old Curiosity Shop, was
to write a short sketch or story for the periodical he edited. Forster had
suggested to him that he should try something in his old way,—something which would recall to the public his youthful achievements in
humorous scenes and characterizations. Dickens replied: "For a little
piece I have been writing—or am writing, for I hope to finish it to-day
—such a very fine, new, and grotesque idea has opened upon me that I
begin to doubt whether I had not better cancel the little paper and
reserve the notion for a new book. You shall judge as soon as I get it
printed. But it so opens out before *me* that I can see the whole of a
serial revolving on it in a most singular and comic manner." This
grotesque idea was, doubtless, the relation established between Pip and
Magwitch, which might easily have been narrated in a few charming
pages, such as those in which he had disposed of the germs of many
other romances, in the series of essays, sketches, and portraitures of life
which he was then writing under the general title of The Uncommercial Traveller. But the idea of an innocent boy establishing unconsciously an immense influence over the mind of a hunted felon, merely
by giving him that assistance which he dared not refuse, haunted
Dickens's imagination until he gathered round it a whole new world of
characters and incidents. He thought at first that it might furnish the
materials for a monthly serial, in twenty numbers, like Dombey and
Son, or Little Dorrit; but the falling off in the circulation of All the

[*] From *The Atlantic Monthly*, XL (September 1877), pp. 327–333.

Year Round induced him to publish it in that weekly, and to confine it to the dimensions of A Tale of Two Cities. It is doubtful if he could have sustained himself in making the story double its present length. As it is, nothing could be better of its kind; but the atmosphere of Old Bailey and Newgate, which penetrates the whole tale, might have become insupportable in a romance as long as Copperfield or Bleak House. The only method by which the interest could have been sustained would have been a forced extension and development of Pip's character through scenes which might have followed the downfall of his "expectations," and which would have led him up to his eventual marriage with Estella in a less curt fashion than that which the romancer eventually employed.

To account for the conclusion of the story as it now stands, where, in a concluding chapter, "the heroine, after being married, reclaimed, and widowed, is in a page or two made love to and remarried to the hero," we must refer to a remonstrance from friends, which was more effectual in the case of Dickens than that which protested against the death of Clarissa Harlowe, in the case of Richardson. Carlyle was among the persons who listened to the reading of advanced sheets of the story, and on one occasion, at a meeting of friends in Dickens's house, called, in his boisterous, laughing way, for more of that "Pip nonsense;" and Bulwer Lytton was so strongly opposed to the conclusion of the story as originally written that Dickens reluctantly altered it. "I have changed the end of Great Expectations," he wrote to Forster, "from and after Pip's return to Joe's, and finding his little likeness there. Bulwer, who has been, as I think you know, extraordinarily taken by the book, so strongly urged it upon me, after reading the proofs, and supported his view with such good reasons, that I resolved to make the change. You shall have it when I come back to town. I have put in as [327/328] pretty a piece of writing as I could, and I have no doubt the story will be more acceptable through the alteration."

The original closing chapter left Pip a solitary man, as much estranged from Estella as he was from all the persons connected with her and his great expectations. He returns to England after an absence of eight years, and finds that Joe and Biddy, happily married, have given his name to their son. He learns that Estella, in marrying Drummle, has endured every outrage that could be inflicted by such a husband's pride, cruelty, and meanness; that she was relieved from her hated bonds by a merciful kick bestowed upon him by a nobler brute, namely, a horse that he had ill-treated; and that she was now married to a Shropshire doctor, who had witnessed and resented, during his professional visits to her dying husband, the outrages that he heaped upon her to the last. Pip is also informed that she and the doctor are living comfortably on her personal fortune. Then come the concluding sentences of the tale: "I was in England again—in London, and walking along Piccadilly with little Pip—when a servant came running after me to ask would I step back to a lady in a carriage, who wished to speak to me. It was a little pony carriage which the lady was driving; and the lady and I looked sadly enough on one another. 'I am greatly changed, I know; but I thought you would like to shake hands with Estella, too, Pip. Lift up that pretty child, and let me kiss it!' (She supposed the child, I think, to be my child.) I was very glad afterwards to have had the interview; for, in her face and in her voice and in her touch, she gave me assurance that suffering had been stronger than Miss Havisham's teaching, and had given her a heart to understand what my heart used to be." This was a natural and artistic conclusion of the story; but Bulwer insisted that Pip should not be left alone in desolate bachelor-hood; that he should marry Estella. It must be confessed that Dickens contrived to give an unprepared, unexpected, and inartistic ending to the romance, satisfying to Bulwer and to ordinary readers of novels, because it promised a marriage between the hero and the heroine; but how dreary, how sepulchral, is this mating of hearts never intended to be matrimonially joined! Better to have left Pip an experienced merchant emancipated from all his old delusions, and leading his little namesake by the hand along Piccadilly, than to have married him to the lady who looked out upon him from her pony carriage as she drove by. Estella had deliberately used her charms for the purpose of winning his heart only to torture it; she had deliberately married a dolt and a brute for money; and she should have been left to the Shropshire doctor, who had softened all the heart she possessed by defending her from the deathbed malignity of her savage husband. Pip, educated into a man of affairs, who had learned the value of the affections he had foolishly sacrificed in his green youth, should also have been left, as Dickens intended to leave him, calmly surveying the woman who had awakened in his youthful breast the passion of love only to deceive it merely as a matron in whom he hoped calamity had developed a heart never revealed to him.

There is much of Dickens's best writing in Great Expectations. The characterization is forcible even when it is least attractive. Thus the weird, ghostly Miss Havisham has more power expended on her than she deserves. Orlick is a savage of the same race as Hugh, in Barnaby Rudge, but is represented as more brutal than his prototype. A broad-shouldered, loose-limbed, swarthy, sullen, hulking ruffian, who "slouches into his work as he slouches out of it," his great physical strength is guided by a low cunning only to the gratification of a low malignity, and he is thoroughly dehumanized in the process by which he is strongly individualized. Magwitch is a criminal of another type, having in him human elements of gratitude and love; and his own account of his miserable life has a rude fervor and pathos which are indescribably affecting. He condenses his biography in what he [328/329] calls "a mouthful of English," namely, "In jail and out of jail, in jail and out of jail, in jail and out of jail. . . . I first became aware of myself, down in Essex, a-thieving turnips for my living. Summun had run away from me,—a man, a tinker,—and he'd took the fire with him, and left me very cold." How did he know his name was Mag-witch? "Much as I know'd the birds' names in the hedges to be chaffinch, sparrer, thrush. I might have thought it all lies together, only as the birds' names come out true, I supposed mine did. So far as I could find, there warn't a soul that see young Abel Magwitch, *with as little on him as in him*, but wot caught fright at him, and either drove him off or took him up. I was took up, took up, took up, to that extent that I reg'larly grow'd up took up." The narrative that succeeds is a compact account of the way in which the criminal classes are constantly recruited by swarms of neglected or abandoned children. Compeyson, the greater rogue of the two, plays an important part in the story, but he is felt rather by the effect his villainy produces on the character and fortunes of others, than by his own personality. The mother of Estella and wife of Magwitch, the murderess whom Mr. Jaggers releases from the grasp of justice and, curiously enough, chooses for his housekeeper, completes the criminal group, though there is not a felon lounging around Mr. Jaggers's office who is not thoroughly individualized by a few brief, discriminating touches, from the red-eyed little Jew "performing a jig of anxiety under a lamp-post, and accompanying himself in a kind of frenzy with the words, 'Oh, Jaggerth, Jaggerth, Jaggerth!'" to the shuffling, one-eyed, weeping Mike, who always seems to have one member of his interesting family up for larceny or burglary, and who is always prepared with a witness ready to swear, "in a general way, anythink."

Mr. Jaggers himself is one of Dickens's most felicitous characterizations in the law department of what we have called Dickens-land. It is astonishing that his limited experience as a reporter and as an apprentice in an attorney's office should have furnished him with so many sharply defined types of the English lawyer, through all the grades of the profession, from Sampson Brass, in The Old Curiosity Shop, all the way up to the bland Lord Chancellor who figures so gracefully in Bleak House. He introduces scores of lawyers into his various romances, and shows a superficial knowledge, at least, of the jargon which distinguishes their language from the English language, and of the moral qualities which distinguish their legal nature from ordinary human nature; but he also discriminates clearly between the different classes into which the profession is divided, and, while preserving the general features of each class, sharply individualizes every person included in it,—that is, every person who seems deserving of a place in his gallery of original characters. Thus Stryver, in A Tale of Two Cities, belongs, like Jaggers, to the class of domineering legal bullies, and they might, upon a superficial observation, be considered as pretty much alike; but, as represented by Dickens, they are very far apart in individual character, and cannot be confounded by any reader whose imagination has once been stamped with the image of either. The variation comes in great part from the fact that the idea, purpose, and atmosphere of the two romances are widely different. Stryver comes into A Tale of Two Cities chiefly as the advocate of an honest man accused of high treason. Jaggers comes into Great Expectations as the legal centre of a story which is saturated with crime, a story where the criminal or worthless characters are in the majority, and where the innocent persons are all involved in a mesh of contradictions, arising from low villainies of which they are the victims. The offenses in the one romance are political: technical crimes which are universally known to be often the highest expression of noble virtues. In the other the crimes are such as all civilized mankind repudiates, and the perpetrators of which are persons who [329/330] can be saved from death or transportation only by the interposition of such lawyers as Mr. Jaggers, exerting their force and ferocity, their ingenuity and knowledge of technical forms, on behalf of the criminal's "legal rights."

Mr. Jaggers is, indeed, the very impersonation of the Old Bailey advocate,—the guardian angel, or at least the protecting genius, of all unfortunate gentlemen afflicted with irresistible tendencies to theft, arson, forgery, and homicide, standing firmly between them and the gallows (provided always that they have previously "seen Wemmick"), and inspiring the whole swell-mob of rascaldom with the well-founded conviction that "Jaggers can do it, if it is to be done." He "always seems to me," says his clerk, Wemmick, "as if he had set a man-trap, and was watching it. Suddenly, click! you're caught!" A poor outcast woman, comforting another outcast whose "Bill" has got into trouble about some matter of housebreaking, says to her, "Jaggers is for him, 'Melia, and what more *could* you have?" Indeed, there is hardly in literature a more finished specimen of the legal bully, perfect in the art of hectoring witnesses, terrifying judges, and bamboozling juries. Even when there is no case to be tried he cannot get rid of the contentiousness of mind and manner he has acquired in the criminal courts. In private conversation, where no point is to be gained, he refuses to admit anything, and cross-examines everything and everybody. When he drops into the village ale-house to inquire after Pip, and inform him of his great expectations, he cannot resist, before proceeding to business, the temptation to demolish poor Mr. Wopsle, who is reading, in his grandest elocutionary tones, to a wondering audience, a thrilling newspaper account of "the last highly popular murder." By a few crushing Socratic interrogatories, as insolent as they are searching, he cross-examines that village luminary into utter silence and insignificance, so that even the rustics around the tavern fire, over whom he has long domineered, feel and see that he is utterly discomfited by this intruding stranger with the big head, deep-set eyes, and bushy, black eyebrows, who lowers upon him from the back of the settle on which Mr. Jaggers is contemptuously leaning. Throughout the book he appears impregnable in every defensive position he takes, and overwhelming whenever he assumes the offensive. He penetrates into the heart of every person with whom he comes in contact or collision, while he himself remains impenetrable. Even Dickens only catches glimpses here and there of his inner self. The one occasion in which he exhibits feeling is that in which Pip implores him to state the facts regarding the parentage of Estella, and then he only gives the information in the form of an imagined case. Both he and Wemmick are so much mortified that they have been betrayed into an expression of sentiment which they consider unprofessional that they become hard and harsh toward each other, and are only prevented from falling into a quarrel by the opportune arrival of Mike, who enters to announce that his eldest daughter is arrested on suspicion of theft. Wemmick detects a tear "twinkling in his eye," and asks him roughly, "What do you come sniveling here for?" "A man can't help his feelings," pleads Mike. "His what?" Wemmick savagely exclaims. "Say that again!" Then Mr. Jaggers advances, points to the door, and, in a voice of thunder, bids this father of an unfortunate family to leave the office. "I'll have no feelings here," he says; "get out." And Pip observes that, after Mike humbly withdraws, "Mr. Jaggers and Wemmick appeared to have reëstablished their good understanding, and went to work again with an air of refreshment upon them, as if they had just had lunch."

Joe Gargery is one of a large class of characters which Dickens delighted to create,—men in whom solid integrity of heart and conduct can find no adequate expression through the brain and the tongue.

Generally the tongue is but too glib in uttering fine sentiments and ideas [330/331] which have no root in feeling or character; if a man has nothing really to say, he finds little difficulty in saying it fluently, coherently, and charmingly; and no hypocrite, conscious or unconscious, would suffer from the impediments which obstruct the utterance of the stalwart Joe, when his great heart stumbles over the usual phrases of affection or disinterestedness in a sort of hopeless confusion. His brain can only stutter when his heart swells to its utmost capacity; and his favorite expression ,"which I meantersay," is more eloquent than the lucid sayings of less simple and noble natures. Dickens was so captivated by Joe Gargery that he undertook the task of devising a new language for him, governed by a novel grammar, and with rules for the construction of sentences which must naturally surprise the student of Blair, Kaimes, Campbell, or Whately. The creator of Joe felt that Christian civilization was based on the real existence of persons resembling Joe in kind; and that political, fashionable, literary, and scientific "society," adorned with any number of fluent, graceful, and highly cultivated men and women, would crumble unless sustained by sturdy workmen of which Gargery is the type. The solid nobility of his nature is all the more apparent when we reflect that the circumstances of his early life were almost as unpropitious as those of Magwitch. In apologizing to Pip for his lack of schooling, this tongue-tied hero—a man whom Carlyle would have rapturously hugged as a realization of his ideal of silent fortitude—gives a pathetic account of his childhood and youth: "My father, Pip, he were given to drink, and when he was overtook with drink, he hammered away at my mother, most onmerciful. It were a'most the only hammering he did, indeed, 'xcepting at myself. . . . Consequence, my mother and me we ran away from my father several times; and then my mother she'd go out to work, and she'd say, 'Joe,' she'd say, 'now, please God, you shall have some schooling, child,' and she'd put me to school. But my father were that good in his hart that he couldn't abear to be without us. So he'd come with a most tremenjous crowd, and make such a row at the doors of the houses where we was that they used to be obligated to have no more to do with us and to give us up to him. And then he took us home and hammered us. Which, you see, Pip, were a drawback on my learning." Joe, under these circumstances, was set hard to work to support the drunken father; and "I kep' him," he adds, "till he went off in a purple'leptic fit. And it were my intentions to have had put upon his tombstone that Whatsume'er the failings on his part, Remember, reader, he were that good in his hart. . . . As I was saying, Pip, it were my intentions to have had it cut over him; but poetry costs money, cut it how you will, small or large, and it were not done. Not to mention bearers, all the money that could be spared were wanted for my mother. She were in poor 'elth, and quite broke. She weren't long of following, poor soul, *and her share of peace come round at last.*" And he then goes on to give the reason why he submits to be so atrociously henpecked by his wife: "I see so much in my poor mother of a woman drudging and slaving and breaking her honest hart, and never getting no peace in her mortal days, that I'm dead afeerd of going wrong in the way of not doing what's right to a woman, and I'd fur rather of the two go wrong the t'other way, and be a little ill-conwenienced myself." There is something almost sublime in the patience of this tender-hearted Vulcan, toiling day after day to support such a vixen Venus, neither expecting nor receiving the slightest recognition of his services, scorned, scolded, derided, and tormented by his termagant wife, and anxious only to save her brother Philip from the worst consequences of her senseless anger when she was on "the rampage." What can be better than his account of his courtship and marriage? "She was a fine figure of a woman, Pip,—a little redness, or a little matter of bone, here or there; what does it signify to me? . . . But when I got acquainted with your sister, it were the talk how she was bringing you [331/332] up by hand. . . . If you could have been aware how small and flabby and mean you was, dear me, you'd have formed the most contemptible opinions of yourself. . . . And when I offered to your sister to keep company, and be asked in church at such times as she was willing and ready to come to the forge, I said to her, 'And bring the poor little child. God bless the poor little child,' I said to your sister, 'there's room for *him* at the forge.' " The essential peculiarity and originality of Joe Gargery is that he is contented with the mere exercise of goodwill toward others. However unworthy may be the objects of his instinctive beneficence, and with whatever ingratitude his service may be requited, he is blind to everything except that the inborn necessity of his nature has found vent in some blundering words or efficient acts which rudely express his benevolent feelings. He is as perfectly unconscious of merit in saying and doing these grand things as he is of merit in breathing, in swinging his arms at his forge, or in exercising any other bodily function. The more the character is studied, the more profound and beautiful in essence it is found to be.

Among the many characters of the book, the uncle of Joe Gargery, the selfish, solemn, windy old donkey, Pumblechook, is deserving of special mention. He is asinine in soul,—a jackass who swindles humanity by assuming the human form, feloniously disregarding the gradual stages which the theory of development exacts in the structural transformation of species. Yet how delicious an ass Pumblechook is! Before Pip comes into his fortune, he is a tyrant; afterwards a sycophant; then again a hypocritical pretender; but always and ever an ass! The different members of the Pocket family who assemble in Miss Havisham's mansion, each toady anxious to excel the other in the grand object of being prominently named in that lady's will, are all well drawn; but we think there is one touch which is original in humorous nomenclature. Camilla is the sentimental lady among the numerous toadies gathered around the ghastly old maid; she suffers, according to her own statement, immense agonies, by night and by day, in thinking of the unhappiness of Miss Havisham; and she constantly appeals to a husband, kept in the background, to sustain her asseverations of the distressing effects on her physical system occasioned by the intensity of her sympathies with the afflicted woman of whom she is ambitious to be the heir. The husband's name is Raymond, and she is legally Mrs. Raymond; but, as she is the dominant force in their domestic establishment, Dickens calls the husband Mr. Camilla. Is not this an entirely original stroke of humor, on a subject which has exercised the humorists of all generations? Certainly no satirist that we can call to mind, in indicating the (doubtless proper) subordination of the husband to the wife, has ever hit before on calling the male animal Mr. Jane, or Mr. Mary, or Mr. Betsy. Then there is Miss Sarah Pocket, "a little dry, brown, corrugated old woman, with a small face that might have been made of walnut-shells, and a large mouth like a cat's, without the whiskers." Mr. Wopsle is another marked character, a man magnificently impotent, with a resounding voice that proclaims his imbecility over a wider area than is reached by the lungs of other fools, and whose performance of Hamlet forms one of the most richly humorous of the many scenes in which Dickens has ridiculed the theatre and the actors of his time. And, finally, there is the father of Herbert Pocket's Clara, old Bill Barley, a bed-ridden, covetous, swearing scamp, who seeks to allay the torments of the gout by copious libations of rum flavored with pepper, and who is naturally indignant that this fiery medicine does not have the curative qualities which might reasonably be expected of it.

But it is needless to call further attention to the felicity with which Dickens instantly individualizes his least important characters. His power of imaginative description is exhibited in this romance in two quite remarkable instances: the first is in the opening chapters, where the boy Pip comes into rela-[332/333]tion with the escaped convict; the second is the account of the defeated attempt, in the fifty-fourth chapter, to get the convict safely out of England. Both are masterly. The incidental remarks, arising naturally in the course of the story, are frequently striking, in their quaint humor of pathos. Thus: "Mrs. Joe was a very clean housekeeper, but had an exquisite art of making her cleanliness more uncomfortable and unacceptable than dirt itself." Pip says: "I was always treated as if I had insisted on being born, in opposition to the dictates of reason, religion, and morality, and against the dissuading arguments of my best friends." Again: "I had seen the damp lying on the outside of my little window, as if some goblin had been crying there all night, and using the window for a pocket-handkerchief." Pip, as a boy, is surprised at the chalk scores against topers on the wall at the side of the door of the village tavern. "They had been there," he says, "ever since I could remember, and had grown more than I had. But there was a quantity of chalk about our country, and perhaps the people neglected no opportunity of turning it to account." Everybody has heard of the rank which the great brewers of England obtain, from the husband of Dr. Johnson's Mrs. Thrale to the present Sir Something Bass. "I don't know," says Herbert Pocket, "why it should be a crack thing to be a brewer, but it is indisputable that while you cannot be genteel and bake, you may be as genteel as never was and brew." Indeed, all the eminent brewers are invariably members of Parliament. Bentley Drummle is described as a fellow so sulky that "he even took up a book as if its writer had done him an injury," a very admirable characterization of a whole class of critics. Pip fears that when Joe Gargery visits him in London the rustic may be seen in his company by Drummle, a person for whom he has the most profound contempt. "So," he says, "throughout our life, our worst weaknesses and meannesses are usually committed for the sake of people whom we most despise." This last remark may have been stated before, but we remember no moralist who has given such pointed expression to a fact of universal experience. A large portion of the comedies and tragedies of life spring from our tendency to live beyond our means; and we live beyond our means merely to keep up a visiting acquaintance with persons whom we either positively hate or for whom we have not the slightest sympathy.

The plot of Great Expectations is more ingeniously complicated than any other of Dickens's novels except Bleak House. As the story came out in weekly installments, the general impression was that the concealed benefactor bent on enriching Pip was Miss Havisham; and when Magwitch, the convicted felon, announced himself as the person who had supplied the funds by which the blacksmith's apprentice had been converted into a fine young gentleman, he surprised most readers of the narrative as much as he surprised, horrified, and disgusted the recipient of his favors. When Dickens was once asked if those who met him daily in society guessed the secret of the story before it was disclosed, he answered that he had succeeded in putting every gentleman of his acquaintance on a false track, but that all the women with whom he conversed divined his purpose before the narrative had gone much beyond the introductory chapters, and were sure, in spite of his denials, that the escaped convict, whom Pip had supplied with a file and with meat and drink, was more likely to be his benefactor than the weird old maid, who used him as a plaything and as a victim. When the novel is read as a whole, we perceive how carefully the author had prepared us for the catastrophe; but, it required feminine sagacity and insight to detect the secret on which the plot turns, as the novel first appeared in weekly parts. It is a pity that some woman has not solved the Mystery of Edwin Drood—a mystery which the author carried with him to the grave—as easily as all women, according to Dickens, solved the mystery of Pip's Great Expectations. [end on 333]

PROBLEMS: Edwin P. Whipple

1. Dickens called the story of *Great Expectations* (from which the novel sprang) a "grotesque idea." What of this "grotesque idea" remains in the novel?

2. What do you suppose the "good reasons" were which Bulwer-Lytton advanced for changing the ending of *Great Expectations?*

3. Why does Whipple think the original ending of the novel was "natural and artistic"? Extend his argument with material from other critics. What reasons would you give for preferring the original ending?

4. What is "dreary" and "sepulchral" about the "new" ending of *Great Expectations?* Do modern critics improve upon Whipple's two words for the second ending? Do they successfully answer Whipple's charges? Which critics?

5. What does "forcible" mean as applied to characterization?

6. Explain Whipple's statement that Miss Havisham "has more power expended on her than she deserves." [p. 328] Do modern critics make an adequate defense of the power Dickens expended on Miss Havisham?

7. Whipple finds it curious that Jaggers should choose Estella's mother for his housekeeper. Can you suggest why he made such a choice? If not, read what some of the later critics have said about Jaggers, and see if they suggest a reason for his employing Molly.

8. Who are the "criminal or worthless characters" in *Great Expectations*? Who are the "innocent characters"? Do you find it difficult to put some of the characters into either class without reservation? Is it hard or easy to classify the characters in this novel?

9. Amplify Whipple's statements about the language of Joe Gargery.

10. Comment upon Whipple's critical method, or upon what his essay added to your understanding of *Great Expectations*.

Great Expectations*

by G. K. CHESTERTON

GREAT EXPECTATIONS, which was written in the afternoon of Dickens's life and fame, has a quality of serene irony and even sadness, which puts it quite alone among his other works. At no time could Dickens possibly be called cynical, he had too much vitality; but relatively to the other books this book is cynical; but it has the soft and gentle cynicism of old age, not the hard cynicism of youth. To be a young cynic is to be a young brute; but Dickens, who had been so perfectly romantic and sentimental in his youth, could afford to admit this touch of doubt into the mixed experience of his middle age. At no time could any books by Dickens have been called Thackerayan. Both of the two men were too great for that. But relatively to the other Dickensian productions this book may be called Thackerayan. It is a study in human weakness and the slow human surrender. It describes how easily a free lad of fresh and decent instincts can be made to care more for rank and pride and the degrees of our stratified society than for old affection and for honour. It is an extra chapter to *The Book of Snobs*.

The best way of stating the change which this book marks in Dickens can be put in one phrase. In this book for the first time the hero disappears. The hero had descended to Dickens by a long line which [197/198] begins with the gods, nay, perhaps if one may say so, which begins with God. First comes Deity and then the image of Deity; first comes the god and then the demi-god, the Hercules who labours and conquers before he receives his heavenly crown. That idea, with

* From the book *Criticisms and Appreciations of Charles Dickens* by G. K. Chesterton. Published by E. P. Dutton & Co., Inc. and reprinted with their permission. (London and New York, 1911). Pages 197–206.

28

continual mystery and modification, has continued behind all romantic tales; the demi-god became the hero of paganism; the hero of paganism became the knight-errant of Christianity; the knight-errant who wandered and was foiled before he triumphed became the hero of the later prose romance, the romance in which the hero had to fight a duel with the villain but always survived, in which the hero drove desperate horses through the night in order to rescue the heroine, but always rescued her.

This heroic modern hero, this demi-god in a top-hat, may be said to reach his supreme moment and typical example about the time when Dickens was writing that thundering and thrilling and highly unlikely scene in *Nicholas Nickleby*, the scene where Nicholas hopelessly denounces the atrocious Gride in his hour of grinning triumph, and a thud upon the floor above tells them that the heroine's tyrannical father has died just in time to set her free. That is the apotheosis of the pure heroic as Dickens found it, and as Dickens in some sense continued it. It may be that it does not appear with quite so much unmistakable youth, beauty, valour, and virtue as it does in Nicholas Nickleby. Walter Gay is a simpler and more careless hero, but when he is doing any of the business of the story he is purely heroic. Kit Nubbles is a humbler hero, but he is a hero; when he is good he is very good. Even [198/199] David Copperfield, who confesses to boyish tremors and boyish evasions in his account of his boyhood, acts the strict stiff part of the chivalrous gentleman in all the active and determining scenes of the tale. But *Great Expectations* may be called, like *Vanity Fair*, a novel without a hero. Almost all Thackeray's novels except *Esmond* are novels without a hero, but only one of Dickens's novels can be so described. I do not mean that it is a novel without a *jeune premier*, a young man to make love; *Pickwick* is that and *Oliver Twist*, and, perhaps, *The Old Curiosity Shop*. I mean that it is a novel without a hero in the same far deeper and more deadly sense in which *Pendennis* is also a novel without a hero. I mean that it is a novel which aims chiefly at showing that the hero is unheroic.

All such phrases as these must appear of course to overstate the case. Pip is a much more delightful person than Nicholas Nickleby. Or to take a stronger case for the purpose of our argument, Pip is a much more delightful person than Sydney Carton. Still the fact remains. Most of Nicholas Nickleby's personal actions are meant to show that he is heroic. Most of Pip's actions are meant to show that he is not heroic. The study of Sydney Carton is meant to indicate that with all his vices Sydney Carton was a hero. The study of Pip is meant to indicate that with all his virtues Pip was a snob. The motive of the literary explanation is different. Pip and Pendennis are meant to show how circumstances can corrupt men. Sam Weller and Hercules are meant to show how heroes can subdue circumstances.

This is the preliminary view of the book which is [199/200] necessary if we are to regard it as a real and separate fact in the life of Dickens. Dickens had many moods because he was an artist; but he had one great mood, because he was a great artist. Any real difference therefore from the general drift, or rather (I apologise to Dickens) the general drive of his creation is very important. This is the one place in his work in which he does, I will not say feel like Thackeray, far less think like Thackeray, less still write like Thackeray, but this is the one of his works in which he understands Thackeray. He puts himself in some sense in the same place; he considers mankind at somewhat the same angle as mankind is considered in one of the sociable and sarcastic novels of Thackeray. When he deals with Pip he sets out not to show his strength like the strength of Hercules, but to show his weakness like the weakness of Pendennis. When he sets out to describe Pip's great expectation he does not set out, as in a fairy tale, with the idea that these great expectations will be fulfilled; he sets out from the first with the idea that these great expectations will be disappointing. We might very well, as I have remarked elsewhere, apply to all Dickens's books the title *Great Expectations*. All his books are full of an airy and yet ardent expectation of everything; of the next person who shall happen to speak, of the next chimney that shall happen to smoke, of the next event, of the next ecstasy; of the next fulfilment of any eager human fancy. All his books might be called *Great Expectations*. But the only book to which he gave the name of *Great Expectations* was the only book in which the expectation was never realised. It was so with the whole of that splendid and [200/201] unconscious generation to which he belonged. The whole glory of that old English middle class was that it was unconscious; its excellence was entirely in that, that it was the culture of the nation, and that it did not know it. If Dickens had ever known that he was optimistic, he would have ceased to be happy.

It is necessary to make this first point clear: that in *Great Expectations* Dickens was really trying to be a quiet, a detached, and even a cynical observer of human life. Dickens was trying to be Thackeray. And the final and startling triumph of Dickens is this: that even to this moderate and modern story, he gives an incomparable energy which is not moderate and which is not modern. He is trying to be reasonable; but in spite of himself he is inspired. He is trying to be detailed, but in spite of himself he is gigantic. Compared to the rest of Dickens this is Thackeray; but compared to the whole of Thackeray we can only say in supreme praise of it that it is Dickens.

Take, for example, the one question of snobbishness. Dickens has achieved admirably the description of the doubts and vanities of the wretched Pip as he walks down the street in his new gentlemanly clothes, the clothes of which he is so proud and so ashamed. Nothing could be so exquisitely human, nothing especially could be so exquisitely masculine as that combination of self-love and self-assertion and even insolence with a naked and helpless sensibility to the slightest breath of ridicule. Pip thinks himself better than every one else, and yet anybody can snub him; that is the everlasting male, and perhaps the everlasting gentleman. Dickens has described perfectly this [201/202] quivering and defenceless dignity. Dickens has described perfectly how ill-armed it is against the coarse humour of real humanity —the real humanity which Dickens loved, but which idealists and philanthropists do not love, the humanity of cabmen and costermongers and men singing in a third-class carriage; the humanity of Trabb's boy. In describing Pip's weakness Dickens is as true and as delicate as Thackeray. But Thackeray might have been easily as true and as delicate as Dickens. This quick and quiet eye for the tremors of mankind is a thing which Dickens possessed, but which others possessed also. George Eliot or Thackeray could have described the weakness of

Pip. Exactly what George Eliot and Thackeray could not have described was the vigour of Trabb's boy. There would have been admirable humour and observation in their accounts of that intolerable urchin. Thackeray would have given us little light touches of Trabb's boy, absolutely true to the quality and colour of the humour, just as in his novels of the eighteenth century, the glimpses of Steele or Boling-broke or Doctor Johnson are exactly and perfectly true to the colour and quality of their humour. George Eliot in her earlier books would have given us shrewd authentic scraps of the real dialect of Trabb's boy, just as she gave us shrewd and authentic scraps of the real talk in a Midland country town. In her later books she would have given us highly rationalistic explanations of Trabb's boy; which we should not have read. But exactly what they could never have given, and exactly what Dickens does give, is the *bounce* of Trabb's boy. It is the real unconquerable rush and energy in a character which was the supreme and quite [202/203] indescribable greatness of Dickens. He conquered by rushes; he attacked in masses; he carried things at the spear point in a charge of spears; he was the Rupert of Fiction. The thing about any figure of Dickens, about Sam Weller or Dick Swiveller, or Micawber, or Bagstock, or Trabb's boy,—the thing about each one of these persons is that he cannot be exhausted. A Dickens character hits you first on the nose and then in the waistcoat, and then in the eye and then in the waistcoat again, with the blinding rapidity of some battering engine. The scene in which Trabb's boy continually overtakes Pip in order to reel and stagger as at a first encounter is a thing quite within the real competence of such a character; it might have been suggested by Thackeray, or George Eliot, or any realist. But the point with Dickens is that there is a rush in the boy's rushings; the writer and the reader rush with him. They start with him, they stare with him, they stagger with him, they share an inexpressible vitality in the air which emanates from this violent and capering satirist. Trabb's boy is among other things a boy; he has a physical rapture in hurling himself like a boomerang and in bouncing to the sky like a ball. It is just exactly in describing this quality that Dickens is Dickens and that no one else comes near him. No one feels in his bones that Felix Holt was strong as he feels in his bones that little Quilp was strong. No one can feel that even Rawdon Crawley's splendid smack across the face of Lord Steyne is quite so living and life-giving as the "kick after kick" which old Mr. Weller dealt the dancing and quivering Stiggins as he drove him towards the trough. This quality, whether expressed intellec-[203/204]tually or physically, is the profoundly popular and eternal quality in Dickens; it is the thing that no one else could do. This quality is the quality which has always given its continuous power and poetry to the common people everywhere. It is life; it is the joy of life felt by those who have nothing else but life. It is the thing that all aristocrats have always hated and dreaded in the people. And it is the thing which poor Pip really hates and dreads in Trabb's boy.

A great man of letters or any great artist is symbolic without knowing it. The things he describes are types because they are truths. Shakespeare may, or may not, have ever put it to himself that Richard the Second was a philosophical symbol; but all good criticism must necessarily see him so. It may be a reasonable question whether the artist should be allegorical. There can be no doubt among sane men that the critic should be allegorical. Spenser may have lost by being less realistic than Fielding. But any good criticism of *Tom Jones* must be as mystical as the *Faery Queen*. Hence it is unavoidable in speaking of a fine book like *Great Expectations* that we should give even to its unpretentious and realistic figures a certain massive mysticism. Pip is Pip, but he is also the well-meaning snob. And this is even more true of those two great figures in the tale which stand for the English democracy. For, indeed, the first and last word upon the English democracy is said in Joe Gargery and Trabb's boy. The actual English populace, as distinct from the French populace or the Scotch or Irish populace, may be said to lie between those two types. The first is the poor man who does not assert [204/205] himself at all, and the second is the poor man who asserts himself entirely with the weapon of sarcasm. The only way in which the English now ever rise in revolution is under the symbol and leadership of Trabb's boy. What pikes and shillelahs were to the Irish populace, what guns and barricades were to the French populace, that chaff is to the English populace. It is their weapon, the use of which they really understand. It is the one way in which they can make a rich man feel uncomfortable, and they use it very justifiably for all it is worth. If they do not cut off the heads of tyrants at least they sometimes do their best to make the tyrants lose their heads. The gutter boys of the great towns carry the art of personal criticism to so rich and delicate a degree that some well-dressed persons when they walk past a file of them feel as if they were walking past a row of omniscient critics or judges with a power of life and death. Here and there only is some ordinary human custom, some natural human pleasure suppressed in deference to the fastidiousness of the rich. But all the rich tremble before the fastidiousness of the poor.

Of the other type of democracy it is far more difficult to speak. It is always hard to speak of good things or good people, for in satisfying the soul they take away a certain spur to speech. Dickens was often called a sentimentalist. In one sense he sometimes was a sentimentalist. But if sentimentalism be held to mean something artificial or theatrical, then in the core and reality of his character Dickens was the very reverse of a sentimentalist. He seriously and definitely loved goodness. To see sincerity and charity satisfied [205/206] him like a meal. What some critics call his love of sweet stuff is really his love of plain beef and bread. Sometimes one is tempted to wish that in the long Dickens dinner the sweet courses could be left out; but this does not make the whole banquet other than a banquet singularly solid and simple. The critics complain of the sweet things, but not because they are so strong as to like simple things. They complain of the sweet things because they are so sophisticated as to like sour things; their tongues are tainted with the bitterness of absinthe. Yet because of the very simplicity of Dickens's moral tastes it is impossible to speak adequately of them; and Joe Gargery must stand as he stands in the book, a thing too obvious to be understood. But this may be said of him in one of his minor aspects, that he stands for a certain long-suffering in the English poor, a certain weary patience and politeness which almost breaks the heart. One cannot help wondering whether that great mass of silent virtue will ever achieve anything on this earth.   [end on 206]

PROBLEMS: G. K. Chesterton

1. Define the term "serene irony." In what way does it fit *Great Expectations*?
2. Chesterton says Dickens had too much vitality to be called cynical. What does he mean? Do you agree?
3. Discuss *Great Expectations* in terms of Chesterton's phrase: "the slow human surrender" [p. 197].
4. Explain the statement by Chesterton that the hero disappears in this novel [p. 197].
5. What does Chesterton add to our understanding of the psychology of Pip?
6. What does Chesterton mean when he speaks of the "real humanity" [p. 202] which idealists and philanthropists do not love, but which Dickens did love?
7. Define more clearly Chesterton's term, the "tremors of mankind" [p. 202], for which Dickens is said to have a quick eye.
8. Comment upon Chesterton's remarks on sentimentalism in Dickens.
9. Explain Chesterton's statement that Joe Gargery must stand as "a thing too obvious to be understood" [p. 206].

[On a Lower Level]*

by STEPHEN LEACOCK

. **.** . BUT EVEN *Great Expectations*, we may expect, could hardly have survived except for its cousinship to still greater.

The opening of the book—the hunted convict among the grave-stones—the churchyard on the marshes by the sea—a picture taken from the view from Gad's Hill—is as wonderful an opening as only Dickens could make. But the story is throughout on a lower level than the greater books, the characters less convincing, the nullities more null, the plot more involved, the fun, what there is of it, apt to sound forced and mechanical. One looks in vain in its pages for world-famous characters. The ending, unexpectedly altered from tragedy to relief, at the suggestion of Bulwer Lytton, is as unconvincing as any end must be when fitted onto the beginning of something else.   [238]

PROBLEMS: Stephen Leacock

1. Leacock finds the characters less convincing in *Great Expectations* than in Dickens's "greater books." Compare the views of other critics.
2. What is forced and mechanical about the fun in *Great Expectations*? Have other critics made this charge? Why, or why not?
3. By alleging that there are no world-famous characters in *Great Expectations*, does Leacock mean that the characterization in the novel is poor? If he does mean this, do you agree? If he doesn't mean that the characterization is poor, what does he mean by this allegation? Does his allegation damage the value of the novel?
4. What do you think Leacock means by "unconvincing" in his last sentence?

* From *Charles Dickens, His Life and Work* (Garden City, New York: Doubleday, Doran and Company, 1936), p. 238.

[A Tale of Adventure]*

by ERNEST A. BAKER

DICKENS NEVER hit upon a finer opening. Here begins the first act in a drama that reaches its logical conclusion on the final page, when years have elapsed, and a number of people have been implicated in the web of fate connecting Pip and the strange fugitive. The earlier auto-biography, *David Copperfield*, had been a straightforward history of childhood and young manhood, with a plot loosely tacked on. This time the plot is fundamental. That other had been in the main a domestic story, with more stirring episodes coming in, as they often do into the most commonplace life. *Great Expectations* is a novel of adventure, the sort of adventure that might well happen to a person who got himself mixed up with questionable characters, in such a spot as this, close to the convict-ships, or in what really were in those days the wilds of London. Pip has narrow [307/308] escapes, and goes through many racking experiences; he has to be prepared for acts of violence, and before the end his manhood is put to the proof in a way unusual in a novel by Dickens. All this is related with a force and terseness equal to that of the initial scene. On the present occasion, Dickens had calculated his effects beforehand, and he secured them without beating about the bush, only once or twice having to fall back upon his regular expedient, barefaced coincidence. The drama has, moreover, what had been a rarity if not quite unexampled in Dickens, an inner side, in the effect of the great expectations and the subsequent contacts with people and events upon the character of Pip. He grows and changes and develops, which cannot be said without many qualifications of any single one in the previous novels. True, David

* From *The History of the English Novel* (London, Witherby, 1936, 10 vols.), vol. 7, pp. 307–313.

37

Copperfield also grew up, and learned from experience how to face a complicated world. But in *David Copperfield* it was a sensitive boy's impressions of a crowd of extraordinary fellow-beings that were so absorbing; David himself left a pleasant but not a very memorable impression.

In *Great Expectations*, those Pip meets with are hardly less wonderful; but Pip himself is interesting, and still more interesting are the ordeals through which he arrives at self-knowledge, realizes the value of what he has slighted in Joe Gargery and Biddy, and puts himself right at last with those faithful friends. It is Dickens's one serious study of the growth of personality; and, though he lets Pip tell the story, he manages with great skill to bring out the true significance and the humour of the strange situations, without showing his own hand, and, notably, without the heavy moralizing which Thackeray put in the mouth of his imaginary autobiographer in *Lovel the Widower*, which appeared this same year.[1] There was much of the same vein of comedy in the tale of David's change of circumstances. Both boys are rescued from poverty, and find themselves in unfamiliar spheres. Both have their [308/309] troubles with manners and deportment. Sitting side by side with the nice boys at Dr Strong's school, David cannot forget that his recent associates were the street urchins, Mick Walker and Mealy Potatoes; and, when years later he writes his reminiscences, he can see the humour of his shyness and confusion at the visit to the Steerforths, how he blushed when the chambermaid brought him his hot water, and was a mere worm in the presence of Littimer, that superfine gentleman's gentleman. But Pip's agonies are much more trying. All the old friends and townsfolk who knew him as the poor boy in the blacksmith's shop have to be duly impressed with the fact that he is now a young gentleman with expectations. He has to flabbergast the old humbug Pumblechook, and show an imperturbable face to the scurrilous Trabb's boy's chaff.

[1] It had come out first in the *Cornhill Magazine*. Some misguided people would make out *Great Expectations* to be a didactic story, whilst others regard it as a satire on snobbishness, in Pip's pretences and uppishness and subsequent humiliations. A moral can, of course, be extracted from almost any story that is tolerably true to life. But Dickens kept clear more than usual here of the temptations to moralize.

Words cannot state the amount of aggravation and injury wreaked upon me by Trabb's boy, when, passing abreast of me, he pulled up his shirt-collar, twined his side-hair, stuck an arm akimbo, and smirked extravagantly by, wriggling his elbows and body, and drawling to his attendant, "Don't know yah, don't know yah, pon my soul don't know yah!"

And Pip is not David. His airs of dignity and condescension make him an easier prey to ridicule, and are the cause of untold anguish when he discovers the odious source of all his great expectations.

At this point the comedy grows serious; and Pip has the shock of his life to find that the rich benefactor is none other than the returned convict, whom he has been patronizing in his genteel chambers and lecturing with priggish superiority. Happily, Magwitch is not over-sensitive, and Pip fights down his abhorrence, comes gradually even to sympathize with the hunted wretch, and at last, cheerfully and with no thought of himself, faces considerable risk in trying to get him out of the country. Nothing Dickens had previously written showed him capable of revealing with such accuracy and delicacy all that went on in Pip's mind, from that midnight interview when Magwitch made himself known, to the terrible moment when Pip and the rest of the boat's crew are flung into the water, and [309/310] presently he finds himself seated beside the recaptured man, who is on the way back to prison and the gallows.

For now my repugnance to him had all melted away, and in the hunted, wounded, shackled creature who held my hand in his, I only saw a man who had meant to be my benefactor, and who had felt affectionately, gratefully, and generously, towards me with great constancy through a series of years. I only saw in him a much better man than I had been to Joe.

For Pip is not yet out of his predicaments. He still has to put himself right with Joe Gargery and Biddy. The great expectations have melted away, and left him resigned; but he cannot rest till he has wiped out his disloyalty to the old friend whose simple-heartedness and greatness of spirit have never even been conscious of it. The end Dickens had in mind for a story in which comedy and tragedy were so closely mixed was not the "happy ever after" which he was persuaded to substitute by Bulwer-Lytton. Pip and Joe were to be the same frank and loving old friends again, as the child and man had been at the beginning, and Pip was to be reconciled to his baffled hopes and to the lot he had earned. That was the right note. Marrying him to Estella after all was a conclusion for which Dickens had not prepared, by the lucid baring of motive which he applied to the other chief characters.

It is remarkable how the characters in *Great Expectations* seem to fall into two divisions, according to their attitude towards Pip: the malignant and the friendly. It is further evidence of Dickens's careful dramatic planning. On the one side, the two half-realized fantasies, Miss Havisham and Estella, stand at the head. It would be rash to pronounce them impossible; Dickens may even have known two such anomalous beings. But he failed to explain and make them credible; they might not have looked so unreal had he gone a little deeper. The difficulty in accepting Miss Havisham is that the blow which unhinged her mind is so lightly and casually intimated. If Dickens comprehended her, she is as great a strain as Rosa Dartle on the comprehension of the reader. And Estella, whom she formed to avenge her on the other sex, is just [310/311] as artificial—a new sort of minx, as impenetrable to the reader as to the unfortunate Pip.[1]

Among the other thorns in the flesh to Pip are that violent governing female, his sister, Mrs Joe; "bullying old Pumblechook," last avatar of the soul of Pecksniff and Chadband, who poses as the boy's deeply injured patron; Mr Wopsle, playing George Barnwell, and identifying Pip with that "ferocious and maudlin" scapegrace; Sarah Pocket, and the rest of the snobs who rage at the boy's elevation; Drummle the "Spider"; and, last not least, his relentless persecutor, Trabb's boy. Orlick and Compeyson, the two murderous ruffians, are enemies of a more fearful brand. All the others who matter much go into the opposite corps. Joe and Biddy come first, from every point of view, and then the unfortunate Magwitch, as chief agent in the strange complication of destinies. Magwitch, it should be noted, in spite of some discrepancies, is no mere automaton; as a study of the operations of a

---

[1] Wright (pp. 298–299) identifies Estella (whose name is said to be manufactured out of the first syllables (*sic*) of the name Ellen Lawless Ternan) with Miss Ternan, supposed to have been just as impenetrable to Dickens.

primitive mind he is not inferior to Joe Gargery. The men of law are the next in importance. Jaggers is a powerful creation; as Wemmick says, "There's only one Jaggers." His terrible clairvoyance! The way he turns you inside out!

> If anybody wouldn't make an admission, he said, "I'll have it out of you!" and if anybody made an admission, he said, "Now I have got you!" The magistrates shivered under a single bite of his finger. Thieves and thief-takers hung in dread rapture on his words, and shrank when a hair of his eyebrows turned in their direction.

It is as daring a figure as Dickens ever imagined, but, like the rest, justified by results. The fault with Wemmick is that he is made too deliberately quaint; he is almost a museum specimen, with his ever-lasting injunction, "Get hold of portable property"; the little castellated mansion where he lives with his Aged P., and the famous "Halloa! Here's a church! Let's go in!" "Here's Miss Skiffins! Let's have [311/312] a wedding." Of the other dramatis personae, hardly one is a mere supernumerary; certainly not that hopeful young fellow, Herbert Pocket, who makes such a practical job of turning Pip into a gentleman; nor the charming Clara, whom he marries. Her father, old Bill Barley, is neutral, an invisible though a very audible character, in his room upstairs, his grog ready mixed in a little tub on the table, and his voice heard at intervals hoarsely growling the refrain, in which Pip says, "I substitute good wishes for something quite the reverse":

> "Ahoy! Bless your eyes, here's old Bill Barley . . . old Bill Barley on the flat of his back, by the Lord. Lying on the flat of his back, like a drifting old dead flounder, here's your old Bill Barley, bless your eyes. Ahoy! Bless you."

But the best of the lot, and the one who would have redeemed a duller story than Dickens ever wrote, is the man with the innocent soul of a child, Joe Gargery, that "worthy, worthy man," as Biddy calls him. Dickens loved integrity and reverenced the beauty of un-selfishness and good-will, and was sometimes wise enough to see that to pay them due honour was better than any formal poetic justice. Never was there a truer example of what has been called a "Nature's gentleman." There is a veritable sublimity in such goodness of heart and utter selflessness, such sweetness of disposition, and humility combined with a proud self-respect. It sounds superhuman. But Joe is credible; the man lives.

"Pip, dear old chap, life is made of ever so many partings welded together, as I may say, and one man's a blacksmith, and one's a whitesmith, and one's a goldsmith, and one's a coppersmith. Divisions among such must come, and must be met as they come. If there's been any fault to-day at all, it's mine. You and me is not two figures to be together in London; nor yet anywheres else but what is private, and beknown, and understood among friends. It ain't that I am proud, but that I want to be right, as you shall never see me no more in these clothes. I'm wrong out of the forge, the kitchen, or off th' meshes. You won't find half so much fault in me if, supposing as you should ever wish to see me, you come and put your head [312/313] in at the forge window and see Joe the blacksmith, there, at the old anvil, in the old burnt apron, sticking to the old work. I'm awful dull, but I hope I've beat out something nigh the rights of this at last. And so God bless you, dear old Pip, old chap, God bless you!"

I had not been mistaken in my fancy that there was a simple dignity in him. The fashion of his dress could no more come in its way when he spoke these words, than it could come in its way in Heaven. He touched me gently on the forehead, and went out. As soon as I could recover myself sufficiently, I hurried out after him and looked for him in the neighbouring streets; but he was gone.

This is not quoted as an example of Joe's gift of simple English, so elemental that it seems to consist of things rather than mere words. It is his one long-winded speech, but it happens to express his homely philosophy. Great Expectations, in comparison with Dickens's besetting carelessness, is a masterpiece of verbal art, whether in narrative and description or in the dialogue. It is not more than half as long as his average novel; and whatever else this thriftiness indicates, it is a sign that Dickens kept his characters in their place, and did not let them display themselves for the sake of display, as was too often his wont, in the novel next to follow, for instance. He evidently saw his ending from the very first, and from time to time put in little hints of what was in store; as when Pip tells Miss Havisham that he only knows how to play beggar my neighbour, and she bids Estella, "Beggar him." It is almost as clear a warning as the later injunction, "Love her, love her, love her!" which is again as ominous as the notice Pip receives when there are other dangers about, "Don't go home!" The presentiments and intuitions, for instance, which somehow convince Pip that Jaggers's housekeeper is Estella's mother, and that her father is Magwitch, are among the links scattered all over the story which hold it firmly together. One thing they make clear and definite, that Estella was meant to be his bane and not his blessing: the altered ending falsified everything.   [end on 313]

PROBLEMS: Ernest A. Baker

1. Baker says that only once or twice does Dickens have to fall back on "barefaced coincidence" in *Great Expectations*. What does Baker mean by "barefaced coincidence"? Why should Dickens have to fall back on coincidence at all?

2. Defend this statement by Baker: "though he [Dickens] lets Pip tell the story, he manages with great skill to bring out the true significance and the humour of the strange situations, without showing his own hand . . ."

3. Do you agree with Baker about what changes take place in Pip and the causes for them? Can you name other critics who agree with Baker?

4. Why does Baker find the characterization of Miss Havisham inadequate? Do you find it inadequate too?

5. Baker claims that Estella is an artificial character. What do you think?

6. If Magwitch is "no mere automaton," what is he?

7. Why does Baker call Jaggers "a powerful creation"?

8. State the case for Wemmick's being more than a "quaint" character.

9. Baker calls Joe Gargery "the best of the lot." What is the fascination Joe has for so many critics? What is the sublimity and credibility of Joe?

10. Explain in detail Baker's statement that *Great Expectations* is a "masterpiece of verbal art."

11. "The altered ending falsified everything," says Baker. But not all critics agree with him. Weigh the pros and cons of the endings, and decide which ending is better.

[Pip's Acquired "Culture"]*

by Humphry House

Dickens was attempting to define within the middle classes some such boundary as he had already accepted in the lower between the respectable and the low. In the last resort he shared Magwitch's belief that money and education can make a 'gentleman', that birth and tradition count for little or nothing in the formation of style. The final wonder of *Great Expectations* is that in spite of all Pip's neglect of Joe and coldness towards Biddy and all the remorse and self-recrimination that they caused him, he is made to appear at the end of it all a really better person than he was at the beginning. It is a remarkable achievement to have kept the reader's sympathy throughout a snob's progress. The book is the clearest artistic triumph of the Victorian bourgeoisie on its own special ground. The expectations lose their greatness, and Pip is saved from the grosser dangers of wealth; but by the end he has gained a wider and deeper knowledge of life, he is less rough, better spoken, better read, better mannered; he has friends as various as Herbert Pocket, Jaggers, and Wemmick; he has earned in his business abroad enough to pay his debts, he has become third partner in a firm that 'had a good name, and worked for its profits, and did very well'. Who is to say that these are not advantages? Certainly not Dickens. But he shirks the implications of the reconciliation with Joe and Biddy: there is one emotional scene with friendliness all round, which shows that in spite of his new accent and new manners Pip is the same decent little fellow after all: but what if he had had no Herbert to fall back on, and had been forced to build his fortunes again from scratch in the old village with Gargerys and Wopsles? Dickens does not face this: he

* From *The Dickens World* (Oxford, Oxford University Press, 1941), pp. 156–160. Reprinted by permission of the Oxford University Press, London, publishers.

takes Pip's new class position as established, and whisks him off to the East, where gentlemen grow like mushrooms. Yet we do not feel [156/157] that this is artistically wrong, as the final marriage to Estella is wrong:[1] for the book is the sincere, uncritical expression of a time when the whole class-drift was upwards and there was no reason to suppose that it would ever stop being so. The social ideals of Pip and Magwitch differ only in taste. Though Pip has shuddered at the convict for being coarse and low, he consoles him on his death-bed with the very thought that first fired and then kept alive his own love for Estella: 'You had a child. . . . She is a lady and very beautiful.'

Here is the story allegorized by Mr. Jackson, writing as a Marxist:

Self-satisfied, mid-Victorian, British society buoyed itself up with as great 'expectations' of future wealth and glory as did poor, deluded Pip. If it had but known, its means of ostentation came from a source (the labour of the depressed and exploited masses) to which it would have been as shocked to acknowledge indebtedness as Pip was to find he owed all his acquired gentility to the patronage of a transported felon. Magwitch differed little from the uncouth monster which respectable society envisaged to itself as the typical 'labouring man'. And in literal truth, good, respectable society owed as much to these working men, and was as little aware of it, as was Pip of the source of his advantages. And respectable society is as little grateful as Pip, whenever the truth is revealed.

This would be very plausible if only the rest of the class distinctions in the novel were what Mr. Jackson makes them out to be:

Such class-antagonism as there is in *Great Expectations* is not that between aristo-crats (as such) and common people, but that between, on the one side, the 'gentlemen' (who are for one reason or another either crazily vengeful or callously [157/158] cold-hearted and corrupt) and with them their sycophants and attendant slum-hooligans and on the other, the honest, working section of the population.

Applied in detail this means Bentley Drummle, Compeyson, and Pumblechook on one side, with Joe, Biddy, Matthew and Herbert Pocket, Jaggers, and Wemmick all lumped together on the other.

[1] The ending was altered to suit Bulwer Lytton, but only 'from and after Pip's return to Joe's, and finding his little likeness there'. Pip's success abroad was thus in the original scheme (Forster, Bk. IX, Chapter III).

This is virtually to say that in the end class distinctions are identical with moral distinctions, without even being particularly nice about morals; it is to ignore all the facts of class difference that Dickens was so subtly analysing. It is in things like Estella's early treatment of Pip, Pip's first weeks with Herbert, Jaggers's treatment of Estella's mother, and the behaviour of Trabb's boy, that these real differences are to be found.

Chesterton professed to find in Trabb's boy the last word upon the triumphant revolutionary sarcasm of the English democracy; you might almost as well find the ultimate English democrat in old Orlick, the soured 'hand' turning to crime because of his inferior status, whom Mr. Jackson just leaves as a 'blackguard'—a man who in another novel might well have been the leader of a no-Popery mob or of physical-force Chartists. The assault of Trabb's boy, which brings Pip's class-consciousness to a head, is more personal than political: Dickens doesn't mean that good clothes are worse than bad or that they are intrinsically funny and that the class that wears them is doomed to die of jeers. . . . [158/159] As things were he [Trabb's boy] was a good pin to prick Pip's conceit; but if he himself had come into a fortune, he would have been just as nasty about it as Pip in his own way; and his way might have been worse.

Great Expectations is the perfect expression of a phase of English society: it is a statement, to be taken as it stands, of what money can do, good and bad; of how it can change and make distinctions of class; how it can pervert virtue, sweeten manners, open up new fields of enjoyment and suspicion. The mood of the book belongs not to the imaginary date of its plot, but to the time in which it was written; for the unquestioned assumptions that Pip can be transformed by money and the minor graces it can buy, and that the loss of one fortune can be repaired on the strength of incidental gains in voice and friends, were only possible in a country secure in its internal economy, with expanding markets abroad: this could hardly be said of England in the 'twenties and 'thirties.

Pip's acquired 'culture' was an entirely bourgeois thing: it came to little more than accent, table manners, and clothes. In these respects a country gentleman with an estate in a remoter part of England would probably have been, even at Queen Victoria's accession, more like the neighbouring farmers than like Mr. Dombey. The process of diffusing standard 'educated', London and Home Counties, speech as the norm expected of a gentleman was by no means complete: its rapid continuance through the Dickens period was an essential part of the increasing social uniformity between the middle and upper classes, helped on by the development of the 'public' schools.[1]   [159/160]

We are told that Pip 'read' a great deal, and that he enjoyed it; but we do not know what he read, or how it affected his mind, or what kind of pleasures he got from it. He knew enough about Shakespeare and acting to realize that Mr. Wopsle turned Waldengarver was ridiculous; but what other delights he found in theatre-going in his prosperous days we are left to judge for ourselves; painting and music certainly had no large part in his life. People like Pip, Herbert Pocket, and Traddles have no culture but domestic comfort and moral decency. They are sensitive, lovable, and intelligent, but their normal activities are entirely limited to a profession and a fireside. When one of their kind extends his activities beyond this range it is in the direction of 'social work', and even that is likely to be governed by his profession, as Allan Woodcourt is a good doctor, and Mr. Milvey a good parson. David Copperfield's other activity is to write novels like *Great Expectations* and *David Copperfield*: so we come full circle.   [end on 160]

PROBLEMS: Humphry House

1. How does House account for the development of Pip's improved character?
2. Formulate an answer to House's question about Pip [bottom of page 156].
3. "The social ideals of Pip and Magwitch differ only in taste" [p. 157]. Write a careful evaluation of this statement.

[1] It is interesting that there is no description of such a school anywhere in Dickens, though he described so many different kinds of private school, and sent his own sons to Eton. The extension of the term 'public school' to an increasing number of boarding schools was a process of the 'forties. (See, for instance, McCulloch's *Account of the British Empire*, 3rd. ed., 1847, Vol. II, p. 329.) It was, of course, the most influential expression of the 'gentleman' idea.

4. Contrast T. A. Jackson's interpretation of the theme of *Great Expectations* with the interpretations of other critics.
5. What quarrel with Chesterton's discussion of Trabb's boy does House offer?
6. Elaborate on House's opinions of *Great Expectations* as a social novel.

[The Ruined Garden]*

by EDGAR JOHNSON

So, WITH the tacked-on addition of a belated marriage to Estella, end Pip's "great expectations." Surely the entire drift of the story reveals how clearly Dickens had at last "come to see that making his living by sticking labels on blacking bottles and rubbing shoulders with boys who were not gentlemen, was as little shameful as being the genteel apprentice in the office of Mr. Spenlow, or the shorthand writer recording the unending twaddle of the House of Commons and its overflow of electioneering bunk on the hustings of all the Eatans-wills in the country."[50a]

In that curious and brilliant novel, *Evan Harrington*, George Meredith does penance for his own snobbery in concealing the fact that he came of a family of naval outfitting tailors in Portsmouth. Paying fictional tribute to the character of his grandfather, portrayed as "the great Mel," the fox-hunting tailor, the story heaps witty scorn on the Countess de Salazar and the other daughters who love the old man and yet hide their relationship to him. *Great Expectations* is Dickens's penance for his subservience to false values. The blacksmith and "the taint of prison and crime"[51] which have so mortified Pip, and of which he comes to feel a remorseful humiliation at ever having been [988/989] ashamed, are both more humbling to genteel thought than the blacking warehouse and the debtors' prison. "The reappearance

---

* From Edgar Johnson, *Charles Dickens: His Tragedy and Triumph* (New York, Simon and Schuster, 1952), 2 vols., vol. 2, pp. 988–994. Copyright, 1952, by Edgar Johnson. Reprinted by permission of Simon & Schuster, Inc.

[50a] Shaw, Introduction to *Great Expectations*. [Footnotes accompanying this selection originally appeared on p. lxxxii.]

[51] G.E., XXXII, 261. [p. 222 in the Chandler Edition].

of Mr. Dickens in the character of a blacksmith's boy," as Shaw remarks, "may be regarded as an apology to Mealy Potatoes."[52]

There is a layer of criticism, however, in *Great Expectations* still deeper than this personal triumph over false social values. It pierces to the very core of the leisure-class ideal that lurks in the heart of a pecuniary society. This is symbolized in Pip's dream of becoming a gentleman living in decorative grandeur on money he has done nothing to earn, supported entirely by the labors of others. It was the dream of nineteenth-century society, willing to base its hopes of comfort and ostentation on the toil of the laboring classes. Pip's "great expectations" were the great expectations of Victorian society, visions of a parastic opulence of future wealth and glory, a materialistic paradise of walnut, plush, gilt mirrors, and heavy dinners. The aim of the fashionable world was an eternal and luxurious ease, the goal of the middle-class businessman to retire to a surburban villa on a fortune.

Although Dickens never expected to be exempt from work himself, and worked hard all his life, earlier in his career he had accepted this ideal. There is no suggestion that Mr. Winkle, Mr. Tupman, or Mr. Snodgrass need ever think of doing anything for a living. Mr. Brownlow and Mr. Grimwig have no occupations. At the close of *Nicholas Nickleby*, Nicholas retires to a country villa and lives upon his share from the profits of the Cheeryble business which others carry on. Little Nell's grandfather sounds the first warning note against the false dream of gaining a luxury one has not earned. Martin Chuzzlewit, after a few abortive efforts to make a living, returns to living on his grandfather. Mr. Dombey leaves to Mr. Carker and a host of subordinates almost all the management of the enterprise from which he derives his wealth. Even the benevolent Mr. Jarndyce seems to be merely a man of property, although Richard Carstone now strikes another warning note against depending upon "expectations" instead of making oneself of use to the world. Stephen Blackpool in *Hard Times*, and Arthur Clennam in *Little Dorrit*, represent the emergence of a new kind of hero in Dickens's novels: the earnest, sober, industrious worker who contributes his share to the efforts of the world.

[52] Shaw, Introduction to *Great Expectations*.

But Pip has no occupation and no ideal save that of an empty good form. He and the "Finches of the Grove,"[53] the club of young men [989/990] of leisure to which he belongs, do nothing but spend money, play cards, drink toasts, buy elaborate wardrobes, drive horses, and go to the theater. They have no culture, no interest in the arts, in music, in the world of reflective thought. Pip "reads" with his tutor and has books on his shelves, but we never learn what he reads or perceive that it has had any effect on him. He has no philosophy, only a set of conventions. The virtues that ultimately save him are mainly those that he unconsciously absorbed from Joe in his childhood. His return to a life of modest usefulness is a repudiation of the ideal of living by the sweat of someone else's brow. And Dickens's analysis of the frivolity, falseness, emptiness, loss of honor, loss of manhood, and sense of futility that the acceptance of that ideal imposed upon Pip is a measure of the rottenness and corruption he now found in a society dominated by it. The system of that society and its grandiose material dreams, he realizes, involve a cheapening, a distortion, a denial of human values.

From another angle, in the portrayal of the lawyer Jaggers, *Great Expectations* conveys the same judgment. It is impossible not to see in him, T. A. Jackson points out, "Dickens' deepening sense that success in business in the bourgeois world can be won only at the expense of everything nobly generous, elevating, sympathetic, and humane."[54] Mr. Jaggers specializes in representing accused criminals, whose unsavory cases he handles with the most unscrupulous and triumphant skill. But with the departure of every felonious visitor he goes to a closet and cleans his hands with scented soap, as if he were washing off the client. On one occasion, Pip remarks, "he seemed to have been engaged on a case of a darker complexion than usual, for we found him with his head butted into this closet, not only washing his hands, but laving his face and gargling his throat. And even when he had done all that, and had gone all round the jack-towel, he took out his penknife and scraped the case out of his nails before he put his coat on."[55]

---

[53] *G.E.*, xxxiv, 271. [p. 230 in the Chandler Edition].
[54] Jackson, *Progress of a Radical*, 196.
[55] *G.E.*, xxvi, 207. [p. 177 in the Chandler Edition].

Though Mr. Jaggers is a highly successful and respected professional man, his own sense of the necessities his life imposes on him is one of degradation and pollution. Could there be a clearer symbolic suggestion that much of the business of such a society is dirty business?

Its consequence is almost to force upon a man of any sensitivity a dual personality, a division and antagonism between the selfish-acquisitive and all that is warmly human. Mr. Jaggers's clerk Wem-[990/991]mick dwells in the kindest domestic affection at Walworth with his deaf and ancient father, "the aged parent,"[56] in a little wooden villa with a narrow moat, a plank drawbridge, a miniature cannon which he fires at night, and a small Gothic entrance door. But all this feeling and imagination he keeps for his home; in the office his mouth is a dry slit like a mailbox, he is dead against Pip's desire to serve his friend Herbert, and harps on the dominant necessity of acquiring "portable property."[57] Only at home will he tell Pip, "This is devilish good of you."[58] "Walworth is one place," he says, "and this office is another."[59]

Both for Wemmick and for Mr. Jaggers, then, their office in Little Britain is a kind of prison in which they lock up their better selves and subdue them to the world of venality. Thus the symbolism of *Great Expectations* develops that of *Little Dorrit* and of *A Tale of Two Cities*. The Marshalsea and Mrs. Clennam in the dark house of greed and Mr. Merdle in the glittering mansion of speculation and the world of "society" are all immured in the same vast outer dungeon of imprisoning ideas. Darnay and Carton are the jailed victims of revenge for past deeds of exploitation and cruelty, and Dr. Manette is driven mad in the Bastille, broken and goaded to a destroying curse by that past injustice. Now, in this last story of the three, Jaggers, Wemmick, Magwitch, Pip, are under like shadows of prison walls; and Miss Havisham, her heart broken by a rapacious adventurer, creates in Estella a living curse, and, surrounded by greedy relatives, wanders self-incarcerated in her dark, decaying house. And intertwined like an iron

---

[56] Ibid., xxv, 202, 203, 204. [p. 172 f. in the Chandler Edition]
[57] Ibid., xxxvi, 289. [p. 246 in the Chandler Edition]
[58] Ibid., xxxvii, 294. [p. 250 in the Chandler Edition]
[59] Ibid., xxxvi, 289. [p. 246 in the Chandler Edition]

chain with all of these is Pip's despairing and disillusioned obsession with Estella, the darkest emotional imprisonment of them all.

It is inevitable that we should associate Pip's helpless enslavement to Estella with Dickens's desperate passion for Ellen Lawless Ternan. The very name "Estella" seems a kind of lawless anagram upon some of the syllables and initials of Ellen's name. The tone of Dickens's unhappy letters to Collins and Forster during all the time between the last night of *The Frozen Deep* and the time of the separation discloses an entirely new intensity of personal misery far exceeding the restlessness of years before. His insistence that since that last night he had "never known a moment's peace or content" centers his distress unmistakably not on the "domestic unhappiness" alone but on a person: "never was a man so seized and rended by one Spirit."[60] His allusion [991/992] in a letter to Mrs. Watson to "the princess I adore—you have no idea how intensely I love her!"[61] points in the same direction, like the desire he there expresses to go "climbing after her, sword in hand," and either win her "or be killed." The words are a kind of desperate playing with his frustration, a half unveiling disguised in ambiguity. And later still there is the black mingling of fear and bitterness and rage in his outburst about the policeman endeavoring to enact the role of a go-between in Berners Street.

With these things must be seen the unprecedently somber hues in which Dickens depicts Pip's feeling for Estella. Never before had he portrayed a man's love for a woman with such emotional depth or revealed its desperation of compulsive suffering. Dolly Varden's capriciousness is a childish coquetry beside Estella's cold obduracy. The unhappiness that breathes in Dickens's youthful letters to Maria Beadnell is the suffering of a boy, whereas Pip's is the stark misery of a man. David Copperfield's heartache for Dora Spenlow is an iridescent dream-grief to this agonized nightmare-reality. Only with Philip Carey's dreadful servitude to the pallid indifference of the sluttish Mildred, in *Of Human Bondage*, or, in Proust's masterpiece, with Swann's craving for Odette, is there anything like Pip's subjection to

---

[60] *Let.*, III, 14, Collins. 3/21/58.
[61] Hunt. MS., Dickens to Mrs. Watson, 12/7/57.

Estella's queenly and torturing disregard. Pip's love is without tenderness, without illusion; it reveals no desire to confer happiness upon the beloved; it is all self-absorbed need. Where in all his past career as a novelist had Dickens painted such passions and in what abyss of personal agony had he learned them?

In love, too, then, Pip's "great expectations," like Dickens's own, have been disappointed and deceived, and ideally the story should have ended on that loss, as Dickens originally planned. Pip's desire for Estella is as selfish as his desire to be a gentleman, not at all the desire to give, only the desire to receive. It is the culminating symbol and the crowning indictment of a society dedicated to selfish ends. It is a bitter revelation of the emptiness of its values and of the distortions they inflict upon all generous feeling, even upon the need to love and to be loved. Pip is not all selfish; he is capable both of generosity and of love. Indeed, at the end he has learned from his experience, learned to work, learned to love, learned to think for others.

Both as art and as psychology it was poor counsel that Lytton gave in urging that the shaping of a lifetime in Estella be miraculously un- [992/993]done. Save for this, though, *Great Expectations* is the most perfectly constructed and perfectly written of all Dickens's works. It should close with that misty moonlight scene in Miss Havisham's ruined garden, but, as Shaw suggests, with Pip and Estella then bidding each other a chastened farewell and Pip saying, "Since that parting I have been able to think of her without the old unhappiness; but I have never tried to see her again, and I know I never shall."[62]

In spite of its theme of disillusion *Great Expectations* is not in its pervading atmosphere a melancholy book. Not merely does it move to an ending of serene and twilight peace, but there are many scenes of high-spirited enjoyment and of the comic gusto Dickens had always been able to command even in the midst of his deepest despair. There is the child Pip's flight into a series of fantastic whoppers when Uncle Pumblechook is badgering him to tell what happened at his first visit to Miss Havisham's and he invents a picture of Miss Havisham sitting in a black velvet coach having cake and wine on gold plates while

[62] Shaw, Introduction to *Great Expectations*.

they feed veal cutlets from a silver basket to four large dogs, wave flags, and shout hurrahs.[63] There is Mr. Wopsle's famous performance of *Hamlet*, with the Danish nobility represented by "a noble boy in the wash-leather boots of a gigantic ancestor, a venerable Peer with a dirty face, who seemed to have risen from the people late in life, and the Danish chivalry with a comb in its hair and a pair of white silk legs presenting on the whole a feminine appearance," and the church in the graveyard scene resembling a "small ecclesiastical wash-house."[64] There is Trabb's boy imitating Pip's progress down the High Street by pulling up his shirt collar, twining his side hair, sticking an arm akimbo, smirking extravagantly, and drawling, "Don't know yah, don't know yah, 'pon my soul don't know yah!"[65] There is Joe's description of how the robbers looted Pumblechook's shop: "and they drinked his wine, and they partook of his wittles, and they slapped his face, and they pulled his nose, and they tied him up to his bedpust, and they giv' him a dozen, and they stuffed his mouth full of flowering annuals to perwent his crying out."[66]

But these joyous moments do not undermine the predominant seriousness of *Great Expectations* and its theme. As Pip and Estella, with linked hands, leave that misty and forlorn garden of their childhood they are reminiscent of the parents of humanity exiled, but not utterly without hope, from another Garden: [993/994]

> *The world was all before them, where to choose*
> *Their place of rest, and Providence their guide.*
> *They hand in hand, with wandering steps and slow,*
> *Through Eden took their solitary way.*[67]   [end on 994]

PROBLEMS: Edgar Johnson

1. What evidences are there in *Great Expectations* that Pip's great expectations are like those of Victorian society? If they are alike,

[63] G. E., IX, 63–4. [pp. 56–57 in the Chandler Edition]
[64] Ibid., XXXI, 251, 252. [pp. 213, 215 in the Chandler Edition]
[65] Ibid., XXX, 243. [p. 207 in the Chandler Edition]
[66] Ibid., LVII, 458. [p. 396 in the Chandler Edition]
[67] Milton, *Paradise Lost*, XII, 646–9.

is Dickens attacking Pip, Victorian society, both, or something else?

2. Is it true, as Johnson says [page 989], that Pip has "no occupation and no ideal save that of an empty good form"? Has anyone in the novel an ideal of work? What reflection does the demonstration of attitudes toward work cast on Dickens's reasons for writing the novel?

3. When Johnson says [page 990] that the Finches of the Grove have no culture, what does he mean by "culture"? What is the importance of Johnson's comments on culture in *Great Expectations*?

4. As a young man in training to be a gentleman, Pip has no philosophy, says Johnson. Does Pip have a philosophy by the end of the novel? Does he have even a point of view? Has he at least learned anything? Has he changed? What do critics say about the development of Pip's character?

5. Drawing on the early events of Pip's life, define the "virtues" which he "unconsciously absorbed from Joe in his childhood" [p. 990]. Give specific references.

6. What are the human values that Pip's "society" seems to deny?

7. Expand Johnson's comments on the relationship of Wemmick's dual life to the social criticism in *Great Expectations*.

8. Fit Biddy and Joe into Johnson's comments on love [p. 992].

9. How does the comic spirit of *Great Expectations* save the novel from being melancholy?

10. What does Johnson imply about the parallel between *Great Expectations* and *Paradise Lost* [pages 993–994]?

On *Great Expectations*[*]

by Dorothy Van Ghent

"The distinguishing quality of Dickens's people," says V. S. Pritchett, is that they are solitaries. They are people caught living in a world of their own. They soliloquize in it. They do not talk to one another; they talk to themselves. The pressure of society has created fits of twitching in mind and speech, and fantasies in the soul . . . The solitariness of people is paralleled by the solitariness of things. Fog operates as a separate presence, houses quietly rot or boisterously prosper on their own . . . Cloisterham believes itself more important than the world at large, the Law sports like some stale and dilapidated circus across human lives. Philanthropy attacks people like a humor or an observable germ. The people and the things of Dickens are all out of touch and out of hearing of each other, each conducting its own inner monologue, grandiloquent or dismaying. By this dissociation Dickens brings to us something of the fright of childhood . . . [1]

Some of the most wonderful scenes in *Great Expectations* are those in which people, presumably in the act of conversation, raptly soliloquize; and Dickens' technique, in these cases, is usually to give the soliloquizer a fantastic private language as unadapted to mutual understanding as a species of pig Latin. Witness Mr. Jaggers' interview with Joe Gargery, in which the dignified lawyer attempts to compensate Joe financially for his part in Pip's upbringing, and Joe swings on him with unintelligible pugilistic jargon.

"Which I meantersay . . . that if you come into my place bullbaiting and badgering me, come out! Which I meantersay as sech if you're a man, come

* From *The English Novel: Form and Function*, by Dorothy Van Ghent. Copyright © 1953 by Dorothy Van Ghent. Reprinted by permission of Holt, Rinehart and Winston, Inc., publishers. New York (1953). Pages 125–138.
[1] *The Living Novel* (New York: Reynal & Hitchcock, 1947), p. 88.

on ! Which I meantersay that what I say, I meantersay and stand or fall by !"
                                                                    [125/126]

Or Miss Havisham's interview with Joe over the question of Pip's wages; for each question she asks him, Joe persists in addressing his reply to Pip rather than herself, and his replies have not the remotest relation to the questions. Sometimes, by sheer repetition of a phrase, the words a character uses will assume the frenzied rotary unintelligibility of an idiot's obsession, as does Mrs. Joe's "Be grateful to them which brought you up by hand," or Pumblechook's mincing "May I?—May I?" The minimal uses of language as an instrument of communication and intellectual development are symbolized by Pip's progress in the school kept by Mr. Wopsle's great-aunt, where the summit of his education consists in his copying a large Old-English "D," which he assumes to be the design for a belt buckle; and by Joe's pleasure in the art of reading, which enables him to find three "J's" and three "O's" and three 'J-O, Joes" in a piece of script.

"Give me [he says] a good book, or a good newspaper, and sit me down afore a good fire, and I ask no better. Lord ! when you *do* come to a J and a O, and says you, 'Here, at last, is a J-O, Joe,' how interesting reading is !"

There is, perhaps, no purer expression of solipsism in literature. The cultivation of the peculiar Dickensian values of language reaches its apogee when the convict Magwitch, with a benefactor's proud delight, asks Pip to read to him from a book in a foreign language, of which he understands no syllable.

From *Don Quixote* on, the novels that we have read in this series of studies have frequently drawn our attention to the ambiguities of language and the varieties of its expressive relationship to life—from the incongruities between Quixote's and Sancho's understanding of the meaning of words, to the hopeless lapse of verbal understanding between Walter and Toby Shandy, and to the subtly threatening divergencies of meaning in the constricted language of Jane Austen's characters. Language as a means of communication is a provision for social and spiritual order. You cannot make "order" with an integer, one thing alone, for order is definitively a relationship among things.

Absolute noncommunication is an unthinkable madness for it negates all relationship and therefore all order, and even an ordinary madman has to create a kind of order for himself by illusions of communication. Dickens' soliloquizing characters, for all their funniness (aloneness is inexorably funny, like the aloneness of [126/127] the man who slips on a banana peel, seen from the point of view of togetherness), suggest a world of isolated integers, terrifyingly alone and unrelated.

The book opens with a child's first conscious experience of his aloneness. Immediately an abrupt encounter occurs—Magwitch suddenly comes from behind a gravestone, seizes Pip by the heels, and suspends him upside down.

"Hold your noise!" cried a terrible voice, as a man started up from among the graves at the side of the church porch. "Keep still, you little devil, or I'll cut your throat!"

Perhaps, if one could fix on two of the most personal aspects of Dickens' technique, one would speak of the strange languages he concocts for the solitariness of the soul, and the abruptness of his tempo. His human fragments suddenly shock against one another in collisions like those of Democritus' atoms or of the charged particles of modern physics. Soldiers, holding out handcuffs, burst into the blacksmith's house during Christmas dinner at the moment when Pip is clinging to a table leg in an agony of apprehension over his theft of the pork pie. A weird old woman clothed in decayed satin, jewels and spider webs, and with one shoe off, shoots out her finger at the bewildered child, with the command: "Play!" A pale young gentleman appears out of a wilderness of cucumber frames, and daintily kicking up his legs and slapping his hands together, dips his head and butts Pip in the stomach. These sudden confrontations between persons whose ways of life have no habitual or logical continuity with each other suggest the utmost incohesion in the stuff of experience.

Technique is vision. Dickens' technique is an index of a vision of life that sees human separatedness as the ordinary condition, where speech is speech *to* nobody and where human encounter is mere collision. But the vision goes much further. Our minds are so constituted that they

insist on seeking in the use of language an exchange function, a delivery
and a passing on of perceptions from soul to soul and generation to
generation, binding them in some kind of order; and they insist on
finding cause and effect, or *motivation*, in the displacements and encounters of persons or things. Without these primary patterns of perception
we would not have what we call minds. And when these patterns are
confused or abrogated by our experience, we are forced, in order to
preserve some kind of psychic equilibrium, to seek them in extraordinary explana-[127/128]tions—explanations again in terms of mutual
exchange and cause and effect. Dickens saw his world patently all in
pieces, and as a child's vision would offer some reasonable explanation
of why such a world was that way—and, by the act of explanation,
would make that world yield up a principle of order, however obscure
or fantastic—so, with a child's literalism of imagination, he discovered
organization among his fragments.

Dickens lived in a time and an environment in which a full-scale
demolition of traditional values was going on, correlatively with the
uprooting and dehumanization of men, women, and children by the
millions—a process brought about by industrialization, colonial im-
perialism, and the exploitation of the human being as a "thing" or an
engine or a part of an engine capable of being used for profit. This was
the "century of progress" which ornamented its steam engines with
iron arabesques of foliage as elaborate as the antimacassars and aspidis-
tras and crystal or cut-glass chandeliers and bead-and-feather portieres
of its drawing rooms, while the human engines of its welfare groveled
and bred in the foxholes described by Marx in his *Capital*. (Hauntingly
we see this discordance in the scene in *Great Expectations* where Miss
Havisham, sitting in her satin and floral decay in the house called Satis,
points her finger at the child and outrageously tells him to "play." For
though the scene is a potent symbol of childish experience of adult
obtuseness and sadism, it has also another dimension as a social symbol
of those economically determined situations in which the human soul
is used as a means for satisfactions not its own, under the gross and
transparent lie that its activity is its happiness, its welfare and fun and
"play"—a publicity instrument that is the favorite of manufacturers

and insurance agencies, as well as of totalitarian strategists, with their common formula, "We're just a happy family.") The heir of the "century of progress" is the twentieth-century concentration camp, which makes no bones about people being "things."

Dickens' intuition alarmingly saw this process in motion, a process which abrogated the primary demands of human feeling and rationality, and he sought an extraordinary explanation for it. People were becoming things, and things (the things that money can buy or that are the means for making money or for exalting prestige in the abstract) were becoming more important than people. People were being de-animated, robbed of their souls, and things were usurping the prerogatives of animate creatures—governing the lives of their owners in the most literal sense. This picture, in which the qualities of things and people were reversed, was a [128/129] picture of a daemonically motivated world, a world in which "dark" or occult forces or energies operate not only in people (as modern psychoanalytic psychology observes) but also in things: for if people turn themselves or are turned into things, metaphysical order can be established only if we think of things as turning themselves into people, acting under a "dark" drive similar to that which motivates the human aberration.

There is an old belief that it takes a demon to recognize a demon, and the saying illustrates the malicious sensibility with which things, in Dickens, have felt out and imitated, in their relationship with each other and with people, the secret of the human arrangement. A four-poster bed in an inn, where Pip goes to spend the night, is a despotic monster that straddles over the whole room,

putting one of his arbitrary legs into the fireplace, and another into the doorway, and squeezing the wretched little washing-stand in quite a Divinely Righteous manner.

Houses, looking down through the skylight of Jaggers' office in London, twist themselves in order to spy on Pip like police agents who presuppose guilt. Even a meek little muffin has to be "confined with the utmost precaution under a strong iron cover," and a hat, set on a mantelpiece, demands constant attention and the greatest quickness of eye and hand to catch it neatly as it tumbles off, but its ingenuity is such that it finally manages to fall into the slop basin. The animation of inanimate objects suggests both the quaint gaiety of a forbidden life and an aggressiveness that has got out of control—an aggressiveness that they have borrowed from the human economy and an irresponsibility native to but glossed and disguised by that economy.

Dickens' fairly constant use of the pathetic fallacy (the projection of human impulses and feelings upon the nonhuman, as upon beds and houses and muffins and hats) might be considered as incidental stylistic embellishment if his description of people did not show a reciprocal metaphor: people are described by nonhuman attributes, or by such an exaggeration of or emphasis on one part of their appearance that they seem to be reduced wholly to that part, with an effect of having become "thinged" into one of their own bodily members or into an article of their clothing or into some inanimate object of which they have made a fetish. Dickens' devices for producing this transposition of attributes are [129/130] various. To his friend and biographer, Forster, he said that he was always losing sight of a man in his diversion by the mechanical play of some part of the man's face, which "would acquire a sudden ludicrous life of its own." Many of what we shall call the "signatures" of Dickens' people—that special exaggerated feature or gesture or mannerism which comes to stand for the whole person— are such dissociated parts of the body, like Jaggers' huge forefinger which he bites and then plunges menacingly at the accused, or Wem- mick's post-office mouth, or the clockwork apparatus in Magwitch's throat that clicks as if it were going to strike. The device is not used arbitrarily or capriciously. In this book, whose subject is the etiology of guilt and of atonement, Jaggers is the representative not only of civil law but of universal Law, which is profoundly mysterious in a world of dissociated and apparently lawless fragments; and his huge forefinger, into which he is virtually transformed and which seems to act like an "it" in its own right rather than like a member of a man, is the Law's mystery in all its fearful impersonality. Wemmick's mouth is not a post-office when he is at home in his castle but only when he is at work in Jaggers' London office, where a mechanical appearance of smiling is required of him. And as Wemmick's job has mechanized him into a grinning slot, so oppression and fear have given the convict Magwitch a clockwork apparatus for vocal chords.

Or this general principle of reciprocal changes, by which things have become as it were daemonically animated and people have been reduced to thing-like characteristics—as if, by a law of conservation of energy, the humanity of which people have become incapable had leaked out into the external environment—may work symbolically in the association of some object with a person so that the object assumes his essence and his "meaning." Mrs. Joe wears a large apron, "having a square impregnable bib in front, that was stuck full of pins and needles" —she has no reason to wear it, and she never takes it off a day in her life. Jaggers flourishes a large white handkerchief—a napkin that is the mysterious complement of his blood-smeared engagements. Estella— who is the star and jewel of Pip's great expectations—wears jewels in her hair and on her breast; "I and the jewels," she says, as if they were interchangeable. This device of association is a familiar one in fiction; what distinguishes Dickens' use of it is that the associated object acts not merely to *illustrate* a person's qualities symbolically—as novelists usually use it—but that it has a necessary metaphysical function in Dickens' universe: in this universe objects ac-[130/131]tually usurp human essences; beginning as fetishes, they tend to—and sometimes quite literally do—devour and take over the powers of the fetish-worshiper.

The process of conversion of spirit into matter that operates in the Dickens world is shown working out with savage simplicity in the case of Miss Havisham. Miss Havisham has been guilty of aggression against life in using the two children, Pip and Estella, as inanimate instruments of revenge for her broken heart—using them, that is, as if they were not human but things—and she is being changed retributively into a fungus. The decayed cake on the banquet table acts, as it were, by homeopathic magic—like a burning effigy or a doll stuck with pins; its decay parallels the necrosis in the human agent. "When the ruin is complete," Miss Havisham says, pointing to the cake but referring to herself, she will be laid out on the same table and her relatives will be invited to "feast on" her corpse. But this is not the only conversion. The "little quickened hearts" of the mice behind the panels have been quickened by what was Miss Havisham, carried off crumb by crumb.

The principle of reciprocal changes, between the human and the nonhuman, bears on the characteristic lack of complex "inner life" on the part of Dickens' people—their lack of a personally complex psychology. It is inconceivable that the fungoid Miss Havisham should have a complex inner life, in the moral sense. But in the *art* of Dickens (distinguishing that moral dialectic that arises not solely from the "characters" in a novel but from all the elements in the aesthetic structure) there is a great deal of "inner life," transposed to other forms than that of human character: partially transposed in this scene, for instance, to the symbolic activity of the speckle-legged spiders with blotchy bodies and to the gropings and pausings of the black beetles on Miss Havisham's hearth. Without benefit of Freud or Jung, Dickens saw the human soul reduced literally to the images occupying its "inner life."

Through the changes that have come about in the human, as humanity has leaked out of it, the atoms of the physical universe have become subtly impregnated with daemonic aptitude. Pip, standing waiting for Estella in the neighbourhood of Newgate, and beginning to be aware of his implication in the guilt for which that establishment stands—for his "great expectations" have already begun to make him a collaborator in the generic crime of using people as means to personal ends—has the sensation of a deadly dust clinging to him, rubbed off on him from the [131/132] environs, and he tries to beat it out of his clothes. Smithfield, that "shameful place," "all asmear with filth and fat and blood and foam," seems to "stick to him" when he enters it on his way to the prison. The nettles and brambles of the graveyard where Magwitch first appears "stretch up cautiously" out of the graves in an effort to get a twist on the branded man's ankles and pull him in. The river has a malignant potentiality that impregnates everything upon it—discolored copper, rotten wood, honeycombed stone, green dank deposit. The river is perhaps the most constant and effective symbol in Dickens, because it establishes itself so readily to the imagination as a daemonic element, drowning people as if by intent, disgorging unforeseen evidence, chemically or physically changing all it touches, and because not only does it act as an occult "force" in itself but it is the common passage and actual flowing element that unites individuals and classes, public persons and private persons, deeds and the results of deeds, however fragmentized and separated. Upon the river, one cannot escape its action; it may throw the murderer and his victim in an embrace. At the end of *Great Expectations*, it swallows Compeyson, while, with its own obscure daemonic motivation, though it fatally injures Magwitch, it leaves him to fulfill the more subtle spiritual destiny upon which he has begun to enter. The river scene in this section, closely and apprehensively observed, is one of the most memorable in Dickens.

It is necessary to view Dickens' "coincidences" under the aspect of this wholesale change in the aptitudes of external nature. Coincidence is the violent connection of the unconnected. Life is full of violent connections of this sort, but one of the most rigorous conventions of fictional and dramatic art is that events should make a logically sequential pattern; for art is the discovery of order. Critics have frequently deplored Dickens' use of coincidences in his plots. But in a universe that is nervous throughout, a universe in which nervous ganglia stretch through both people and their external environment, so that a change in the human can infect the currents of the air and the sea, events and confrontations that seem to abrogate the laws of physical mechanics can logically be brought about. In this sense, the apparent coincidences in Dickens actually obey a causal order—not of physical mechanics but of moral dynamics.

What connection can there be [Dickens asks in another novel] between many people in the innumerable histories of this world, who, [132/133] from opposite sides of great gulfs, have, nevertheless, been very curiously brought together!

What brings the convict Magwitch to the child Pip, in the graveyard, is more than the convict's hunger; Pip (or let us say simply "the child," for Pip is an Everyman) carries the convict inside him, as the negative potential of his "great expectations"—Magwitch is the concretion of his potential guilt. What brings Magwitch across the "great gulfs" of the Atlantic to Pip again, at the moment of revelation in the story, is their profoundly implicit compact of guilt, as binding as the convict's leg iron which is its recurrent symbol. The multiplying likenesses in the street as Magwitch draws nearer, coming over the sea, the mysterious warnings of his approach on the night of his reappearance, are moral projections as "real" as the storm outside the windows and as the crouched form of the vicious Orlick on the dark stairs. The conception of what brings people together "coincidentally" in their seemingly uncaused encounters and collisions—the total change in the texture of experience that follows upon any act, public or private, external or in thought, the concreteness of the effect of the act not only upon the conceiving heart but upon the atoms of physical matter, so that blind nature collaborates daemonically in the drama of reprisal—is deep and valid in this book.

In a finely lucid atmosphere of fairy tale, Dickens uses a kind of montage in *Great Expectations*, a superimposing of one image upon another with an immediate effect of hallucination, that is but one more way of representing his vision of a purely nervous and moral organization of reality. An instance is the scene in which Estella walks the casks in the old brewery. Estella's walking the casks is an enchanting ritual dance of childhood (like walking fence rails or railroad ties), but inexplicably present in the tableau is the suicidal figure of Miss Havisham hanging by her neck from a brewery beam. Accompanying each appearance of Estella—the star and the jewel of Pip's expectations—is a similarly disturbing ghost, an image of an unformed dread. When Pip thinks of her, though he is sitting in a warm room with a friend, he shudders as if in a wind from over the marshes. Her slender knitting fingers are suddenly horribly displaced by the marred wrists of a murderess. The technique of montage is that of dreams, which know with awful precision the affinities between the guilt of our desires and the commonplace of our immediate perceptions.   [133/134]

This device, of doubling one image over another, is paralleled in the handling of character. In the sense that one implies the other, the glittering frosty girl Estella, and the decayed and false old woman, Miss Havisham, are not two characters but a single one, or a single essence with dual aspects, as if composed by montage—a spiritual continuum, so to speak. For inevitably wrought into the fascinating jewel-likeness of Pip's great expectations, as represented by Estella, is the falsehood and degeneracy represented by Miss Havisham, the soilure on the un-purchased good. The boy Pip and the criminal Magwitch form another such continuum. Magwitch, from a metaphysical point of view, is not outside Pip but inside him, and his apparition is that of Pip's own unwrought deeds: Pip, having adopted "great expectations," will live by making people into Magwitches, into means for his ends. The relation-ship between Joe Gargery, saintly simpleton of the folk, and Orlick, dark beast of the Teutonic marshes (who comes "from the ooze"), has a somewhat different dynamics, though they too form a spiritual con-tinuum. Joe and Orlick are related not as two aspects of a single moral identity, but as the opposed extremes of spiritual possibility—the one unqualified love, the other unqualified hate—and they form a frame within which the actions of the others have their ultimate meaning. A commonplace of criticism is that, as Edmund Wilson puts it, Dickens was usually unable to "get the good and bad together in one charac-ter."[2] The criticism might be valid if Dickens' were a naturalistic world, but it is not very relevant to Dickens' daemonically organized world. In a naturalistic world, obeying mechanical laws, each character is organically discrete from every other, and presumably each contains a representative mixture of the "the good and bad." But in Dickens' thoroughly nervous world, that does not know the laws of mechanics but knows only spiritual law, one simple or "flat" character can be superimposed upon another so that together they form the representa-tive human complexity of good-in-evil and evil-in-good.

Two kinds of crime form Dickens' two chief themes, the crime of parent against child, and the calculated social crime. They are formally analogous, their form being the treatment of persons as things; but they are also inherent in each other, whether the private will of the parent is to be considered as depraved by the operation of a public institution, or the social institution is to be considered as a bold concert of the de-pravities of individual "fathers." In *Great Expectations* the private crime against [134/135] the child is Mrs. Joe's and Pumblechook's and Wopsle's, all "foster parents" either by necessity or self-conceit; while

[2] *The Wound and the Bow* (Boston: Houghton Mifflin Company, 1941), p. 65.

the social crime is the public treatment of Magwitch. That the two kinds of crime are inherent in each other we are made aware of as we are led to identify Magwitch's childhood with Pip's; the brutality exercised toward both children was the same brutality, though the "parents" in the one case were private persons, and in the other, society itself. Complicating the meaning of "the crime" still further, Magwitch also has taken upon himself the role of foster parent to Pip, and whether, as parent, he acts in charity or impiousness, or both, is a major ambiguity which the drama sets out to resolve.

"The crime," in Dickens, is evidently a permutation of multiple motivations and acts, both public and private, but always with the same tendency to convert people into things, and always implying either symbolically or directly a child-parent situation. The child-parent situation has been disnatured, corrupted, with the rest of nature; or rather, since the child-parent situation is the dynamic core of the Dickens world, the radical disnaturing here is what has corrupted the rest. His plots seldom serve to canalize, with the resolution of the particular set of plotted circumstances, the hysteria submerged in his vision of a nature gone throughly wrong; the permutations of the crimes are too many, and their ultimate cause or root is evasive, unless one would resort to some dramatically unmanageable rationale such as original sin. The Dickens world requires an act of redemption. A symbolic act of this kind is again and again indicated in his novels, in the charity of the uncherished and sinned-against child for the inadequate or criminal father—what might be called the theme of the prodigal father, Dickens' usual modification of the prodigal son theme. But the redemptive act should be such that it should redeem not only the individual "fathers," but society at large. One might almost say—thinking of Dickens' caricatures of the living dead, with their necrotic members and organs, their identifications of themselves with inanimate objects—that it should be such as to redeem the dead. *Great Expectations* is an exception among his novels in that here the redemptive act is adequate to and structural for both bodies of thematic material—the sins of individuals and the sins of society.

Pip first becomes aware of the "identity of things" as he is held suspended heels over head by the convict; that is, in a world literally turned upside down. Thenceforth Pip's interior landscape is inverted by his guilty knowledge of this man "who had been soaked in water, and [135/136] smothered in mud, and lamed by stones, and cut by flints, and stung by nettles, and torn by briars." The apparition is that of all suffering that the earth can inflict, and that the apparition presents itself to a child is as much as to say that every child, whatever his innocence, inherits guilt (as the potential of his acts) for the condition of man. The inversion of natural order begins here with first self-consciousness: the child is heir to the sins of the "fathers." Thus the crime that is always pervasive in the Dickens universe is identified in a new way—not primarily as that of the "father," nor as that of some public institution, but as that of the child—the original who must necessarily take upon himself responsibility for not only what is to be done in the present and the future, but what has been done in the past, inasmuch as the past is part and parcel of the present and the future. The child is the criminal, and it is for this reason that he is able to redeem his world; for the world's guilt is his guilt, and he can expiate it in his own acts.

The guilt of the child is realized on several levels. Pip experiences the psychological *form* (or feeling) of guilt before he is capable of voluntary evil; he is treated by adults—Mrs. Joe and Pumblechook and Wopsle —as if he were a felon, a young George Barnwell (a character in the play which Wopsle reads on the night when Mrs. Joe is attacked) wanting only to murder his nearest relative, as George Barnwell murdered his uncle. This is the usual nightmare of the child in Dickens, a vision of imminent incarceration, fetters like sausages, lurid accusatory texts. He is treated, that is, as if he were a thing, manipulable by adults for the extraction of certain sensations: by making him feel guilty and diminished, they are able to feel virtuous and great. But the psychological *form* of guilt acquires spiritual *content* when Pip himself conceives the tainted wish—the wish to be like the most powerful adult and to treat others as things. At the literal level, Pip's guilt is that of snobbery toward Joe Gargery, and snobbery is a denial of the human value of others. Symbolically, however, Pip's guilt is that of murder; for he steals the file with which the convict rids himself of his leg iron, and it is this leg iron, picked up on the marshes, with which Orlick attacks Mrs. Joe; so that the child does inevitably overtake his destiny, which was, like George Barnwell, to murder his nearest relative. But the "relative" whom Pip, adopting the venerable criminality of society, is, in the widest symbolic scope of intention, destined to murder is not Mrs. Joe but his "father," Magwitch—to murder in the socially chronic fashion of the Dickens world, which consists in the [136/137] dehumanization of the weak, or in moral acquiescence to such murder. Pip is, after all, the ordinary mixed human being, one more Everyman in the long succession of them that literature has represented, but we see this Everyman as he develops from a child; and his destiny is directed by the ideals of his world—toward "great expectations" which involve the making of Magwitches—which involve, that is, murder. These are the possibilities that are projected in the opening scene of the book, when the young child, left with a burden on his soul, watches the convict limping off under an angry red sky, toward the black marshes, the gibbet, and the savage lair of the sea, in a still rotating landscape.

In Dickens' modification of the folk pattern of the fairy wishing, Magwitch is Pip's "fairy godfather" who changes the pumpkin into a coach. Like all the "fathers," he uses the child as a thing in order to obtain through him vicarious sensations of grandeur. In relation to society, however, Magwitch is the child, and society the prodigal father; from the time he was first taken for stealing turnips, the convict's career has duplicated brutally and in public the pathos of the ordinary child. Again, in relation to Pip, Magwitch is still the child; for, spiritually committed by his "great expectations" to that irresponsibility which has accounted for the Magwitches, Pip is projectively, at least, answerable for Magwitch's existence and for his brutalization. Pip carries his criminal father within him; he is, so to speak, the father of his father. The ambiguities of each term of the relationship are such that each is both child and father, making a fourfold relationship; and the act of love between them at the end is thus reinforced fourfold, and the redemption by love is a fourfold redemption: that is to say, it is symbolically infinite, for it serves for all the meanings Dickens finds it possible to attach to the central child-father situation, the most profound and embracing relationship that, in Dickens' work, obtains among men.

As the child's original alienation from "natural" order is essentially mysterious, a guilty inheritance from the fathers which invades first awareness, so the redemptive act is also a mysterious one. The mysterious nature of the act is first indicated, in the manner of a motif, when Mrs. Joe, in imbecile pantomime, tries to propitiate her attacker, the bestial Orlick. In Orlick is concretized all the undefined evil of the Dickens world, that has nourished itself underground and crept along walls, like the ancient stains on the house of Atreus. He is the lawlessness implied in the unnatural conversions of the human into the nonhuman, the retributive [137/138] death that invades those who have grown lean in life and who have exercised the powers of death over others. He is the instinct of aggression and destruction, the daemonism of sheer external Matter as such; he is pure "thingness" emerging without warning from the ooze where he has been unconsciously cultivated. As Orlick is one form of spiritual excess—unmotivated hate—Joe Gargery is the opposed form—love without reservation. Given these terms of the spiritual framework, the redemptive act itself could scarcely be anything but grotesque—and it is by a grotesque gesture, one of the most profoundly intuitive symbols in Dickens, that Mrs. Joe is redeemed. What is implied by her humble propitiation of the beast Orlick is a recognition of personal guilt in the guilt of others, and of its dialectical relationship with love. The motif reappears in the moment of major illumination in the book. Pip "bows down," not to Joe Gargery, toward whom he has been privately and literally guilty, but to the wounded, hunted, shackled man, Magwitch, who has been guilty toward himself. It is in this way that the manifold organic relationships among men are revealed, and that the Dickens world—founded in fragmentariness and disintegration—is made whole. [end on 138]

PROBLEMS: Dorothy Van Ghent

1. Many critics of Dickens speak, in one way or another, of the fact that the characters in *Great Expectations* and other Dickens novels

soliloquize, even when in conversation with each other. Explain how Mrs. Van Ghent deals with this problem and why she considers the problem important in discussing *Great Expectations*. Why is Joe Gargery a good character with which to begin the discussion?

2. Why does Mrs. Van Ghent say [p. 126], "there is, perhaps, no purer expression of solipsism in literature"? What other expressions of solipsism are there in *Great Expectations*'

3. Explain the statement [p. 126], "The cultivation of the peculiar Dickensian values of language reaches its apogee when the convict Magwitch . . . asks Pip to read to him from a book in a foreign language, of which he understands no syllable." In what ways are Dickens's values of language peculiar?

4. Is loneliness a motif in *Great Expectations*? Has this any connection with the soliloquies of characters? What is the relationship between loneliness and the theme of the novel?

5. Discuss in detail the strange languages Dickens concocts for *Great Expectations*, explaining how and why he devises them.

6. Mrs. Van Ghent uses the word *incohesion* [p. 127]. What does that word mean as applied to *Great Expectations*? What has incohesion to do with the theme of the novel?

7. Discuss the animation of inanimate objects in *Great Expectations*. Does Dickens also make animate objects inanimate? Why would he do either or both? Do other critics mention this transference? How important to an understanding of the novel is the interchange of the animate and inanimate?

8. How well unified does Mrs. Van Gent think *Great Expectations* is? What does she think the unifying principles are? Are other critics in agreement with her?

9. Discuss doubling or superimposing of images in *Great Expectations*.

10. Compare Mrs. Van Ghent's idea of the role of Orlick with Moynahan's idea. Which do you prefer?

11. Mrs. Van Ghent says two kinds of crime form Dickens's two chief themes. Do you agree? Do other critics?

12. Analyze the roles of love and guilt in *Great Expectations*.

13. Miss Vande Kieft disagrees with portions of Mrs. Van Ghent's argument. Which writer offers the more persuasive argument? Be specific about the area of disagreement.

Expectations Well Lost:
Dickens' Fable for His Time*

by G. ROBERT STANGE

GREAT EXPECTATIONS is a peculiarly satisfying and impressive novel. It is unusual to find in Dickens' work so rigorous a control of detail, so simple and organic a pattern. In this very late novel the usual features of his art—proliferating sub-plots, legions of minor grotesques —are almost entirely absent. The simplicity is that of an art form that belongs to an ancient type and concentrates on permanently significant issues. *Great Expectations* is conceived as a moral fable; it is the story of a young man's development from the moment of his first self-awareness, to that of his mature acceptance of the human condition.

So natural a theme imposes an elemental form on the novel: the over-all pattern is defined by the process of growth, and Dickens employs many of the motifs of folklore. The story of Pip falls into three phases which clearly display a dialectic progression. We see the boy first in his natural condition in the country, responding and acting instinctively and therefore virtuously. The second stage of his career involves a negation of child-like simplicity; Pip acquires his "expectations," renounces his origins, and moves to the city. He rises in society, but since he acts through calculation rather than through instinctive charity, his moral values deteriorate as his social graces improve. This middle phase of his career culminates in a sudden fall, the beginning of a redemptive suffering which is dramatically concluded by an attack of brain fever leading to a long coma. It is not too fanciful to regard this

* From *College English*, XVI, 1 (October 1954), pp. 9–17. Reprinted with the permission of the National Council of Teachers of English.

illness as a symbolic death; Pip rises from it regenerate and percipient. In the final stage of growth he returns to his birthplace, abandons his false expectations, accepts the limitations of his condition, and achieves a partial synthesis of the virtue of his innocent youth and the melancholy insight of his later experience.

Variants of such a narrative are found in the myths of many heroes. In Dickens' novel the legend has the advantage of providing an action which appeals to the great primary human affections and serves as unifying center for the richly conceived minor themes and images which form the body of the novel. It is a signal virtue of this simple structure that it saves *Great Expectations* from some of the startling weaknesses of such excellent but inconsistently developed novels as *Martin Chuzzlewit* or *Our Mutual Friend*.

The particular fable that Dickens elaborates is as interesting for its historical as for its timeless aspects. In its [9/10] particulars the story of Pip is the classic legend of the nineteenth century: *Great Expectations* belongs to that class of education or development-novels which describe the young man of talents who progresses from the country to the city, ascends in the social hierarchy, and moves from innocence to experience. Stendhal in *Le Rouge et le Noir*, Balzac in *Le Père Goriot* and *Les Illusions perdues*, use the plot as a means of dissecting the post-Napoleonic world and exposing its moral poverty. This novelistic form reflects the lives of the successful children of the century, and usually expresses the mixed attitudes of its artists. Dickens, Stendhal, Balzac communicate their horror of a materialist society, but they are not without admiration for the possibilities of the new social mobility; *la carrière ouverte aux talents* had a personal meaning for all three of these energetic men.

Pip, then, must be considered in the highly competitive company of Julien Sorel, Rubempré, and Eugène de Rastignac. Dickens' tale of lost illusions, however, is very different from the French novelists'; *Great Expectations* is not more profound than other development-novels, but is more mysterious. The recurrent themes of the genre are all there: city is posed against country, experience against innocence; there is a search for the true father; there is the exposure to crime and the acceptance of guilt and expiation. What Dickens' novel lacks is the clarity and, one is tempted to say, the essential tolerance of the French. He could not command either the saving ironic vision of Stendhal or the disenchanted practicality and secure Catholicism of Balzac. For Dickens, always the Victorian protestant, the issues of a young man's rise or fall are conceived as a drama of the individual conscience; enlightenment (partial at best) is to be found only in the agony of personal guilt.

With these considerations and possible comparisons in mind I should like to comment on some of the conspicuous features of *Great Expectations*. The novel is interesting for many reasons: it demonstrates the subtlety of Dickens' art; it displays a consistent control of narrative, imagery, and theme which gives meaning to the stark outline of the fable, and symbolic weight to every character and detail. It proves Dickens' ability (which has frequently been denied) to combine his genius for comedy with his fictional presentation of some of the most serious and permanently interesting of human concerns.

The principal themes are announced and the mood of the whole novel established in the opening pages of *Great Expectations*. The first scene with the boy Pip in the graveyard is one of the best of the superbly energetic beginnings found in almost all Dickens' mature novels. In less than a page we are given a character, his background, and his setting; within a few paragraphs more we are immersed in a decisive action. Young Pip is first seen against the background of his parents' gravestones—monuments which communicate to him no clear knowledge either of his parentage or of his position in the world. He is an orphan who must search for a father and define his own condition. The moment of this opening scene, we learn, is that at which the hero has first realized his individuality and gained his "first most vivid and broad impression of the identity of things." This information given the reader, the violent meeting between Pip and the [10/11] escaped convict abruptly takes place.

The impression of the identity of things that Pip is supposed to have received is highly equivocal. The convict rises up like a ghost from among the graves, seizes the boy suddenly, threatens to kill him, holds him upside down through most of their conversation, and ends by forcing the boy to steal food for him. The children of Dickens' novels always receive rather strange impressions of things, but Pip's epiphany is the oddest of all, and in some ways the most ingenious. This encounter in the graveyard is the germinal scene of the novel. While he is held by the convict, Pip sees his world upside down; in the course of Dickens' fable the reader is invited to try the same view. This particular change of viewpoint is an ancient device of irony, but an excellent one: Dickens' satire asks us to try reversing the accepted senses of innocence and guilt, success and failure, to think of the world's goods as the world's evils.

A number of ironic reversals and ambiguous situations develop out of the first scene. The convict, Magwitch, is permanently grateful to Pip for having brought him food and a file with which to take off his leg-iron. Years later he expresses his gratitude by assuming in secrecy an economic parenthood; with the money he has made in Australia he will, unbeknownst to Pip, make "his boy" a gentleman. But the money the convict furnishes him makes Pip not a true gentleman, but a cad. He lives as a *flâneur* in London, and when he later discovers the disreputable source of his income is snobbishly horrified.

Pip's career is a parable which illustrates several religious paradoxes: he can gain only by losing all he has; only by being defiled can he be cleansed. Magwitch returns to claim his gentleman, and finally the convict's devotion and suffering arouse Pip's charity; by the time Magwitch has been captured and is dying Pip has accepted him and come to love him as a true father. The relationship is the most important one in the novel: in sympathizing with Magwitch Pip assumes the criminal's guilt; in suffering with and finally loving the despised and rejected man he finds his own real self.

Magwitch did not have to learn to love Pip. He was naturally devoted to "the small bundle of shivers," the outcast boy who brought him the stolen food and the file in the misty graveyard. There is a natural bond, Dickens suggests, between the child and the criminal; they are alike in their helplessness; both are repressed and tortured by established society, and both rebel against its incomprehensible authority. In the first scene Magwitch forces Pip to commit his first "criminal" act, to steal the file and food from his sister's house. Though this theft produces agonies of guilt in Pip, we are led to see it not as a sin but as an instinctive act of mercy. Magwitch, much later, tells Pip: "I first become aware of myself, down in Essex, a thieving turnips for my living." Dickens would have us, in some obscure way, conceive the illicit act as the means of self-realization.

In the opening section of the novel the view moves back and forth between the escaped criminal on the marshes and the harsh life in the house of Pip's sister, Mrs. Joe Gargery. The "criminality" of Pip and the convict is contrasted with the socially approved cruelty and injustice of Mrs. Joe and her respectable friends. The elders who come to the Christmas feast at the [11/12] Gargerys' are pleased to describe Pip as a criminal: the young are, according to Mr. Hubble, "naterally wicious." During this most bleak of Christmas dinners the child is treated not only as outlaw, but as animal. In Mrs. Joe's first speech Pip is called a "young monkey"; then, as the spirits of the revellers rise, more and more comparisons are made between boys and animals. Uncle Pumblechook, devouring his pork, toys with the notion of Pip's having been born a "Squeaker":

"If you had been born such, would you have been here now? Not you. . . ."

"Unless in that form," said Mr. Wopsle, nodding towards the dish.

"But I don't mean in that form, sir," returned Mr. Pumblechook, who had an objection to being interrupted; "I mean, enjoying himself with his elders and betters, and improving himself with their conversation, and rolling in the lap of luxury. Would he have been doing that? No, he wouldn't. And what would have been your destination?" turning on me again. "You would have been disposed of for so many shillings according to the market price of the article, and Dunstable the butcher would have come up to you as you lay in your straw, and he would have whipped you under his left arm, and with his right he would have tucked up his frock to get a penknife from out of his waistcoat-pocket, and he would have shed your blood and had your life. No bringing up by hand then. Not a bit of it!"

This identification of animal and human is continually repeated in the opening chapters of the novel, and we catch its resonance throughout the book. When the two convicts—Pip's "friend" and the other fugitive, Magwitch's ancient enemy—are captured, we experience the horror of official justice, which treats the prisoners as if they were less than human: "No one seemed surprised to see him, or interested in seeing him, or glad to see him, or sorry to see him, or spoke a word, except that somebody in the boat growled as if to dogs, 'Give way, you!'" And the prison ship, lying beyond the mud of the shore, looked to Pip "like a wicked Noah's ark."

The theme of this first section of the novel—which concludes with the capture of Magwitch and his return to the prison ship—might be called "the several meanings of humanity." Only the three characters who are in some way social outcasts—Pip, Magwitch, and Joe Gargery the child-like blacksmith—act in charity and respect the humanity of others. To Magwitch Pip is distinctly not an animal, and not capable of adult wickedness: "You'd be but a fierce young hound indeed, if at your time of life you could help to hunt a wretched warmint." And when, after he is taken, the convict shields Pip by confessing to have stolen the Gargerys' pork pie, Joe's absolution affirms the dignity of man:

"God knows you're welcome to it—so far as it was ever mine," returned Joe, with a saving remembrance of Mrs. Joe. "We don't know what you have done, but we wouldn't have you starved to death for it, poor miserable fellow-creatur.—Would us, Pip?"

The next section of the narrative is less tightly conceived than the introductory action. Time is handled loosely; Pip goes to school, and becomes acquainted with Miss Havisham of Satis House and the beautiful Estella. The section concludes when Pip has reached early manhood, been told of his expectations, and has prepared to leave for London. These episodes develop, with variations, the theme of childhood betrayed. Pip himself renounces his childhood by coming to accept the false social values of middle-class society. His perverse development is expressed by persistent images of the opposition [12/13] between the human and the non-human, the living and the dead.

On his way to visit Miss Havisham for the first time, Pip spends the night with Mr. Pumblechook, the corn-chandler, in his lodgings behind his shop. The contrast between the aridity of this old hypocrite's spirit and the viability of his wares is a type of the conflict between natural growth and social form. Pip looks at all the shop-keeper's little drawers filled with bulbs and seed packets and wonders "whether the flower-seeds and bulbs ever wanted of a fine day to break out of those jails and bloom." The imagery of life repressed is developed further in the descriptions of Miss Havisham and Satis House. The first detail Pip notices is the abandoned brewery where the once active ferment has ceased; no germ of life is to be found in Satis House or in its occupants:

> . . . there were no pigeons in the dove-cot, no horses in the stable, no pigs in the sty, no malt in the storehouse, no smells of grains and beer in the copper or the vat. All the uses and scents of the brewery might have evaporated with its last reek of smoke. In a by-yard, there was a wilderness of empty casks. . . .

On top of these casks Estella dances with solitary concentration, and behind her, in a dark corner of the building, Pip fancies that he sees a figure hanging by the neck from a wooden beam, "a figure all in yellow white, with but one shoe to the feet; and it hung so, that I could see that the faded trimmings of the dress were like earthly paper, and that the face was Miss Havisham's."

Miss Havisham *is* death. From his visits to Satis House Pip acquires his false admiration for the genteel; he falls in love with Estella and fails to see that she is the cold instrument of Miss Havisham's revenge on human passion and on life itself. When Pip learns he may expect a large inheritance from an unknown source he immediately assumes (incorrectly) that Miss Havisham is his benefactor; she does not un-deceive him. Money, which is also death, is appropriately connected with the old lady rotting away in her darkened room.

Conflicting values in Pip's life are also expressed by the opposed imagery of stars and fire. Estella is by name a star, and throughout the novel stars are conceived as pitiless: "And then I looked at the stars, and considered how awful it would be for a man to turn his face up to them as he froze to death, and see no help or pity in all the glittering multitude." Estella and her light are described as coming down the dark passage of Satis House "like a star," and when she has become a woman she is constantly surrounded by the bright glitter of jewelry.

Joe Gargery, on the other hand, is associated with the warm fire of the hearth or forge. It was his habit to sit and rake the fire between the lower bars of the kitchen grate, and his workday was spent at the forge. The extent to which Dickens intended the contrast between the warm and the cold lights—the vitality of Joe and the frigid glitter of Estella— is indicated in a passage that describes the beginnings of Pip's dis- illusionment with his expectations:

When I woke up in the night . . . I used to think, with a weariness on my spirits, that I should have been happier and better if I had never seen Miss Havisham's face, and had risen to manhood content to be partners with Joe in the honest old forge. Many a time of an evening, when I sat alone looking at the fire, I thought, after all, there was no fire like the forge fire and the kitchen fire at home.   [13/14]
      Yet Estella was so inseparable from all my restlessness and disquiet of mind, that I really fell into confusion as to the limits of my own part in its production.

At the end of the novel Pip finds the true light on the homely hearth, and in a last twist of the father-son theme, Joe emerges as a true parent —the only kind of parent that Dickens could ever fully approve, one that remains a child. The moral of this return to Joe sharply contradicts the accepted picture of Dickens as a radical critic of society: Joe is a humble countryman who is content with the place in the social order he has been appointed to fulfill. He fills it "well and with respect"; Pip learns that he can do no better than to emulate him.

The second stage of Pip's three-phased story is set in London, and the moral issues of the fiction are modulated accordingly. Instead of the opposition between custom and the instinctive life, the novelist treats the conflict between man and his social institutions. The topics and themes are specific, and the satire, some of it wonderfully deft, is more social than moral. Not all Dickens' social message is presented by means that seem adequate. By satirizing Pip and his leisure class friends (The Finches of the Grove, they call themselves) the novelist would have us realize that idle young men will come to a bad end. Dickens is here expressing the Victorian Doctrine of Work—a pervasive notion that both inspired and reassured his industrious contemporaries.

The difficulty for the modern reader, who is unmoved by the objects of Victorian piety, is that the doctrine appears to be the result, not of moral insight, but of didactic intent; it is presented as statement, rather than as experience or dramatized perception, and consequently it never modifies the course of fictional action or the formation of character. The distinction is crucial: it is between the Dickens who *sees* and the Dickens who *professes*; often between the good and the bad sides of his art.

The novelist is on surer ground when he comes to define the nature of wealth in a mercantile society. Instead of moralistic condemnation we have a technique that resembles parable. Pip eventually learns that his ornamental life is supported, not by Miss Havisham, but by the labor and suffering of the convict Magwitch:

> "I swore afterwards, sure as ever I spec'lated and got rich, you should get rich. I lived rough, that you should live smooth; I worked hard that you should be above work. What odds, dear boy? Do I tell it fur you to feel a obligation? Not a bit. I tell it, fur you to know as that there dunghill dog wot you kep life in, got his head so high that he could make a gentleman—and, Pip, you're him!"

The convict would not only make a gentleman but own him. The blood horses of the colonists might fling up the dust over him as he was walking, but, "I says to myself, 'If I ain't a gentleman, nor yet ain't got no learning, I'm the owner of such. All on you owns stock and land; which on you owns a brought-up London gentleman?'"

In this action Dickens has subtly led us to speculate on the connections between a gentleman and his money, on the dark origins of even the most respectable fortunes. We find Magwitch guilty of trying to own another human being, but we ask whether his actions are any more sinful than those of the wealthy *bourgeois*. There is a deeper [14/15] moral in the fact that Magwitch's fortune at first destroyed the natural gentleman in Pip, but that after it was lost (it had to be forfeited to the state when Magwitch was finally captured) the "dung-hill dog" did actually make Pip a gentleman by evoking his finer feelings. This ironic distinction between "gentility" and what the father of English poetry meant by "gentilesse" is traditional in our literature and our mythology. In

Great Expectations it arises out of the action and language of the fiction; consequently it moves and persuades us as literal statement never can.

The middle sections of the novel are dominated by the solid yet mysterious figure of Mr. Jaggers, Pip's legal guardian. Though Jaggers is not one of Dickens' greatest characters he is heavy with implication; he is so much at the center of this fable that we are challenged to interpret him—only to find that his meaning is ambiguous. On his first appearance Jaggers strikes a characteristic note of sinister authority:

> He was a burly man of an exceedingly dark complexion, with an exceedingly large head and a correspondingly large hand. He took my chin in his large hand and turned up my face to have a look at me by the light of the candle. . . . His eyes were set very deep in his head, and were disagreeably sharp and suspicious. . . .
>
> "How do *you* come here?"
>
> "Miss Havisham sent for me, sir," I explained.
>
> "Well! Behave yourself. I have a pretty large experience of boys, and you're a bad set of fellows. Now mind!" said he, biting the side of his great forefinger, as he frowned at me, "you behave yourself."

Pip wonders at first if Jaggers is a doctor. It is soon explained that he is a lawyer—what we now ambiguously call a *criminal* lawyer—but he is like a physician who treats moral malignancy, with the doctor's necessary detachment from individual suffering. Jaggers is interested not in the social operations of the law, but in the varieties of criminality. He exudes an antiseptic smell of soap and is described as washing his clients off as if he were a surgeon or a dentist.

Pip finds that Jaggers has "an air of authority not to be disputed . . . with a manner expressive of knowing something secret about every one of us that would effectually do for each individual if he chose to disclose it." When Pip and his friends go to dinner at Jaggers' house Pip observes that he "wrenched the weakest parts of our dispositions out of us." After the party his guardian tells Pip that he particularly liked the sullen young man they called Spider: " 'Keep as clear of him as you can. But I like the fellow, Pip; he is one of the true sort. Why if I was a fortune-teller. . . . But I am not a fortune-teller,' he said. . . . 'You know what I am don't you?' " This question is repeated when Pip is being shown through Newgate Prison by Jaggers' assistant, Wemmick. The turnkey says of Pip: "Why then . . . he knows what Mr. Jaggers is."

But neither Pip nor the reader ever fully knows what Mr. Jaggers is. We learn, along with Pip, that Jaggers has manipulated the events which have shaped the lives of most of the characters in the novel; he has, in the case of Estella and her mother, dispensed a merciful but entirely personal justice; he is the only character who knows the web of secret relationships that are finally revealed to Pip. He dominates by the strength of his knowledge the world of guilt and sin—called *Little Britain*—of which his office is the center. He has, in brief, the powers that an artist [15/16] exerts over the creatures of his fictional world, and that a god exerts over his creation.

As surrogate of the artist, Jaggers displays qualities of mind—complete impassibility, all-seeing unfeelingness—which are the opposite of Dickens', but of a sort that Dickens may at times have desired. Jaggers can be considered a fantasy figure created by a novelist who is forced by his intense sensibility to re-live the sufferings of his fellow men and who feels their agonies too deeply.

In both the poetry and fiction of the nineteenth century there are examples of a persistent desire of the artist *not to care*. The mood, which is perhaps an inevitable concomitant of Romanticism, is expressed in Balzac's ambivalence toward his great character Vautrin. As arch-criminal and Rousseauistic man, Vautrin represents all the attitudes that Balzac the churchman and monarchist ostensibly rejects, yet is presented as a kind of artist-hero, above the law, who sees through the social system with an almost noble cynicism.

Related attitudes are expressed in the theories of art developed by such different writers as Flaubert and Yeats. While—perhaps because —Flaubert himself suffered from hyperaesthesia, he conceived the ideal novelist as coldly detached, performing his examination with the deft impassivity of the surgeon. Yeats, the "last Romantic," found the construction of a mask or anti-self necessary to poetic creation, and insisted that the anti-self be cold and hard—all that he as poet and feeling man was not.

Dickens' evocation of this complex of attitudes is less political than Balzac's, less philosophical than Flaubert's or Yeats'. Jaggers has a complete understanding of human evil but, unlike the living artist, can wash his hands of it. He is above ordinary institutions; like a god he dispenses justice, and like a god displays infinite mercy through unrelenting severity:

> "Mind you, Mr. Pip," said Wemmick, gravely in my ear, as he took my arm to be more confidential; "I don't know that Mr. Jaggers does a better thing than the way in which he keeps himself so high. He's always so high. His constant height is of a piece with his immense abilities. That Colonel durst no more take leave of *him*, than that turnkey durst ask him his intentions respecting a case. Then between his height and them, he slips in his subordinate—don't you see? —and so he has 'em soul and body."

Pip merely wishes that he had "some other guardian of minor abilities."

The final moral vision of *Great Expectations* has to do with the nature of sin and guilt. After visiting Newgate Pip, still complacent and self-deceived, thinks how strange it was that he should be encompassed by the taint of prison and crime. He tries to beat the prison dust off his feet and to exhale its air from his lungs; he is going to meet Estella, who must not be contaminated by the smell of crime. Later it is revealed that Estella, the pure, is the bastard child of Magwitch and a murderess. Newgate is figuratively described as a greenhouse, and the prisoners as plants carefully tended by Wemmick, assistant to Mr. Jaggers. These disturbing metaphors suggest that criminality is the condition of life. Dickens would distinguish between the native, inherent sinfulness from which men can be redeemed, and that evil which destroys life: the sin of the hypocrite or oppressor, the smothering wickedness of corrupt institutions. The last stage of Pip's progression is reached [16/17] when he learns to love the criminal and to accept his own implication in the common guilt.

Though Dickens' interpretation is theologically heterodox, he deals conventionally with the ancient question of free will and predestination. In one dramatic paragraph Pip's "fall" is compared with the descent of the rock slab on the sleeping victim in the Arabian Nights tale: Slowly,

slowly, "all the work, near and afar, that tended to the end, had been accomplished; and in an instant the blow was struck, and the roof of my stronghold dropped upon me." Pip's fall was the result of a chain of predetermined events but he was, nevertheless, responsible for his own actions; toward the end of the novel Miss Havisham gravely informs him: "You have made your own snares. *I* never made them."

The patterns of culpability in *Great Expectations* are so intricate that the whole world of the novel is eventually caught in a single web of awful responsibility. The leg-iron, for example, which the convict removed with the file Pip stole for him is found by Orlick and used as a weapon to brain Mrs. Joe. By this fearsome chain of circumstance Pip shares the guilt for his sister's death.

Profound and suggestive as is Dickens' treatment of guilt and expiation in this novel, to trace its remoter implications is to find something excessive and idiosyncratic. A few years after he wrote *Great Expectations* Dickens remarked to a friend that he felt always as if he were wanted by the police—"irretrievably tainted." Compared to most of the writers of his time the Dickens of the later novels seems to be obsessed with guilt. The way in which his development-novel differs from those of his French compeers emphasizes an important quality of Dickens' art. The young heroes of *Le Rouge et le Noir* and *Le Père Goriot* proceed from innocence, through suffering to learning. They are surrounded by evil, and they can be destroyed by it. But Stendhal, writing in a rationalist tradition, and Balzac displaying the worldliness that only a Catholic novelist can command, seem astonishingly cool, even callous, beside Dickens. *Great Expectations* is outside either Cartesian or Catholic rationalism; profound as only an elementally simple book can be, it finds its analogues not in the novels of Dickens' English or French contemporaries, but in the writings of that other irretrievably tainted artist, Fyodor Dostoevski.   [end on 17]

PROBLEMS: G. Robert Stange

1. Stange says that the pattern of this novel is simple. Is this the opinion of all the critics you have read? Which critics? What does Stange mean by "simple" as he applies it to *Great Expectations?*

2. What are the "great primary human affections" [p. 9] to which *Great Expectations* may be said to appeal?

3. Trace out some of the minor themes of the novel, and show how they relate to the main theme as Stange outlines it.

4. Comment on the historical or on the timeless aspects of *Great Expectations*.

5. What does Stange mean when he says that Pip "must search for a father"?

6. Add to the list of "criminal" things Pip does in his childhood, and see if you can, as Stange does, show the essential goodness of these acts.

7. In the second section of the novel, says Stange, Pip renounces the humanity of his childhood: "His perverse development is expressed by persistent images of the opposition between the human and the nonhuman, the living and the dead" [pp. 12–13]. What other critic speaks at length of these images? Support the above statement by citing and analyzing several such images.

8. Stange refers [p. 13] to the image of Miss Havisham hanging in the abandoned brewery. Collect several interpretations which critics have made of this scene, note the similarities and differences, and decide which interpretation is most helpful to your understanding of the novel.

9. Stange says that Joe's emerging as a parent of Pip is the "last twist of the father-son theme" [p. 14] in the novel. Trace this theme from beginning to end, and decide its exact meaning.

10. What is "mysterious" about Mr. Jaggers?

11. Stange finds "something excessive and idiosyncratic" [p. 17] in Dickens's treatment of the remoter implications of guilt and expiation. Do Stange's reasons convince you? Refute or support his arguments.

The Poor Labyrinth: The Theme of Social Injustice in Dickens's "Great Expectations"*

by JOHN H. HAGAN, JR.

I

ON THE surface *Great Expectations* is simply another very good example of that perennial *genre*, the education novel. In particular, it is the story of a restless young boy from the lower classes who comes into possession of a fortune he has done nothing to earn, founds a host of romantic aspirations upon it at the cost of becoming a snob, comes to be disappointed both romantically and socially, and, finally, with a more mature knowledge of himself and the world, works out his regeneration. As such, the novel is what G. K. Chesterton once called it, "an extra chapter to 'The Book of Snobs.'" But while admitting that Pip is a fairly good specimen of a certain type of mentality so dear to Dickens's satirical spirit, we cannot overlook the fact that Dickens is using his character to reveal some still more complex truths about society and its organization.

Though its shorter length and more compact organization have prevented it from being classed with *Bleak House*, *Little Dorrit*, and *Our Mutual Friend*, *Great Expectations* is really of a piece with that great social "trilogy" of Dickens's later years. In the briefer novel Dickens is attempting only a slightly less comprehensive anatomization of social

* Reprinted from *Nineteenth-Century Fiction*, IX, 3 (December 1954), pp. 169–178. Copyright © 1954 The Regents of the University of California.

evil; thematically, the implications of Pip's story are almost as large. Consider, for instance, how many different strata of society are gotten into the comparatively small number of pages that story takes up. In the first six chapters alone we meet members of the criminal, the military, and the artisan classes, together with a parish clerk and two well-to-do entrepreneurs. The [169/170] principal difference between *Great Expectations* and the more massive panoramic novels lies more in the artistic means employed than in the intellectual content. In *Great Expectations* Dickens strips the larger novels to their intellectual essentials. The point of one line of action in *Bleak House*, we remember, was to show how Lady Dedlock had been victimized by social injustice operating in the form of conventional morality and its hypocrisies. But into that novel Dickens also packed a great deal else; the Lady Dedlock action was but part of a gigantic network. In *Great Expectations* all such additional ramifications are discarded. Dickens concentrates with great intensity upon a single line of development, and, to our surprise, this line turns out to be remarkably similar in its theme to that of Lady Dedlock's story. For Pip's career shows not only a hapless young man duped by his poor illusions, but a late victim in a long chain of widespread social injustice.

The story's essential features make this fact plain. We learn in Chapter XLII that the prime mover, so to speak, of the entire course of events which the novel treats immediately or in retrospect is a man by the name of Compeyson, a cad who adopts the airs of a "gentleman." Significantly, he remains throughout the book shrouded in mist (literal and figurative), vague, remote, and terrifying, like some vast impersonal force. Through his actions two people once came to grief. First, after stripping her of a great deal of her fortune, he jilted the spoiled and naïve Miss Havisham, and thereby turned her wits against the whole male sex. Secondly, he further corrupted a man named Magwitch who had already been injured by poverty, and revealed to him how easily the law may be twisted into an instrument of class. The trial of Magwitch and Compeyson is so important a key to the novel's larger meanings that the former's description of it in the later pages of the book should be read in entirety. What the passage reveals is that impartiality in the courts is often a myth. Judges and jury alike may be swayed by class prejudice. The whole judicial system may tend to perpetuate class antagonism and hostility. In short, an important [170/171] element at the root of Magwitch's career is great social evil: the evil of poverty, and the evil of a corruptible judicial system. Though not entirely so, Magwitch is certainly, in part, a victim. The conventional words Pip speaks over his corpse at the end—" 'O Lord, be merciful to him a sinner' "—remain merely conventional, for the man was more sinned against than sinning. From his very first appearance in the novel, when we see him shivering on the icy marshes, he is depicted with sympathy, and by the time we get to the end, he has risen to an almost heroic dignity.

The connection of all this with Pip is plain. The young boy becomes for both Magwitch and Miss Havisham a means by which, in their different ways, they can retaliate against the society that injured them. One of Miss Havisham's objects is, through Pip, to frustrate her greedy relatives who, like Compeyson himself, are interested in her for her money alone, and who, again like Compeyson, typify the rapacious and predatory elements of society at large. Magwitch, on the other hand, retaliates against society by striving to meet it on the ground of its own special prejudices. Though deprived from childhood of the opportunity to become a "gentleman" himself, he does not vow destruction to the "gentleman" class. Having seen in Compeyson the power of that class, the deference it receives from society, he fashions a gentleman of his own to take his place in it. He is satisfied to live vicariously through Pip, to show society that he can come up to its standards, and, by raising his pawn into the inner circle, to prove that it is no longer impregnable.

Thus Pip, in becoming the focal point for Miss Havisham's and Magwitch's retaliation—the one who is caught in the midst of the cross fire directed against society by two of the parties it injured, who, in turn, display in their desire for proprietorship some of the very tyranny and selfishness against which they are rebelling—becomes society's scapegoat. It is he who must pay the price for original outrages against justice, who must suffer for the wider injustices of the whole society of which he is but a humble part. The result is that he too takes on society's vices, its selfishness, ingrati-[171/172]tude, extravagance, and pride. He, too, becomes something of an impostor like Compeyson himself, and thereby follows in the fatal footsteps of the very man who is indirectly the cause of his future misery. Thus the worst qualities of society seem inevitably to propagate themselves in a kind of vicious circle. Paralleling the case of Pip is that of Estella. As Pip is the creation of Magwitch, she is the creation of Miss Havisham. Her perversion has started earlier; as the novel opens, it is Pip's turn next. He is to be the latest heir of original injustice, the next to fall victim to the distortions that have already been forced upon Magwitch, Miss Havisham, and Estella. He is to be the latest product of Compeyson's evil as it continues to infect life.

But injustice does not come to bear upon Pip through Magwitch and Miss Havisham alone. There is injustice under the roof of his own house. Throughout the first stage of Pip's career, Dickens presents dramatically in scene after scene the petty tyranny exercised over the boy by his shrewish sister, Mrs. Gargery, and some of her friends, particularly Mr. Pumblechook, the blustering corn merchant, and Wopsle, the theatrically-minded parish clerk. It is the constant goading Pip receives from these people that makes him peculiarly susceptible to the lure of his "great expectations" with their promise of escape and freedom. But more important is the fact that it is Pumblechook and Mrs. Gargery who first put the treacherous idea into Pip's head that Miss Havisham is his secret patroness. One of the very reasons they insist upon his waiting on the old woman in the first place is their belief that she will liberally reward him, and thereafter they never let the idea out of the boy's mind. In short, Mrs. Gargery, Pumblechook, and Wopsle do as much as Magwitch and Miss Havisham to turn Pip into his erring ways. To be sure, the novel is not an essay in determinism. But despite the legitimacy of the reproaches of Pip's conscience, we cannot forget how early his impressionable mind was stamped with the images of greed and injustice—images that present a small-scale version of the greedy and unjust world of "respectability" as a [172/173] whole. The tyranny exercised over Pip by his sister,

Pumblechook, and their like is a type of the tyranny exercised by the conventionally "superior" elements of society over the suffering and dispossessed. Theirs is a version in miniature of the society that tolerates the existence of the dunghills in which Magwitch and his kind are spawned, and then throws such men into chains when they violate the law. When Pumblechook boasts of himself as the instrument of Pip's wealth, he is truthful in a way he never suspects or would care to suspect. For the obsequious attitude toward money he exemplifies is, indirectly, at the root of Pip's new fortune. It was just such an attitude that resulted in the debasing of Magwitch below Compeyson at their trial, and thus resulted in the former's fatal determination to transform Pip into a "gentleman."

Injustice is thus at the heart of the matter—injustice working upon and through the elders of Pip and Estella, and continuing its reign in the children themselves. With these children, therefore, we have a theme analogous to one deeply pondered by another great Victorian novelist: the idea of "consequences" as developed by George Eliot. Both she and Dickens are moved by a terrifying vision of the wide extent to which pollution can penetrate the different, apparently separate and unrelated, members of society. Once an act of injustice has been committed, there is no predicting to what extent it will affect the lives of generations yet unborn and of people far removed in the social scale from the victims of the original oppression. Though on a smaller scale, Dickens succeeds no less in *Great Expectations* than in his larger panoramic novels in suggesting a comprehensive social situation. No less than in *Bleak House*, *Little Dorrit*, and *Our Mutual Friend*—and in *A Tale of Two Cities* as well—the different levels of society are brought together in a web of sin, injustice, crime, and destruction. The scheme bears an analogy to the hereditary diseases running throughout several generations in Zola's *Les Rougons-Macquarts* series. Dickens compresses his material more than Zola by starting *in medias res*, and showing Pip as the focal point for the past, present, [173/174] and future at once. In him are concentrated the effects of previous injustice, and he holds in himself the injustice yet to come. The interest of the novel is never restricted merely to the present. Dickens opens a great vista, a "poor labyrinth," through which we may see the present as but the culmination of a long history of social evil. Society is never able to smother wholly the facts of its injustice. As Dickens shows in novel after novel, somehow these facts will come to light again: Bounderby's mother in *Hard Times* rises to reveal her son's hypocrisy to the crowd he has bullied for so many years; the facts of Mrs. Clennam's relationship to the Dorrit family, and of society's injury to Lady Dedlock, her lover, and her child, are all unearthed in the end. Immediate victims may be skillfully suppressed, as Magwitch, returning from exile, is finally caught and imprisoned again. But the baleful effects of social evil go on in a kind of incalculable chain reaction. It is the old theme of tragic drama read into the bleak world of Mid-Victorian England: the sins of the fathers will be visited upon the heads of their children; the curse on the house will have to be expiated by future generations of sufferers.

Thus it is fair to say that Pip's story is more than a study of personal development. In his lonely struggle to work out his salvation, he is atoning for the guilt of society at large. In learning to rise above selfishness, to attain to a selfless love for Magwitch, he brings to an end the chain of evil that was first forged by the selfish Compeyson. His regeneration has something of the same force as Krook's "spontaneous combustion" in *Bleak House*, or the collapse of the Clennam mansion in *Little Dorrit*, or even the renunciation of his family heritage by Charles Darnay in *A Tale of Two Cities*. Just as Darnay must atone for the guilt of his family by renouncing his property, so Pip must atone for the evils of the society that has corrupted him by relinquishing his unearned wealth. And as Darnay marries the girl whose father was one of the victims of his family's oppression, so Pip desires to marry the girl whose father, Magwitch, is the victim of the very society whose values Pip himself has embraced.   [174/175]

II

In giving his theme imaginative embodiment Dickens used what are perhaps some of the most ingenious and successful devices of his entire career. With disarming suddenness, for example, *Great Expectations* opens with the presentation of a physical phenomenon almost as memorable as that of the fog in *Bleak House*: the marshes. More than a Gothic detail casually introduced to give the story an eerie beginning, the marshes reappear again and again, not only in the first six chapters, where indeed they figure most prominently, but throughout the book. They haunt the novel from start to finish, becoming finally one of its great informing symbols. The variety of ways in which Dickens manages unobtrusively to weave them, almost like a musical motif, into the texture of his tale is remarkable. At one time they may flicker briefly across the foreground of one of Pip's casual reveries; at another they may provide the material of a simile; or Pip may return to them in fact when he is summoned there late in the story by Orlick; or, again, he may see them from a distance when he is helping Magwitch make his getaway down the Thames. "It was like my own marsh country," Pip says of the landscape along the part of the river he and Magwitch traverse:

. . . some ballast lighters, shaped like a child's first rude imitation of a boat, lay low in the mud; and a little squat shoal-lighthouse on open piles, stood crippled in the mud on stilts and crutches: and slimy stakes stuck out of the mud, and slimy stones stuck out of the mud, and red landmarks and tidemarks stuck out of the mud, and an old landing-stage and an old roofless building slipped into the mud, and all about us was stagnation and mud.

Mud is a peculiarly appropriate symbol for the class of society that Magwitch represents—the downtrodden and oppressed of life, all those victims of injustice whom society has tried to submerge. It is a natural image of the social dunghill in which violence and rebellion are fomented, the breeding place of death. Likewise, it is the condition of death itself upon which certain forms of life must feed. It is no accident on Dickens's part that when Pip and his com-[175/176] panions stop at a public house on their journey down the river, they meet a "slimy and smeary" dock attendant whose clothes have all been taken from the bodies of drowned men. In fact, the motif of life thriving upon death is underlined more than once throughout the novel in a number of small but brilliant ways. On his first trip to Newgate, Pip meets a man wearing "mildewed clothes, which had evidently not belonged to him originally, and which, I took it into my head, he had bought cheap of the executioner." Trabb, the haberdasher and funeral director of Pip's village, is still another kind of scavenger. He, too, like the many undertakers in Dickens's other novels and Mrs. Gamp in *Martin Chuzzlewit*, profits hideously by the misfortunes of others. It is this condition that Dickens sums up most effectively in the repulsive image of mud.

But together with the marshes, he uses still another symbol to keep the idea of social injustice and its consequences before us. Chapter I opens with a description of the graveyard in which Pip's parents and several infant brothers are buried. Though less prominent as an image than the marshes, that of the grave presents much more explicitly the idea of the death-in-life state to which Magwitch and others in his predicament are condemned. We remember that it is from among the tombstones that Magwitch first leaps forth into the story; and when, at the end of the chapter, he is going away, Pip has been so impressed by his likeness to a risen corpse that he imagines the occupants of the graveyard reaching forth to reclaim him. This is not a merely facetious or lurid detail. The grave imagery suggests in a highly imaginative way the novel's basic situation. Magwitch, in relation to the "respectable" orders of society, is dead; immured in the Hulks or transported to the fringes of civilization, he is temporarily removed from active life. But when in the opening scene of the book he rises from behind the tombstone, he is figuratively coming back to life again, and we are witnessing the recurrence of an idea Dickens made a central motif of *A Tale of Two Cities*, the idea of resurrection and revolution. When Magwitch looms up from the darkened stairwell of Pip's [176/177] London lodging house at the end of the second stage of the boy's career, we are witnessing, as in the case of Dr. Manette's being "recalled to life" from the Bastille, an event of revolutionary implications. For what this means is that one whom society has tried to repress, to shut out of life, has refused to submit to the edict. He has come back to take his place once more in the affairs of men, and to influence them openly in a decisive way. The injuries society perpetrates on certain of its members will be thrust back upon it. Society, like an individual, cannot escape the consequences of its injustice; an evil or an injury once done continues to infect and poison life, to pollute the society responsible for it.

This is suggested by the very way in which the material of the novel is laid out. Within the first six chapters, Dickens regularly alternates outdoor and indoor scenes, each one of which is coincident with a chapter division. There is a steady movement back and forth between the shelter and warmth of the Gargery's house and the cold misery and danger of the marshes. Thus, while getting his plot under way, Dickens is at the same time vividly impressing upon us his fundamental idea of two worlds: the world of "respectability" and the world of ignominy; of oppressors and of oppressed; of the living and of the dead. In the first six chapters these worlds are separate; it is necessary to come in or to go out in order to get from either one to the other. But in his excursions from the house to the marshes and back again, Pip is already forging the link that is to bring them together at the end of the second stage of his adventures when Magwitch, refusing to be left out in the cold any longer, actually becomes an inhabitant of Pip's private rooms. The clearest hint of this coming revolution is given when the soldiers burst from the marshes into Joe's house, and disrupt the solemn Christmas dinner. The breaking in upon it of the forces of another world shows on what a sandy foundation the complacency of Pumblechook and his kind is based. Beneath the self-assured crust of society, the elements of discontent and rebellion are continually seething, continually threatening to erupt. Thus the alternation be-[177/178] tween worlds that gives the novel's first six chapters their order supplies the reader at once with the basic moral of the book as a whole: the victims of injustice cannot be shut out of life forever; sooner or later they will come into violent contact with their oppressors.

Moving from the early pages of the book to the larger pattern, we discover that alternation between two different locales is basic to the whole. Pip tries to make his home in London, but he is forced a number of times to return to the site of his former life, and each return brings him a new insight into the truth of his position, one progressively more severe than another. The alternation between London and the old village becomes for Dickens a means of suggesting what the alternation between outdoor and indoor scenes in the first six chapters suggested: pretend as one will, reality will eventually shatter the veil of self-deception. Like the individual who has come to sacrifice his integrity for society's false values only to find it impossible to deny indefinitely his origins and the reality upon which his condition rests, society cannot effectively stifle all the victims of its injustice and oppression. There will always be men like Jaggers—men to connect the dead with the living, to act as the link between the underground man and the rest of society. As a defender of criminals, Jaggers is the great flaw in society's repression of its victims; he is their hope of salvation and resurrection. Like Tulkinghorn, the attorney in *Bleak House*, he knows everybody's secrets; he is the man to whom the lines between the high and the low, the men of property and the dispossessed, are no barrier. A wise and disillusioned Olympian, Jaggers comments like a tragic chorus on the two great worlds that are the product and expression of social injustice, for the existence of which Pip and others must suffer the terrible consequences.   [end on 178]

PROBLEMS: John H. Hagan, Jr.

1. Does Hagan mean to say [pp. 169–170] that *Great Expectations* is more tightly unified and better structured than *Bleak House* and other "big" novels by Dickens? Or does he mean to say something else about the novel?

2. According to Hagan, what is the role of Compeyson in *Great Expectations*? Do you agree with Hagan? If not, what do you think is the function of Compeyson? If you agree with Hagan, explain how important Compeyson is in the novel. Why have so few critics said more than a few words about this character if he is important?

3. What does Hagan think Magwitch represents in the novel? How does this opinion differ from those of other critics (for instance, Dorothy Van Ghent)?

4. Why does Hagan call Pip "society's scapegoat" [p. 171]? Define the phrase.

5. Hagan says, "Mrs. Gargery, Pumblechook, and Wopsle do as much as Magwitch and Miss Havisham to turn Pip into his erring ways" [p. 172]. Do you agree? Do other critics?

6. Analyze fully Pumblechook's contribution to Pip's snobbery.

7. Contrast Hagan's use of the word "labyrinth" with J. Hillis Miller's use of it.

8. In addition to the characters mentioned by Hagan, show how "the chain of evil that was first forged by the selfish Compeyson" encircles the lives of other characters in the novel.

9. Do you think Hagan would approve of the revised ending of *Great Expectations*? Would he prefer the original ending?

10. Discuss the marshes as a symbol in *Great Expectations*.

11. Discuss the grave as a symbol in *Great Expectations*.

Technique in *Great Expectations*[*]

by THOMAS E. CONNOLLY

IN STRUCTURE *Great Expectations* is notable among Dickens's works for
its compression and the balanced proportion of its parts. It is ex-
ceptional, too, in its treatment of the pedagogical theme. It is natural
in Dickens to find that the influencing factors which affect the life of
the hero are outside the person himself. *Great Expectations* is no
exception in this respect. However, in the earlier pedagogical novels—
in *David Copperfield*, for example,—the hero emerges as essentially the
same person who was introduced in the first pages of the novel.
Spiritually he is relatively unchanged by these external forces, however
much he may have prospered materially. But this is not true of Pip.
He is altered in character by these forces, and it is this alteration which
gives us the informing idea of the novel. Once this informing idea had
been developed in the author's mind, the novel flowed structurally and
thematically from it. The idea is, of course, the effect upon Pip's life
of the lure of unearned money and false prosperity. It is not only,
however, the story of one Philip Pirrip. Pip assumes a much larger
rôle than that of an individual. Consequently, when we study the
three phases of Pip's life, we must think not only of *his* expectations,
illusions, and disillusionment, but also of the general malaise which
gripped the entire nineteenth century. It is the life of the *parvenu*. We
must consider the story of Pip's life as a social criticism of the illusion
of fortune which was sweeping society of the day into a whirlwind
of falsity, sham, pretense, and social corruption.

It is not the purpose of this study, however, to go into the social
implications of this novel. That subject has been admirably treated a

[*] From *Philological Quarterly*, XXXIV (January 1955), pp. 48–55. Reprinted by permission of the author and the publisher.

number of times, by Humphry House, T. A. Jackson, and George Orwell among others. Rather, I intend to examine Dickens's technique in structure and presentation to show the unique position which this novel holds among his works.

It is sometimes said that *Great Expectations* lacks diversity. Admittedly it does not have the whole range of the author's resources included in it. *Bleak House*, for example, is a much more complex [48/49] novel. In manipulating the plot and the social criticism of that novel in terms of the mystery and its detection, Dickens has created a framework of unusual diversity. But there is a wide variety of material present in *Great Expectations*, though it does not draw attention to itself because the various minor topics or themes are always carefully subordinated to the unity of the whole. The lengthy passages of social criticism which appeared in other novels are not to be found in this one. Each element of the action is made to carry the weight of the implicit theme of the novel. Hence, when Dickens introduces a minor theme, such as education (seen in the absurd school run by Mr. Wopsle's great aunt and in Mr. Pocket's tutoring system), it has no existence apart from the plot. It is all part of Pip's development and also part of the implicit social criticism that is his life. In a similar manner the prison theme becomes an intrinsic part of Pip's life. It is refreshing to discover in the usually extravagant Dickens such economy as the rowing episodes. Part of Pip's social snobbishness is the impulse to learn boating so that he may keep up with those two Joneses, Drummle and Startop. Even this minor detail is stored away carefully so that it can be used later in the Magwitch escape sequence. It is thus in many other instances that the minor themes which cover a wide range of subjects— prisons, child abuse, education, social stratification, bungling police, murder, corrupt legal practice, Jellyby-like family neglect, toadyism, middle-class love of property, religion, the theater, debts, and even Victorian funerals—these minor themes have no place in the novel except insofar as they contribute to the main plot. Lurking over the entire work like a huge black spider which draws all threads of the material into a single, unified, web-like pattern, is the symbol of money. It is to money, either positively by acquisitiveness, or negatively by influence, that all persons and things in the novel are subject.

In presentation or point of view, as well as in structure, the novel is controlled by the three phases of Pip's life. Narration in the first person was not new in Dickens at this time. *David Copperfield* and *Bleak House*, among his longer works, both make use of this method of presentation. In *David Copperfield* the narration is straight history, and the style is not complicated by changing phases of life. In *Bleak House* there are two points of view used: Esther's highly sentimental, first-person, past-tense narrative is set over against the highly ironical third-person, present-tense por-[49/50]tion of the novel. The result is that these two points of view present a two-dimensional critical commentary both upon each other and upon the social institutions which form the nucleus of the novel. The point of view in *Great Expectations* is that of the first person, but it divides into three parts which correspond to the three structural parts of the novel.

Perhaps one of the greatest talents which Dickens possessed was that of accurate representation of the state of mind of childhood. In this part of his work there is usually none of the artificiality of Victorian convention which sometimes detracts from his representation of adult emotional life. The early chapters of this novel reveal Dickens's sympathy for and understanding of the psychology of childhood. The spirit of childhood experience is skilfully suggested in the scenes of Pip's theft of the food and his delivery of it to the convict. The childish mingling of emotions—generosity, pity, fear, guilt, and the belief in the omniscience of the adult world—is seen in the most perfect form. It reaches its peak in a weird flight of childish imagination when Pip comes upon the cattle on his way to the convict with the stolen food:

The mist was heavier yet when I got out upon the marshes, so that instead of my running at everything, everything seemed to run at me. This was very disagreeable to a guilty mind. The gates and dykes and banks came bursting at me through the mist, as if they cried as plainly as could be, "A boy with Somebody else's pork pie! Stop him!" The cattle came upon me with like suddenness, staring out of their eyes, and steaming out of their nostrils, "Halloa, young thief!" One black ox, with a white cravat on—who even had to my awakened conscience something of a clerical air—fixed me so obstinately with his eyes, and moved his blunt head round in such an accusatory manner as I moved round, that I blubbered out to him, "I couldn't help it, sir! It wasn't for myself I took it!" Upon which he put down his head, blew a cloud of smoke out of his nose, and vanished with a kick-up of his hind legs and a flourish of his tail.[1]

It will be noticed that at the same time that this evocation of the childhood mood is accomplished, there is no departure from legitimate, cultured, adult language. The spirit of childhood has been generated and the adult language of the representation of that mood does not detract, generally, from the psychological effect. I can think of only one passage, and that a very brief one, in which the words attributed to Pip are quite out of character. He has just met the terrifying convict who has him perched on a tombstone and is tilting him over backwards to emphasize his demands. Pip's answer somehow seems just a bit too proper for a terrorized boy: [50/51]

I was dreadfully frightened, and so giddy that I clung to him with both hands, and said, "If you would kindly please to let me keep upright, sir, perhaps I shouldn't be sick, and perhaps I could attend more."[2]

One other citation will be sufficient to demonstrate Dickens's understanding of child psychology and his achievement of the childish point of view. Upon his return from his first visit to Miss Havisham, Pip is cross-questioned by his sister and Pumblechook. In his fear of revealing the truth and his reluctance to satisfy their morbid curiosity, he resorts to sheer invention. The childish imagination is given free play to the obvious delight of the two examiners, who are willing to believe anything about the fantastic Miss Havisham. His inventions are really no more fantastic than the actuality, but to the childish mind they are more fascinating, and even Joe, who is so much a child himself in his simplicity, though disappointed by the fact that Pip lied, is much more upset when he discovers that there weren't any black coaches or huge dogs in the house. This resort to deception in dealing with an unsympathetic adult world is as natural to childhood as marble-playing and leap-frog.[3]

---

[1] Charles Dickens, *Great Expectations* (London, 1907), p. 14. [pp. 12–13 in the Chandler Edition]

[2] *Ibid.*, p. 3. [p. 3 in the Chandler Edition]

[3] Compare this episode (Chapter IX) with the more serious deception practiced by David Copperfield when faced with the oppression of the Murdstones.

In the second part of the novel the method of presentation becomes more complex. Here it is necessary to have Pip recount with true feeling and objectively the period of his illusions. To do this after the realization of the falseness and irony of the illusions, and still not to permit later disillusionment to be felt in the telling, is a difficult task. It is made more difficult by the absence of a third-person narrator to furnish the commentary. Dickens manages to give a true picture of Pip's priggishness and social vanity by the rigid suppression of anything which might resemble commentary on the part of the narrator. Had he permitted this to creep into Pip's narrative the effect would not have been nearly so striking as it is. The result amounts to tragic irony, the reproduction of the reality of an experience at a time when the realization of the folly of it is known. There is a doubleness of vision in those pages devoted to Joe's visit to Barnard's Inn in which both the cruelty and the horror of Pip's rejection and his realization of the full meaning of what he is doing become apparent.

In the last part of the novel both childhood psychology and snobbish duality are left behind. Pip arrives at his final state of mind, [51/52] and the resulting narration is much more simple. There is no childish distortion; there is no egotistical dislocation. Hence, melodrama replaces psychology in the reduction to essentials. The Magwitch escape plot, Compeyson's horrible death, Orlick's attempt on Pip's life, Miss Havisham's destruction, are all sheer melodrama and are all crowded into this last section. Disillusionment is the theme, but there is also the consolation of truth-facing in this final part. The novel ends sombrely, but the bitterness is relieved by the heightened melodramatic action.

In character development, too, *Great Expectations* represents a high point in Dickens's development. Ever since *Dombey and Son* he had been consciously striving to draw a more perfect hero. In that novel, instead of letting Walter Gay "go bad" as he had originally planned, he kept him stalwart, pure, and unrealistic. It was necessary for David Copperfield to awaken to certain realities before his life could be considered complete. Though he does, it is essentially an unchanged David who is last seen, dandling small Copperfields on his knee, and basking in the warm comfort of a cozy fire. He is almost completely a portrait of a boy from beginning to end. There is scarcely any David, the man, to be seen. Richard Carstone, in *Bleak House*, is permitted to disintegrate under the blighting influence of Chancery Court, but Dickens, at the time of *Bleak House*, was well on the way toward the creation of a realistic hero in Rick, even though he failed to give a full psychological insight into the mind of the man. Even in his complete collapse he appears to be a rather unreal, papier-mâché figure. Arthur Clennam, of *Little Dorrit*, is the most convincing hero in Dickens before the coming of Pip. Clennam displays his humanity in the frequent periods of reflection in which he is seen. But even in Clennam the entire psychological man was not developed. Pip's character is traced in its development from boy to man. It is a full portrait. The reason for the realistic presentation of this hero is to be found in the fact that we are taken within the hero's mind. We are no longer external observers, left to judge the character of the observed solely from the evidence of his speech and actions. In presenting Pip, Dickens shows the detailed growth of a man from the internal vantage point of the man's own feelings. Pip is a great stride forward in the development of the type of character later seen in Bradley Headstone or in John Jasper, the man [52/53] who combines within himself good and evil, the modern bifurcated hero.

In a like manner, *Great Expectations* gives us an example of Dickens's advance in the creation of female characters. Shaw, in his preface to *Saint Joan*, condemns Mark Twain's Joan and says: "Like Esther Summerson she makes her creator ridiculous." Almost all of Dickens's heroines make him look a bit ridiculous. His goody-goody girls, Mary Graham, Florence Dombey, Agnes Wickfield, Esther Summerson, Amy Dorrit, Lucie Manette, are always even-tempered, long-suffering, and virtuous *ad nauseam*. In *Little Dorrit* Miss Wade shows some of the traits which are incorporated into Estella and which serve to make her such a radical departure from the usual Dickens heroine. Estella's training by Miss Havisham has warped and twisted her. To the extent that love has never been permitted to grow in her heart she is not a normal human being, and cannot be called a realistic heroine. But

Dickens's women are growing up. Shaw's comments on Estella in his preface to the Limited Editions Club edition of *Great Expectations* reveal the truth about her character:

It is not surprising that the unfortunate Bentley Drummle, whom she marries in the stupidity of sheer perversity, is obliged to defend himself from her clever malice with his fists; a consolation to us for Pip's broken heart, but not altogether a credible one; for the real Estellas can usually intimidate the real Bentley Drummles. At all events the final sugary suggestion of Estella redeemed by Bentley's thrashings and waste of her money, and living happily with Pip for ever after, provoked even Dickens's eldest son to rebel against it, most justly.[4]

Had the process of her humanization after her exposure to Bentley Drummle been shown, we might have seen a more perfect delineation of a credible human being. As it is, she is a close approach.

Of the rest of the characters in the novel, perhaps the most curious is Miss Havisham. She presents several critical problems. She and Wopsle and Pumblechook are echoes from the older period of fantasy. In Miss Havisham there is also a large share of Dickens's love of theatrical effects. Although these characters are remnants of an earlier period, they appear without the old spontaneity amidst the realistic seriousness of the novel. There is a heaviness about them. In Miss Havisham there is not only the abnormality of her fantastic existence to be considered, there is also the abnormal acceptance of her by the townspeople. Their matter-of-fact acceptance is not the usual reaction of average people to a deranged [53/54] mind. It is evidently another example of the distortion of normal lives brought about by social position and wealth. In *Bleak House*, Krook was surely a fantastic creature, both in life and in his death by spontaneous combustion. But as far as the action went he was relatively a minor character and, despite Dickens's prefatory scientific interest in him, served almost entirely as pure symbolism. Miss Havisham, however, is different. She holds a far more important position in this work than Krook did in his. Her symbolic function is diminished in proportion to the importance of her part in the action. It is natural to find in the world

[4] G. B. Shaw, "Preface to *Great Expectations*," (Edinburgh, 1937), p. xix.

such deranged people who are driven to extremes by obsessions, but it is questionable whether the grotesque or the fantastic should be used as a keystone in the structure of a serious work. The question reduces itself to this: was it necessary or desirable that Miss Havisham be presented in such a weird fashion in order that her function be performed? Could not the same important position be occupied, and similar results be attained by a less fantastic figure? Even though she is a grotesque element, Miss Havisham, it must be admitted, has been skilfully used. Dickens so manages her that the average reader of his day (like the casual reader of today) was willing to accept her along with the realistic elements of the novel, the average reader being far more willing to suspend his disbelief than some critics are ready to admit.

Herbert Pocket, Joe Gargery and Trabb's boy serve in varying degrees as norms against which Pip's life can be measured. Herbert has a duality of character, of which each half serves as a commentary on Pip. One side of his character is level, steady, and substantial. This is the Herbert who acts as Pip's social tutor, who comforts and cares for him when he has been injured, who is manager of the plans for Magwitch's escape. There is, however, another side of his nature which is similar to that second phase of Pip's life, the period of illusion. This is the Herbert who is even more outlandish in his expectations than Pip. This is the Herbert who is more hopelessly lost in his air castles because they have not even the insecure foundation of an unknown patron. According to Herbert, all he has to do to become an insurer of ships is to look about him for the necessary capital. The closest he comes to disillusionment is the realization "that an opening won't come to one, but one must go to it—so I have been."[5] He has walked [54/55] on 'Change during a busy time with a careful eye peeled for any capital that might come his way. This is the Herbert whom Pip rescues in the one decent act of his period of snobbery. Had there been no Pip to save him with the actuality of a partnership, Herbert would have remained in his world of illusion.

Joe Gargery, in a different fashion, also serves as a commentary on

---

[5] *Great Expectations*, p. 256. [p. 232 in the Chandler Edition]

Pip. He is a recurrence of the Dickens "good" earthy character. He represents in one human frame all the best elements of human nature. When he appears in Pip's rooms he becomes the most damning evidence of Pip's degeneration. The irony of the rejection is made all the more evident by Joe's consciousness of the system of social stratification. "Diwisions among such must come, and must be met as they come."[6] It is the fatalistic acceptance which points up the evil of the system.

Trabb's boy is almost pure demon. He is a demon who serves a delightful purpose, and I can conceive of no reader who does not feel like cheering him on as he capers on High Street and, shred by shred, strips Pip down to the disgusting bone. To make him "the joy of life felt by those who have nothing else but life," as Chesterton does,[7] is to stretch him a little beyond his capacity. Humphry House has summarized his rôle and character quite well:

As things were he was a good pin to prick Pip's conceit; but if he himself had come into a fortune, he would have been just as nasty about it as Pip in his own way; and his way might have been worse.[8]

Jaggers, Wemmick, Magwitch, Wopsle, Pumblechook, Belinda Pocket, Matthew Pocket and Biddy are all interesting and well-drawn characters whose casual listing should in no way imply that they are not each worth a serious and detailed investigation. They all show the extent to which Dickens had advanced in character delineation. In *Great Expectations* almost no character serves but a single purpose. Dickens had learned how to make his characters complex so that they function economically both in the basic plot and in the thematic presentation. *Great Expectations* is a novel which treats the social fable in terms of the life of one man. A wealth of material and characterization is present in the work, but it is so closely controlled by the author that no individual element or part exists which does not carry its proportionate share of the main plot and theme.   [end on 55]

[6] *Ibid.*, p. 209. [p. 189 in the Chandler Edition]
[7] *Ibid.*, p. xi.
[8] Humphry House, *The Dickens World* (London, 1941), p. 159.

PROBLEMS: Thomas E. Connolly

1. What are the parts of *Great Expectations*, and how are they balanced?

2. "It is sometimes said that *Great Expectations* lacks diversity," observes Connolly [p. 48]. Who has said this about the novel, and why have they said it?

3. Choose several of the minor themes which Connolly lists [p. 49], and show how they become a part of the main plot.

4. Extend, by using the views of other critics and by your own observations, Connolly's statement that "one of the greatest talents which Dickens possessed was that of accurate representation of the state of mind of childhood" [p. 50].

5. Connolly says that in the second section of the novel Dickens rigidly suppresses "anything which might resemble commentary on the part of the narrator" [p. 51]. Review this section carefully, and comment on this statement.

6. Is Biddy one of Dickens's "goody-goody girls" [p. 53]? If not, why not? If so, why doesn't she hurt the novel?

7. Would *Great Expectations* be better or worse if Miss Havisham were less fantastic?

8. What is the main thesis of this article? How successfully has it been defended? What contribution has it made to general critical comment on *Great Expectations*?

The Sense of Self*

by Monroe Engel

THE END of the first part of *Great Expectations* suggests a context for the entire novel: [156/157]

> I walked away at a good pace, thinking it was easier to go than I had supposed it would be, and reflecting that it would never have done to have an old shoe thrown after the coach, in sight of all the High-Street. I whistled and made nothing of going. But the village was very peaceful and quiet, and the light mists were solemnly rising, as if to show me the world, and I had been so innocent and little there, and all beyond was so unknown and great, that in a moment with a strong heave and sob I broke into tears. . . .

> So subdued I was by those tears, and by their breaking out again in the course of the quiet walk, that when I was on the coach, and it was clear of the town, I deliberated with an aching heart whether I would not get down when we changed horses and walk back, and have another evening at home, and a better parting. We changed, and I had not made up my mind, and still reflected for my comfort that it would be quite practicable to get down and walk back, when we changed again. . . .

> We changed again, and yet again, and it was now too late and too far to go back, and I went on. And the mists had all solemnly risen now, and the world lay spread before me.

No over-subtlety is required at this point to remember the departure of Adam and Eve from Eden—behind them the cherubim on the ground looking, Milton tells us, like mist risen from the marshes, while the other way, "The World was all before them."

The usefulness of this suggestion depends on caution. The suggestion is slight, and *Great Expectations* is no formal allegory. It would not

* Reprinted by permission of the publishers from Monroe Engel, *The Maturity of Dickens*. (Cambridge, Mass.: Harvard University Press.) Copyright, 1959, by the President and Fellows of Harvard College. Pages 156–168.

have occurred to Dickens that one book could or should stand upon another. Obviously, however, the departure from Eden belongs in no exlusive way to Milton, but has become one of those great general metaphors by which man explains his rea-[157/158]sonably inexplicable condition. The slight verbal parallel between the end of the first part of *Great Expectations* and the end of *Paradise Lost* may only be happy chance, but it exercises an imaginative control nonetheless over this perhaps most controlled of Dickens' novels.

The Eden from which young Philip Pirrip departs does not conform much to our idea of the garden: the marshes extending from the river where the prison ships are perpetually anchored; the warning gibbet on the shore; the mists and fogs and damp, cold weather; the un-promising village with its merchant rulers of the High-Street, its rough inn and pub, its tight provincial society; and the uncomfortable house by the forge where Mrs. Gargery brings up not only her young brother, but her husband too, "by hand." None of this is much to the point except that it has the quality of being a place apart, isolated largely, though not completely, from the world.

What figures most here is not the cosmography of place, but the innocence of Pip's soul and mind in this place, an innocence which leads him to infer the characters and appearances of his parents and brothers from their tombstones; to love Joe "because the dear fellow let me love him"; to pity the desolation of the escaped convict and be glad that he enjoys his stolen food; to believe that the exhortation of his catechism, "to walk in the same all the days of my life," binds him to take the same route without variation whenever he leaves his house to walk through the village. This innocence, too, enables him to discriminate justly between good and bad, and wisely among people as to those who are his friends and those who are not. Pip's innocence is fractured by expectation—planted by his sister and Pumblechook, encouraged by [158/159] the secret plans of Magwitch and of Miss Havisham. The objects of his expectation are, conventionally enough, property and love, scarcely distinguishable in his thinking, but each considered in detailed variation in this novel.

The evil of property lies in its tendency to use its possessors instead of being used by them. The point is made unambiguously and with force. Pip's first genuine act in *Great Expectations*, and an act from which ensue the consequences that in good part make the novel, is to steal food and a file from his home for the starving escaped convict Magwitch. It is notable that the guilt that haunts his mind has nothing to do with the genuinely serious matter of aiding an escaped and dangerous convict. It is his own theft he worries about, and not so much the stolen file as the stolen food, the broken vittles. Joe Gargery, who remains in the Eden of innocence throughout the novel, and is the control or fixed point in relation to which Pip's wandering is measured, makes overt the moral significance of this theft, when the escaped convict, to protect Pip, says that it was he who stole the food from the Gargerys' house: " 'God knows you're welcome to it—so far as it was ever mine,' returned Joe, with a saving remembrance of Mrs. Joe. 'We don't know what you have done, but we wouldn't have you starved to death for it, poor miserable fellow creature—Would us, Pip?' "

Joe tries to bolster Pip in his innocence, but Mrs. Joe is another matter. For her, property is sacred and uncomfortable, like some people's religion. Her preparations for Christmas dinner blight the holiday, and when she walks to town, she carries "a basket like the Great [159/160] Seal of England in plaited straw, a pair of pattens, a spare shawl, and an umbrella, though it was a fine bright day." Pip was not clear whether "these articles were carried penitentially or ostentatiously," but he thought they were probably "displayed as articles of property—much as Cleopatra or any other soverign lady on the Rampage might exhibit her wealth in a pageant or procession."

Pumblechook (a good example of Dickens' genius for fitting names) is far worse than Mrs. Gargery, and it is he who pushes Pip into the Havisham connection, bullies and maltreats him, flatters him when his fortunes are risen, and turns on him self-righteously and full of injury when they fall. But the real nightmare of property is provided by Miss Havisham in Satis House. A rough irony of names is used frequently in *Great Expectations*, starting with the title itself; of the name of the Havisham house, Estella says: "It meant when it was given, that whoever had this house, could want nothing else. They must have been easily satisfied in those days, I should think." In a ruin of old symbolic goods, Miss Havisham lives a living death, and plots her vicarious vengeance on victims who have only a token culpability for her tragedy. It is her goods, her wealth, that have ruined her in the first place by attracting Compeyson to her, and now she will have the goods work in reverse, by making Estella rich, impregnable, heart-breaking.

To Pip at first she seems, quite accurately, a waxwork or a skeleton amidst her goods, but this perception does not save him from becoming a victim to his expectations of property, and of property as a means of access to love. Miss Havisham encourages his delusion that she is his patroness, the cause and source of his expectations, and [160/161] that, as she intends him to have fortune, she intends him to have Estella too, and to be prepared for her and made more worthy of her by this money. So he is least prepared for the ultimate revelation of the true source of his expectations. In fact, he thinks his bond of complicity with Magwitch to be reduced, almost written off by his fortune:

If I had often thought before, with something allied to shame, of my companionship with the fugitive whom I had once seen limping among those graves, what were my thoughts on this Sunday, when the place recalled the wretch, ragged and shivering, with his felon iron and badge! My comfort was, that it happened a long time ago, and that he had doubtless been transported a long way off, and that he was dead to me, and might be veritably dead into the bargain.

No more low wet grounds, no more dykes and sluices, no more of these grazing cattle—though they seemed, in their dull manner, to wear a more respectful air now, and to face round, in order that they might stare as long as possible at the possessor of such great expectations—farewell, monotonous acquaintances of my childhood, henceforth I was for London and greatness: not for smith's work in general and for you! I made my exultant way to the old Battery, and, lying down there to consider the question whether Miss Havisham intended me for Estella, fell asleep.

But it is the fortune that makes Pip's bond to Magwitch indissoluble. In the world of this novel, property is harmless only when it is allowed no false aura of dignity or pretense, when it is clearly useful, and bears clear and preferably comic marks of human contrivance and effort. Of such property Wemmick's little estate at Walworth is the chief example; and in this setting there is a happy, loving society.   [161/162]

Of Pip's second expectation, love, Dickens draws an equally forbidding and infrequently relieved picture. It is useful to remember Dickens' own life at this point, though not to elaborate on it tenuously. By 1860, his marriage had ended in a legal separation, but was still a source of unrest and bitterness to him; and his relationship with Ellen Ternan too, now well past its first flush, had settled into some sort of disappointing resolution of its own. At least two critics[2] have found verbal plays and echoings of Ellen Ternan's name in the names of a number of Dickens' late heroines, including the Estella of *Great Expectations*. These heroines reflect too, they think, Ellen Ternan's failing in her relationship with Dickens: coldness, frigidity. Be this as it may—and the evidence gives the speculation great weight—it is clear enough that Estella is as cold and distant, as removed, as the stars her name suggests. She warns Pip herself that she has "no heart"; and, unable to manage a normal response to love, she has the decency to reserve herself from anyone capable of better, and gives herself instead to Bentley Drummle, who is as unfeeling as she, but a sensual brute in addition.

In some really frightful way here, anything like normal sexuality always makes for terror and tragedy. Miss Havisham falls passionately in love with Compeyson and is victimized by her love. The love of Magwitch and his wife ends in violence. Orlick, who desires Biddy, kills Mrs. Gargery and tries to kill Pip too. Mr. Pocket is victimized by his early love for Mrs. Pocket, and Joe by his for Pip's sister. The only relationships between [162/163] men and women that work out are reasonable, nonpassionate relationships: the middle-aged love of Wemmick and Miss Skiffins; Joe's fatherly love for Biddy, and her motherly love for him; the patient domestic attachment of Herbert and Clara; and the final rapprochement of Pip and Estella after their misspent youths are well behind them.

It is no wonder, then, that with his great expectations of property and love, Pip comes a cropper. There is no doubt that these bad

---

[2] Edmund Wilson; and Ada Nisbet in *Dickens and Ellen Ternan* (Berkeley, California, 1952).

expectations seem to make inevitable his disappointments. Yet again, here as in *David Copperfield*, fate is beyond good or bad choice, beyond prudence or prodigality. Pip's profoundest fate works by indirection, in which good comes out of bad and bad out of good. The basic first action in the novel is the encounter with Magwitch in the cemetery. Out of a mixture of fear and compassion, Pip helps the escaped convict, bringing him food, and a file with which to remove his fetters. Initially, everything seems to condone Pip's actions as simple charity toward someone in distress.

But the situation is not this simple. Magwitch is an escaped convict, a man both capable and guilty of great violence. After his escapade, Pip is in fear of the police, and feels guilty for his failure of openness with Joe. But these are comparatively minor matters, only the direct consequences of his complicity with Magwitch. The indirect consequences are more dire. When his sister is struck over the head with a heavy object, that object turns out to be "a convict's leg-iron . . . filed asunder." Pip is certain it is Magwitch's iron, filed off with the file with which he provided him. Still Pip temporizes and does not disclose what he knows to Joe. He contains it, [163/164] even as he kept his council when the strange man in the pub stirred a drink with a file, and presented him with a shilling wrapped in two one-pound notes, and when he had bad dreams at night, and thought—rather insufficiently to the point—what a "guiltily coarse and common thing it was, to be on secret terms of conspiracy with convicts."

The richest morality and realism of *Great Expectations* depends on the figure of Magwitch. The convict is a dangerous, violent man, and unregenerate in his violence, as his final murder of Compeyson shows. His wife, Molly, too, with her strong scarred wrists, is a woman whose violence is kept down only by strong restraint, her own and Jaggers'. Yet the violence of these two (and of many others, it is suggested) is not spontaneous, or not always and entirely so. In part at least, they are the victims of poverty and of a class system that fosters and gives protection to weak or evil villains like Miss Havisham's brother or Compeyson. Official justice, the justice of the courts and prisons, is an unfeeling and corrupt justice whose drunken ministers sell good seats in court for half-a-crown, and buy second-hand clothes cheap from the executioner.

The nature of this justice is made clear in the account of Magwitch's trial:

The trial was very short and very clear. Such things as could be said for him, were said—how he had taken to industrious habits, and had thriven lawfully and reputably. But, nothing could unsay the fact that he had returned, and was there in the presence of the Judge and Jury. It was impossible to try him for that, and do otherwise than find him guilty.

At that time it was the custom (as I learnt from my terrible [164/165] experience of that Sessions) to devote a concluding day to the passing of Sentences, and to make a finishing effect with the Sentence of Death. But for the indelible picture that my remembrance now holds before me, I could scarcely believe, even as I write these words, that I saw two-and-thirty men and women put before the Judge to receive that sentence together. Foremost among the two-and-thirty was he; seated, that he might get breath enough to keep life in him.

The whole scene starts out again in the vivid colours of the moment, down to the drops of April rain on the windows of the court, glittering in the rays of April sun. Penned in the dock, as I again stood outside it at the corner with his hand in mine, were the two-and-thirty men and women; some defiant, some stricken with terror, some sobbing and weeping, some covering their faces, some staring gloomily about. There had been shrieks from among the women convicts, but they had been stilled, and a hush had succeeded. The sheriffs with their great chains and nosegays, other civic gewgaws and monsters, criers, ushers, a great gallery full of people—a large theatrical audience—looked on, as the two-and-thirty and the Judge were solemnly confronted. Then, the Judge addressed them. Among the wretched creatures before him whom he must single out for special address, was one who almost from infancy had been an offender against the laws. . . .

The sun was striking in at the great windows of the court, through the glittering drops of rain upon the glass, and it made a broad shaft of light between the two-and-thirty and the Judge, linking both together, and perhaps reminding some among the audience, how both were passing on, with absolute equality, to the greater Judgment that knoweth all things and cannot err. Rising for a moment, a distinct speck of face in this way of light, the prisoner said, "My Lord, I have received my sentence of Death from the Almighty, but I bow to yours," and sat down again. There was some hushing, and the Judge went on with what he had to say to the rest. [165/166] Then, they were all formally doomed, and some of them were supported out, and some of them sauntered out with a haggard look of bravery, and a few nodded to the gallery, and two or three shook hands, and others went out chewing the fragments of herb they had taken from the sweet herbs lying about. He went last of all, because of having to be helped from his chair and to go very slowly; and he held my hand while all the others were removed, and while the audience got up (putting their dresses right, as they might at church or elsewhere) and pointed down at this criminal or that, and most of all at him and me.

In contrast to this justice of mass reprisal and of brutalizing public spectacle, Magwitch's administration of a personal justice that rewards good and punishes evil and takes the consequences for its own acts has its splendor and dignity, even though it cannot be allowed.

Pip, after visiting Newgate with Wemmick, thinks how strange it is that the taint of prison and crime should pervade his fortune and advancement. He thinks, too, what a contrast all this is to "the beautiful young Estella." But what he must still learn, of course, is that Estella is in fact the daughter of Magwitch and Molly. Eventually, he not only knows but is also reconciled. He comes not only to be unashamed of the dying Magwitch, but genuinely to love him, and just before Magwitch dies, Pip is able to tell him that his daughter whom he thought dead is alive, that she is a lady and very beautiful, and that he loves her. As Miss Havisham's foster-daughter and her false heir, Estella and Pip cannot come together. As Magwitch's true daughter and his deprived heir, they will.

There are no triumphantly happy endings in Dickens' later novels. Instead, there is the second chance that [166/167] comes after chastening and acceptance. In *David Copperfield* still, the happiness that comes after chastening seems almost able to disregard its own past—it is a virtually uninjured, full happiness. But in the later books, life is made more consequential, and people are what they are because of what they have been. Their happiness is a reconciliation to knowledge, and in these later books too, knowledge without reconciliation produces the riven mind, as in the case of Flora Finching. The alternatives Dickens offers, with increasing exclusiveness, are either madness, or the muted happiness that comes after acceptance.

The actual reconciliation of Pip and Estella at the end of *Great Expectations* was, as everyone knows, not in the original draft of the novel, but was added when Bulwer-Lytton objected to the unrelievedly somber tone of the original ending. But the limited optimism of the resolution of the novel does not depend on, and is not modified by, the changed ending. Pip has lost all his property, and has only such money as he earns by his own labors. Estella too has lost all her property. The Estella whom Pip had loved, and expected, really exists no longer, nor has he won the relatively romantic consolation of Biddy. And he is reconciled to his losses. Both he and Estella, we are told, have paled but grown better with age.

So after many years they meet again on a misty early evening on the grounds of Miss Havisham's old house—in the ruined garden, in fact, to return to the metaphor of the loss of Eden. Now Estella has a heart, and can confess to Pip's place in it. She, of course, has her place still in his heart, too. It is reasonable then to suggest that Pip has reentered the ruined Eden in order to leave again, [167/168] as Adam had left, chastened and with his chastened Eve: "I took her hand in mine, and we went out of the ruined place; and, as the morning mists had risen long ago when I first left the forge, so, the evening mists were rising now, and in all the broad expanse of tranquil light they showed to me, I saw no shadow of another parting from her."

Great Expectations provides a correction to the conventional optimism of *David Copperfield*. Pip must learn that fortune is not the way to happiness. Perhaps, too, Dickens is celebrating the losses that accompanied his success and the consequences of his will to forget his past. Certainly, to the modern reader, *Great Expectations* seems the more adult book—in its view of love, of success, of society; and its tighter structure and allegorical overtones are likely to please the chaste and intellectual modern taste more than the loose structure and folk tale elements of *David Copperfield*.

Yet though opinions and views may change, the basic vision of the individual imagination is relatively constant, and the greater the work of art, the more it founds the changing appearances dictated in part by view and opinion on the obsessional configurations of the imagination. Both *David Copperfield* and *Great Expectations* bear the profound marks of Dickens' imagination, and despite the many important ways in which one denies the other, essentially they reveal the same vision of life. Each of these books—*David Copperfield* as well as *Great Expectations*—is subversive, and the power of each depends on a response to the rendering of loss, of the beauty of hazard, of the horror of social injustice, and of the preposterous comedy of hypocrisy and self-delusion.   [end on 168]

PROBLEMS: Monroe Engel

1. Note the number of critics who make reference to the conclusion of *Paradise Lost* in connection with *Great Expectations*; what relationship between the two do you see?
2. In what ways does Pumblechook's name fit him, as Engel suggests?
3. Develop the comments Engel makes concerning Pumblechook.
4. To what extent is it fair to say that "Miss Havisham encourages his [Pip's] delusion that she is his patroness"?
5. Extend or refute the remarks on Magwitch [p. 164].
6. Engel makes a case for the alternate ending which Dickens provided for the novel at the urging of Bulwer-Lytton. Evaluate his defense in the light of other criticism.
7. Summarize Engel's article in terms of his concluding remark that *Great Expectations* is subversive.

Great Expectations[*]

by J. HILLIS MILLER

I

MY FIRST most vivid and broad impression of the identity of things, seems to me to have been gained on a memorable raw afternoon towards evening. At such a time I found out for certain, that this bleak place overgrown with nettles was the churchyard; and that Philip Pirrip, late of this parish, and also Georgiana wife of the above, were dead and buried; and that Alexander, Bartholomew, Abraham, Tobias, and Roger, infant children of the aforesaid, were also dead and buried; and that the dark flat wilderness beyond the churchyard, intersected with dykes and mounds and gates, with scattered cattle feeding on it, was the marshes; and that the low leaden line beyond was the river; and that the distant savage lair from which the wind was rushing, was the sea; and that the small bundle of shivers growing afraid of it all and beginning to cry, was Pip.(1)[1]

Great Expectations is the most unified and concentrated expression of Dickens' abiding sense of the world, and Pip might be called the archetypal Dickens hero. In Great Expectations Dickens' particular view of things is expressed with a concreteness and symbolic intensity he never surpassed. Perhaps the restrictions of shorter length and of weekly rather than monthly publication led Dickens to present his story more in symbolic than in discursive form. The result is not a narrowing and rarefying of meaning, but rather a large increase in intensity and complexity. What it took Dickens in 1850 the first hundred pages of David Copperfield to say is presented far [249/250] more powerfully in the first few pages of Great Expectations: the lonely boy becoming aware of his desolation on the dark marshes in the

---

* Reprinted by permission of the publishers from J. Hillis Miller, *Charles Dickens: The World of His Novels.* (Cambridge, Mass.: Harvard University Press.) Copyright, 1958, by The President and Fellows of Harvard College. Pages 249–278.

1 Numbers in parentheses refer to chapters in *Great Expectations.*

midst of a hostile universe, standing by the graves of his mother, father, and brothers, aware that he will be beaten by his foster mother when he returns home, and suddenly terrified by the apparition of the "fearful man" "starting up from among the graves" (1). What had been presented seriatim in the earlier novels is here said with poetic compression. And in following Pip's adventures we perhaps come closest to the intimate center of Dickens' apprehension of the world and of his mode of existence within it. *Great Expectations* makes available, as does no other of Dickens' novels, the central experiences of the universal Dickensian hero.

Never, perhaps, was the form of a great novel conceived as the response to so practical a demand. In the early fall of 1860 the sales of *All the Year Round* were dropping sadly because of the unpopularity of Charles Lever's *The Day's Ride*. Dickens "dashed" in (*Let.*, III, 183) with *Great Expectations* in order to save circulation. At first *Great Expectations* was a "little piece" (*ibid.*, p. 182). Then, as the idea grew— "such a very fine, new, and grotesque idea" (*ibid.*)—it was planned as a monthly serial of twenty numbers, like *Bleak House* or *Little Dorrit*. Then, because of the falling-off of the sales of *All the Year Round*, Dickens decided to write it in the much briefer form of a serial in weekly numbers for that journal.

Dickens' own language for what he was doing scarcely reveals its importance. The central motif of *Great Expectations*, the *donnée* with which Dickens began, was the secret manipulation of Pip's life by Magwitch the convict—a striking idea, which goes to the roots of several key nineteenth-century notions about human existence. Dickens' phrase for it was "the grotesque tragi-comic conception that first encouraged me" (*ibid.*, p. 186). We have only one important sign of the depths which Dickens was plumbing in the conception of the basic motif of *Great Expectations*: "To be quite sure I had fallen into no unconscious repetitions, I read David Copperfield again the other day, and was affected by it to a degree you would hardly believe" (*ibid.*). This is a valuable reinforcement of the sense [250/251] we get from the novel itself that Dickens was here drawing again, as in *David Copperfield*, on his most intimate personal experiences. They are transformed into a "fable," perhaps, but still retain the essential form of Dickens' sense of the meaning of his own life.

What form does this meaning take?

Great Expectations, like most of Dickens' novels, does not begin with a description of the perfect bliss of childhood, the period when the world and the self are identified, and the parents are seen as benign gods whose care and whose overlooking judgment protect and justify the child. Like Oedipus, who, as a newborn baby, was put out in the fields to die, Dickens' heroes and heroines have never experienced this perfect security. Each becomes aware of himself as isolated from all that is outside of himself. The Dickensian hero is separated from nature. The world appears to him as cold and unfriendly, as a "wilderness" or a graveyard. In Dickens there is no Wordsworthian theory of the child's filial bond with nature. There is no moment of primitive or infantile identification of subject and object, self and world, followed by a "fall" into the cruel realm of time and division. The self is not initially the plenitude of a union with the entire universe, but is already down to "the small bundle of shivers growing afraid of it all and beginning to cry." The Dickensian hero is also alienated from the human community. He has no familial tie. He is an orphan, or illegitimate, or both. He has no status in the community, no inherited role which he can accept with dignity. He is characterized by desire, rather than by possession. His spiritual state is one of an expectation founded on a present consciousness of lack, of deprivation. He is, in Wallace Stevens' phrase, "an emptiness that would be filled."

Furthermore, the Dickensian hero becomes aware of himself as guilty. His very existence is a matter of reproach and a shameful thing. Esther Summerson's foster mother tells her that it would have been better if she had never been born, and Pip says of himself: "I was always treated as if I had insisted on being born in opposition to the dictates of reason, religion, and morality, and against the dissuading arguments of my best [251/252] friends" (4). It is mere accident that he is alive at all, and is not buried beside his brothers in the lonely church-yard by the sea. "As to you," says Joe of his first glimpse of the infant Pip, "if you could have been aware how small and flabby and mean you was, dear me, you'd have formed the most contemptible opinions of yourself!"(7). And Mrs. Joe recalls "all the times she had wished [Pip] in [his] grave, and [he] had contumaciously refused to go there" (4). The typical Dickens hero, like Pip, feels guilty because he has no given status or relation to nature, to family, or to the community. He is, in everyone's eyes, in the way, superfluous. He is either ignored by society altogether, thrown into the streets to beg or starve, or he is taken care of by the state or by his foster parents in an impersonal way which deprives him of any real identity. To submit to this "care" is to be transformed into an object. He may, alternatively, accept a job as a functionary in the vast system of money-getting which dominates urban society. This will as effectively dehumanize him as going to the poorhouse. Dickens shows that, for his characters at least, no "natural right" exists, no "state" in the sense that Rousseau and Matthew Arnold meant it: something above all hereditary legitimacies and distinctions, something to which the individual may tie himself and submit, as to his own best self. For Dickens, such submission means to lose all one's specifically human qualities of self-consciousness and freedom. Submission to the collective process of making and selling, of "beggaring your neighbor" lest he "beggar" you, is to be in danger of becoming dehumanized, like Wemmick, who is "a dry man, . . . with a square wooden face, whose expression seem[s] to have been imperfectly chipped out with a dull-edged chisel" (21). Or, even worse, the individual may be destroyed altogether by society, and remain behind only as the trophy of somebody's successful manipulations, like Jaggers' clients, who have been transformed into "dreadful casts on a shelf, of faces peculiarly swollen, and twitchy about the nose" (20).

Since the Dickensian hero has initially no real role, any status he attains in the world will be the result of his own efforts. He will be totally responsible, himself, for any identity [252/253] he achieves, and thus "guilty" in the sense of being the source of his own values. He has no hope of ever being justified by any external approval. He will be, whatever he does, a "self-made man," a man who has made himself his own goal and end. This will be true in spite of any efforts on his part to escape his superfluity. The world has simply refused to give him any assigned place, and any place he gets will have to be seized.

Given such a situation, the hero can remove himself from the world in which he has no place, withdraw into a solitary enclosure. Suicide is not really an option for Dickens' characters, except for those who are completely evil, but withdrawal and passivity are possible. In different ways, for example, Arthur Clennam, Mrs. Clennam, John Harmon, and Miss Havisham attempt to escape from the threat of dehumanization by willing not to will, by abnegation, by a passive drifting which will, they vainly hope, relieve them of the guilt of action. On the other hand, the Dickensian hero can submit to the complete dehumanization which society or his stepparents would practice upon him, or, finally, he can take upon himself the responsibility and guilt of a selfhood which is to be made, not accepted from the outside. In one case, he tries to hide from himself his freedom by submitting to the role society would have him play. He thus becomes one of Dickens' comic automatons, like Wemmick, who at first seems to be a wooden puppet manipulated by external forces, wholly lacking in real human qualities, mouthing the dead language of cliché and slogan: "My guiding star," says Wemmick, "is: Get hold of Portable Property." In the other case, he consciously sets himself up as an end in himself. He is then in danger of becoming, like Blandois in *Little Dorrit*, a demonic individualist whose hand is against his neighbor, and who hopes to achieve personal identity by the destruction of everything that is. But Dickens' true heroes and heroines, those characters at the centers of his novels, seek some intermediary between these extremes. They seek some way out that will make possible the achievement of true selfhood, while not necessitating the extreme of anarchic individualism. These protagonists try various ways, some proper, some improper, of attaining the reconciliation of free-[253/254]dom and security. The single great development in Dickens' world view is the change in the kinds of expedients which are deemed to be proper or possible. *Great Expectations* is the novel in which the various alternatives are most clearly presented and opposed.

II

In a world where the only possible relation to other people seems to be that of oppressor to oppressed, or oppressed to oppressor, those who are born into oppression may try to seize the role of oppressor. If one must be either master or slave, it seems better to be master than slave. But the choice of Blandois, in *Little Dorrit*, the choice of an open attempt to be master ("It is my character to dominate," says Blandois), is not possible without the consciousness of guilt. Only those who are born members of the upper class can rule guiltlessly, by "divine right," as it were, and the outcast knows that neither God nor the collective approval of society will justify any open attempts on his part to reverse the role, and to become oppressor rather than oppressed. So he tries various ways to attain the same movement up in the social scale without incurring guilt for it.

He may simply dominate those beneath him in the social chain of being, as Wemmick, himself a victim of the great legal organization, treats those beneath him, Jaggers' clients, condemned jailbirds, as though they were the plants in his flower garden, or as Abel Magwitch, escaped convict, at the extreme point of his exclusion from society, coerces Pip into feeding him. He is "beneath" everyone in the world except Pip, whom he seizes and turns upside down, as though to reverse their roles. Much later in the novel, when Pip is being browbeaten by Jaggers (surely "master" rather than "slave" in the world of the novel), he says: "I felt at a disadvantage, which reminded me of that old time when I had been put upon a tombstone" (36). The inadequacies of this expedient are obvious. The "exploiter" cannot hide from himself the fact that he has unjustifiably seized power over another human being.

But two other more surreptitious ways are attempted by characters in *Great Expectations*. In the first case, one person [254/255] manipulates another not as his victim, but as the agent of his revenge on society. In one way or another several characters in *Great Expectations* try to "make" other characters. They do not try to make them into mere dehumanized tools, but to make them into members of the upper class who will have all the prerogatives of justified exploitation which they themselves lack. Thus Magwitch boasts that Pip is "the gentleman what I made." If he cannot himself ever by anything but a transported felon, "hunted dunghill dog," perhaps he can secretly create a gentleman through whom he will vicariously enjoy all the powers he could never attain himself: "I says to myself, 'If I ain't a gentleman, nor yet ain't got no learning, I'm the owner of such. All on you owns stock and land; which on you owns a brought-up London gentleman?'" (39). Magwitch is a nightmare permutation of Mr. Brownlow and Mr. Jarndyce. He is the benevolent guardian, secretly manipulating the fortunes of the hero and protecting him, turned into a condemned felon who, like a horrible old dog, gloats over his victim.

There is at least one comic parody of this theme: Pumblechook boasts that he is the "founder" of Pip's fortune, and he shakes Pip's hand again and again on the day his great expectations are announced. Pumblechook's action is an ominous anticipation of Magwitch's symbolic gesture of appropriation when he appears at Pip's door, and grasps his hands. Indeed, as John H. Hagan, Jr. has observed, Pumblechook, as one of those who have schooled Pip in the attitudes which prepare him for his delusion, can claim with justice to be the founder of Pip's fortune.[1]

But Miss Havisham is a more important parallel to Magwitch. Her heart has been broken by Compeyson, the archvillain who lies behind all the evil in the story. She has withdrawn forever from the world, and has renounced all attempts to act in her own person. Miss Havisham has attempted to stop time at the moment she received the news that her bridegroom-to-be had deceived and deserted her. She does not try to stop [255/256] time at the moment *before* she heard the news. No, she does not want to escape the harsh reality of her betrayal, and return to the time when she was living in an illusory world of innocence, security, and, as she thought, reciprocal love. She wants, rather, to crystallize her grief and bereavement into an eternal moment of shock and sorrow, like those of Faulkner's characters who remain

[1] See pp. 172, 173 of "The Poor Labyrinth: The Theme of Social Injustice in Dickens's 'Great Expectations,'" *Nineteenth-Century Fiction*, IX (1954), 169–178.

immobilized with their backs to the future, facing some terrible event in the past which has determined the meaning of their lives.

Miss Havisham has two motives for her attempt to freeze time. She wants to make certain that her betrayal will be the whole meaning of her life, that nothing more will happen to change her destiny as it existed at the moment of betrayal. She does not want it to be possible for her to stop suffering, to forget, to turn her attention to other things and other people, and so cease to be the Miss Havisham who was cruelly abandoned on the day of her wedding. If she allows herself to change at all that self may become a thing of the past, a matter of history, a self she no longer is. She may slip back into time, which means to slip back into a human existence which is conditioned in its essence by temporality. And to be essentially conditioned by time means never to reach a stopping place in one's life, to be "ever more about to be," to be not yet what one is going to be, and never finally what one is. Miss Havisham's attempt to freeze time implies a recognition of the same harsh truth that drove Quentin Compson in Faulkner's *The Sound and the Fury* to suicide: "You are not thinking of finitude," says Quentin's father, "you are contemplating an apotheosis in which a temporary state of mind will become symmetrical above the flesh and aware both of itself and of the flesh it will not quite discard you will not even be dead . . . you cannot bear to think that someday it will no longer hurt you like this . . . no man ever does that [commits suicide] under the first fury of despair or remorse or bereavement he does it only when he has realised that even the despair or remorse or bereavement is not particularly important to the dark diceman."[2] [256/257] Miss Havisham, like Quentin, wants to achieve an inhuman fixity, to escape time and to live as if her life were finished, as if she had survived herself, and could look back at her life as everyone else does, regarding it as a "destiny" and as a completed meaning. Dickens judges Miss Havisham as harshly as any of his characters, though he abandons his apparent intention to have her hang herself (8): "in shutting out the light of day, she had shut out infinitely more; . . . in seclusion, she had

---

[2] William Faulkner, *The Sound and the Fury & As I Lay Dying* (Modern Library ed., New York, n.d.), pp. 195, 196.

secluded herself from a thousand natural and healing influences; ...
her mind, brooding solitary, had grown diseased, as all minds do and
must and will that reverse the appointed order of their Maker ..." (49).
Moreover, Miss Havisham's attempt is doomed to failure. For in
willing to freeze her life at the moment the annihilating blow came
from the outside, she changes her abandonment from a "cruel fate" to
a chosen role. It is Miss Havisham herself who chooses to make her
betrayal the central event and meaning of her life. And in so choosing
she makes herself responsible for it. She tries to flee forever out of the
realm of freedom, unpredictability, and change, but she only succeeds
in making herself responsible for ruining her own life, and for nearly
ruining Estella's and Pip's.

Miss Havisham's second motive for attempting to freeze time at the
moment of her betrayal is the motive of revenge. She had loved
Compeyson with a love she herself defines as "blind devotion, un-
questioning self-humiliation, utter submission, trust and belief against
yourself and against the whole world, giving up your whole heart and
soul to the smiter..." (29). "There is no doubt," says Herbert Pocket, "that
she perfectly idolised him" (22). Miss Havisham tries to carry the same kind
of all or nothing quality into her new life. Her revenge is to make her
betrayal into the very meaning of her life, and to make her resulting
death-in-life a curse on her heartless lover: " 'When the ruin is complete,' said she, with a ghastly look, 'and when they lay me dead, in
my bride's dress on the bride's table—which shall be done, and which
will be the finished curse upon him—so much the better if it is done
on this day!' " (11). ("This day" is the anniversary of her betrayal.) If she
slips one instant in her determination to make her whole [257/258] life
a reproach and a curse on Compeyson, her revenge will be incomplete.
Her frozen life is not the result of a failure of will, but of a will strong
as iron to "reverse the appointed order of [her] Maker" by closing
every last aperture of her life through which change might come, just
as she has closed all the windows and doors in Satis House through
which the natural light and air might enter.

Miss Havisham's other method of revenge is Estella. "... with my
praises, and with my jewels, and with my teachings, and with this

figure of myself always before her," says Miss Havisham of Estella, "... I stole her heart away and put ice in its place" (49). Just as Magwitch, another victim of Compeyson, creates in Pip an "instrument" of his revenge on society, so Miss Havisham "mould[s] [Estella] into the form that her wild resentment, spurned affection, and wounded pride, found vengeance in" (49). Estella will draw men as a candle attracts moths, but, being without a heart, she will treat them as Compeyson treated Miss Havisham: "How does she use you, Pip, how does she use you?" asks Miss Havisham. She had deluded herself into thinking she is taking no direct revenge on mankind, but only letting her state of abandonment be a punishment. Through Estella she will take an indirect and therefore guiltless revenge, and break a hundred hearts for her own one heart that was broken.

This transformation of the master-slave relation is apparently a reconciliation of irreconcilables. Miss Havisham and Magwitch hope to attain vicariously all that they lack. They will enjoy the power of the oppressor without being guilty of having unjustifiably seized that power. No one will be able to blame Magwitch for the arrogance of Pip the gentleman, and no one will blame Miss Havisham for the cruelties Estella practices on her suitors. Since the low origin of his great expectations is hidden from Pip, he will have the sense of "divine right" that is enjoyed by a gentleman born. His transformation from "common" blacksmith's boy to London gentleman will seem to him like a "destiny," something at any rate for which he is not guiltily responsible. And Estella will be brought up to feel that men are her natural enemies. She will experience no re-[258/259]morse for breaking their hearts because she will have no heart herself. She will be like a superhuman goddess, unable to understand the sorrows of mere mortals.

This attempt to transcend isolation without guilt, by paradoxically both being and not being another person whom one has created, in both cases fails.

For Miss Havisham love reduces itself to the extreme of masochistic submission to the iron heel of the lover. For her, human relations are inevitably a conflict, a war to the death, and love to her is simply an extreme form of that possession and manipulation of another person which we see in the relations of Magwitch and Pip, Miss Havisham and Estella, Jaggers and his clients, and so on. Love, for Miss Havisham, is another form of "fettering," and cannot escape from the universal law which says, "I shall either dehumanize my neighbor, or be dehumanized by him, either be master or slave." But Miss Havisham proves in her own experience the hard truth that the relation of master and slave is frustration, suffering, and alienation for master as well as for slave. For if the master succeeds in driving away all the human qualities of his victim, as Miss Havisham has succeeded with Estella, then in a single stroke the victim as human being evaporates, and with him the validation of selfhood which the master had structured on his relation to the slave. "You stock and stone! . . . You cold, cold heart!" says Miss Havisham in the anguish of her realization that as a result of her upbringing Estella is altogether incapable of returning her "burning love, inseparable from jealousy at all times" (38). Miss Havisham is not telling all the truth earlier when she says her motive in attaching Estella to herself is to make possible a perfect revenge on men for her betrayal. She also wants to create between herself and her creature Estella a perfect relation as a substitute for the one which so failed her when her lover abandoned her. Then she had set her whole heart on Compeyson, and had been reduced to spiritual nothingness when he betrayed her. Now she still wants a perfect relation to another person, a relation which will fill up the void left in her heart by the tragedy of her youth. But she wants to achieve that relation without risk. Miss Havisham imagines [259/260] that she can escape the uncertainty of all authentic human relationships if she takes a young girl, before her personality has been formed, and brings her up to look only to her guardian for protection and love. She wants Estella to love her only, so that in the dark, airless confines of Satis House they may dwell safe from all the world, and be sufficient to one another. Miss Havisham succeeds in making Estella wholly her "creation," but, at the same time, she destroys any possibility of a return of her love. The kind of relation Miss Havisham wants cannot be achieved without risk, without an acceptance of the unpredictability and insecurity of all real human relations. At the very moment Miss Havisham makes sure of Estella, Estella will, paradoxically, reverse roles and become Miss Havisham's master: " 'But to be proud and hard to *me*!' Miss Havisham quite shrieked, as she stretched out her arms. 'Estella, Estella, Estella, to be proud and hard to *me*!' "(38).

In the same way Magwitch cannot resist the temptation to return from New South Wales, even at the risk of his life, to see with his own eyes the gentleman he has made: "I've come to the old country fur to see my gentleman spend his money *like* a gentleman. That'll be *my* pleasure. *My* pleasure 'ull be fur to see him do it. And blast you all! . . . blast you every one, from the judge in his wig, to the colonist a stirring up the dust, I'll show a better gentleman than the whole kit on you put together!" Magwitch has returned to let Pip know the real source of his transformation into a gentleman. His project cannot succeed because Pip must both know and not know that Magwitch has "made" him. He must not know, in order to remain a true gentleman, conscious of enjoying his status by right. He must know in order really to be Magwitch's representative, the creature he has manufactured to wreak his vengeance on society: "Once more he took me by both hands and surveyed me with an air of admiring proprietorship . . ." (40). Magwitch wants to enjoy directly his sense of power, and he wants Pip to know that all his acts are as the vicar of Magwitch. But of course as soon as Pip knows the source of his great expectations he no longer thinks of himself as a gentleman. Rather he repudiates with horror his connection with [260/261] Magwitch, and looks upon himself as Magwitch's dupe, manipulated, as Magwitch was by Compeyson, for his criminal assault upon society. Neither Estella nor Pip can embody in their own persons the contradictory needs of their creators' projects for them.

III

She had adopted Estella, she had as good as adopted me, and it could not fail to be her intention to bring us together. She reserved it for me to restore the desolate house, admit the sunshine into the dark rooms, set the clocks a going and the cold hearths a blazing, tear down the cobwebs, destroy the vermin—in short, do all the shining deeds of the young Knight of romance, and marry the Princess (29).

Neither way out of alienation will work, neither the attempt to become an oppressor of those below even while being oppressed from above, nor the attempt to endow someone else with the power to be an oppressor while one remains innocently passive oneself. One other way remains, a way that even more subtly than the others hides its radical defect: The disinherited one may accept "great expectations." That is, he may believe that, in spite of his apparent lack of status, and of any real reason for existing, there is a hidden place for him, a destined role among those who enjoy the dignity and security of being masters. Pip repudiates what he is now with the utmost horror: He denies that he is an orphan, "brought up by hand," destined to be apprenticed to Joe and to spend the rest of his life as a country black-smith. No, he is not what he appears to be. He is really the secret self which lies unfulfilled in the future, beyond the shadowy mists of his great expectations. Now, he is not what he is, and he is what he is not. Pip's acceptance of great expectations does not mean seizing recogni-tion of his usefulness by force. It means believing that he will be miraculously given a place in society as though it were his natural right, as though the world had for some unaccountable reason conspired to keep his real place hidden, only to bestow it at last as a free gift. Such are Pip's hopes. He believes that Estella and all the privileges possessed by a gentleman are destined for [261/262] him by Miss Havisham. He will not need to dirty his hands with the crime of appropriating a place among the oppressors. He will suddenly be transformed from the class of the exploited to the class of the exploiters. There will be an absolute discontinuity between his initial given condition of alienation and isolation, and the suddenly attained possession of a secure place in society. The new man will be both free (cannot Pip buy anything he wants?), and at the same time wholly consecrated in his new role by the approval of society.

Although Pip is of course the main example of the theme of "great expectations," a number of other characters are comic parodies of Pip's attempt to transcend his first situation. If Pip seeks escape in the unconditioned possession of Estella and the rights of a gentleman, Wemmick's goal is the unlimited possession of "Portable Property." Wopsle lives in the unquenchable expectation of reviving the drama, with himself as a famous actor, receiving the applause of multitudes. Mrs. Pocket is the daughter of a very small nobleman, and has been "brought up from her cradle as one who in the nature of things must marry a title" (23). As a result she has "grown up highly ornamental, but perfectly helpless and useless" (23). And Herbert Pocket has even greater expectations than Pip does. Although he is a mere miserable apprentice in a counting house, in his own mind he has already made his fortune, and is "a capitalist—an Insurer of Ships" (22).

Pip might have moved beyond awareness that the family and the social order are based on the notion that there are two distinct kinds of being. He might have rejected the whole structure. But no; he accepts the situation, and simply "expects" to move from one status to the other. When Jaggers announces the great expectations, he tells Pip what he has been hoping for all along: his benefactor wishes "that he be immediately removed from his present sphere of life and from this place, and be brought up as a gentleman—in a word, as a young fellow of great expectations" (18). When Joe and Biddy express "wonder" at the notion of Pip as a gentleman, he doesn't "half like it" (18). To him the good fortune is merely the recognition of the true Pip, the Pip who has heretofore by accident been hid-[262/263]den from view. The new Pip feels, like a supernatural being, a "sublime compassion for the poor creatures who were destined to go there [to the country church], Sunday after Sunday, all their lives through, and to lie obscurely at last among the low green mounds" (19). To the new godlike Pip the country people seem less than human. They are like beasts of the field who live a merely natural life, unconsciously passing on to an obscure death, like the "mute inglorious" countrymen of Gray's "Elegy." Pip plans a great feast for the village, in which he, the *grand seigneur*, will stoop from his godlike height and bestow "a dinner of roast-beef and plum-pudding, a pint of ale, and a gallon of condescension, upon everybody in the village" (19). As for Pip: "henceforth [he is] for London and greatness" (19).

It is at first difficult to see why Pip's great expectations do not seem to him another form of the degrading manipulation by society, another subtler form of alienation. They do appear that way to Joe and Biddy, who accept their status with the proud independence of the lower class. When Pip suggests to Biddy that he might "remove Joe into a higher sphere" (19) (a parody of what Jaggers said when he announced the great expectations), she says, "He may be too proud to let any one take him out of a place that he is competent to fill, and fills well and with respect" (19). Why then does Pip accept so readily a change in status which to Joe seems an affront to his pride and independence? It is a very different thing to have as one's given place in society the status of a gentleman rather than the status of a blacksmith. It approaches the reconciliation of freedom and security which Pip seeks. Moreover, the circumstances of mystery which surround the great expectations make it possible to manipulate their meaning ambiguously. Pip thinks they come from Miss Havisham, but he is not certain, and this uncertainty allows him to interpret them as at once a willful choice on someone's part to change his place in society, or as a reward for faithful service, or as recognition that he has too noble a nature to be a blacksmith. Because of the mystery about the gift Pip can look upon his great expectations as at once earned and gratuitously bestowed. The more pleasant interpretation is the one which makes them the recognition by society of what [263/264] his inmost nature has been all along. The flattering Pumblechook chooses this interpretation of Pip's rise in the world: "I give you joy of your good fortune," he says. "Well deserved, well deserved!" (19). And he tells Pip he has always said of him: "That boy is no common boy, and mark me, his fortun' will be no common fortun'" (19). The word "common" here has a good deal of nuance. "Coarse and common" was what Estella had called him; these were the words that made him dissatisfied with his lot as a blacksmith's apprentice.

Indeed, Pip's first visit to Miss Havisham's determines everything which follows in his life, because it determines the way he reacts to everything which happens to him thereafter: "That was a memorable day to me, for it made great changes in me. But it is the same with any

life. Imagine one selected day struck out of it, and think how different
its course would have been. Pause you who read this, and think for a
moment of the long chain of iron or gold, of thorns or flowers, that
would never have bound you, but for the formation of the first link
on one memorable day" (9). Pip is "bound" by his reaction to the
experiences of this day, as firmly as he is bound apprentice to Joe, and
as firmly as the captured Magwitch is bound by his fetters. On this
day he makes the original choice of a desired self, and binds his destiny
inextricably to Estella. Pip is able to understand this only much later,
on the day when, aware that he has lost Estella, he first confesses his
love for her: "You are part of my existence, part of myself. You have
been in every line I have ever read, since I first came here, the rough
common boy whose poor heart you wounded even then. You have
been in every prospect I have ever seen since—on the river, on the sails
of the ships, on the marshes, in the clouds, in the light, in the darkness,
in the wind, in the woods, in the sea, in the streets. You have been the
embodiment of every graceful fancy that my mind has ever become
acquainted with. The stones of which the strongest London buildings
are made, are not more real, or more impossible to be displaced by
your hands, than your presence and influence have been to me, there
and everywhere, and will be" (44). Pip's desire to possess Estella, in spite
of his recognition of her nature, is identified with his [264/265] deepest
project of selfhood. It is, he says, "the clue by which I am to be
followed into my poor labyrinth" (28), "the innermost life of my
life" (29). In choosing Estella, Pip alters and defines the entire world, and
gives it a permanent structure pervaded by her presence. He is true to the
determining choice of his life, the choice that was made when,
"humiliated, hurt, spurned, offended, angry, sorry"(8), he reacted to the
taunts of Estella not by hating and rejecting her, but by accepting her
judgment of him, and by spontaneously rejecting all the pieties of the
forge. Before he went to Satis House the forge had been sacred. His
prospective relation to it had justified his life as completely as a Christian
is justified by his conversion and by his sense of receiving God's grace:
"I had believed in the best parlour as a most elegant saloon; I had
believed in the front door, as a mysterious portal of the Temple of

State whose solemn opening was attended with a sacrifice of roast fowls; I had believed in the kitchen as a chaste though not magnificent apartment; I had believed in the forge as the glowing road to manhood and independence"(14). Now all that is changed. The old gods have been rejected, and Pip is ashamed of home: "Within a single year all this was changed. Now, it was all coarse and common, and I would not have had Miss Havisham and Estella see it on any account"(14). It is only in response to his acceptance of Estella's judgment of him that Pip's great expectations come into existence. It is only because Estella has become part of "every prospect" that Pip makes the otherwise unlikely mistake of assuming Miss Havisham is the source of his great expectations and intends Estella for him. Just as he has rejected as far as possible his relation to Magwitch—being "on secret terms of conspiracy with convicts" is to Pip a "guiltily coarse and common thing," "a feature in [his] low career that [he] had previously forgotten" (10)—so he interprets everything that happens to him in terms of Estella and Miss Havisham. He is not fooled; he fools himself: "All other swindlers upon earth are nothing to the self-swindlers, and with such pretences did I cheat myself" (10).

Pip's love of Estella is by its very nature a self-deception, because it is a love which is based on its own impossibility. It de-[265/266]pends in its intimate nature on the fact that it can never be satisfied. On the one hand, Pip says, "... I loved her against reason, against promise, against peace, against hope, against happiness, against all discouragement that could be"(29), and, on the other hand, he can say, "Then, a burst of gratitude came upon me, that she should be destined for me, once the blacksmith's boy"(29). From the beginning Estella is the judge who scornfully labels Pip "a common labouring-boy," who looks down on him from a great height like a cold star, and fixes everything eternally in its place, as everything seems eternally immobilized under the winter stars. To Pip, Estella seems always "immeasurably above [him]," and treats him "as insolently as if [he] were a dog in disgrace"(8). But he does not wish to escape from this relationship to Estella, any more than he wishes to escape from his submission to society in those "wretched hankerings after money and gentility" which cannot be dissociated from "her presence" (29). Rather, he imagines that when Estella is given to him as his wife he will succeed in possessing his judge. She is "destined" for him, and therefore he expects to bring down his star from the sky, to have in Estella at once judge and submissive wife.

Pip has succeeded through Estella, if not in escaping his initial state, then at least in defining himself as the lack of something particular. His essence is defined entirely by negations (he lacks the education, language, manners, and fine clothes of a gentleman; he fails to possess Estella—she is "inaccessible"), but even a definition in terms of what he is not is better than no definition at all. Pip in his relation to Estella achieves the only kind of definiteness, it may be, which is available to man: the definition of a desired future self. In spite of her infinite distance and inaccessibility, and in a way because of them, Estella is the source of all the meaning and coherence of Pip's life. To Pip it is a great relief to be judged. The criminal seeks out his own punishment. If his crime remains a secret and he is accepted by everyone as hough he were still the person he was before the crime, he has a horrible sense of his own unreality. The gap between what he is for himself, and what other people think he is, causes intolerable suffering. The crim-[266/267]inal will give himself up in order to be reintegrated into the human community, even if being reintegrated means to be condemned to death. In the same way, Pip never hesitates a moment to accept Estella's judgment of him, even though it means accepting a much less admirable self than he is in the eyes of Biddy. To Biddy he is an honest blacksmith's apprentice faithful to his duty. But to accept Biddy's judgment rather than Estella's means accepting the role which has become identified for Pip with his initial state of isolation and subjection. On the other hand, Estella's judgment that he is coarse and common implies a very definite self which he fails to be, and which would transcend his first state if he could reach it. It is no wonder that he repudiates Herbert's suggestion that he give her up because she will never make him happy. To give up Estella would be to give up the very meaning of his life. Pip can abandon this relationship to Estella only when the entire structure of his world has been destroyed by the return of Magwitch.

But why did Dickens choose to have his hero enchanted by such a person as Miss Havisham? What is the relation between Pip and Miss Havisham? And why should Estella be identified with the desolation of Satis House? Satis House is an elaborate example of a figurative technique constantly employed by Dickens: the use of houses to symbolize states of soul. Again and again in Dickens' novels we find houses which are the mirror images of their masters or mistresses. But Satis House expresses far more than merely Miss Havisham's nature. Miss Havisham and her house are the images of a fixed social order, the power which can judge Pip at first as coarse and common, and later as a gentleman. The name "Satis House," as Estella tells Pip, "meant, when it was given, that whoever had this house, could want nothing else" (8). That Pip becomes fascinated by such a vision of the upper class and of its norms is all the stronger testimony to the falsity of his desire to be a gentleman. Miss Havisham's house of darkness, decay, and frozen time is a symbol of the upper class, paralyzed in its codified mores and prejudices, as much as it is a symbol of the spiritual condition of Miss Havisham. When Pip sees in "the stopped clock, . . . the withered articles of bridal dress upon [267/268] the table and the ground, . . . in the falls of the cobwebs from the centre-piece, in the crawlings of the spiders on the cloth," "in everything the construction that [his] mind [has] come to, repeated and thrown back to [him]" (38), he is confessing to the effect of his infatuation with the idea of being a gentleman as much as to the effect of his submission to Miss Havisham or to Estella as persons. Pip in London, living in the eternally un-satisfied pursuit of Estella and of the "pleasure" of London high society, is as much the victim of his desire to be a gentleman as he is of his love for Estella, or of his "enchantment" by Miss Havisham. Miss Havisham and her house, then, are the concrete symbols of that place in the upper class Pip has been led to want by Estella's judgment of him. They express his fatuity as no abstract analysis could do. Pip is willing to barter all the spontaneity and charity of his relations to Joe for the coldness, formality, and decay of Miss Havisham's house, and for the life as a gentleman he thinks she has given him.

But Pip finds that being a gentleman is no escape from uncertainty and guilt. One of the conditions of his great expectations is that he shall still go by the name of Pip, the name he gave himself in his early childhood. This is a symbol of the fact that he cannot make a full break with the past, and in a way hints of the terrible revelation which will shatter his expectations. But even when he has received his expectations, is living as a gentleman in London, and has not received the blow which will destroy his hopes, he is not at peace: "I cannot tell you how dependent and uncertain I feel, and how exposed to hundreds of chances" (30); "I lived in a state of chronic uneasiness respecting my behaviour to Joe" (34); "... a weariness on my spirits" (*ibid.*); "... restlessness and disquiet of mind" (*ibid.*). This is partly, no doubt, because of Pip's uncertainty about Estella, but it is also part of the very condition of being a gentleman—as Dickens showed in his other portraits of idle and uneasy aristocrats (such as Eugene Wrayburn or Henry Gowan). These young gentlemen all suffer from ennui, and from an inability to choose a course of ac-[268/269]tion. Paralysis of will seizes them precisely because they have unlimited possibilities. There are so many courses open to them that they are wholly unable to choose one. Far from realizing the peace of a reconciliation of freedom and security, Pip's transformation into a gentleman only plunges him into deeper disquietude and weariness of spirits—deeper because he is even further than ever away from the discovery of some externally imposed duty which will tell him what to do and who he is.

IV

There comes a moment, then, when Pip discovers the futility and hollowness of his expectations. Already he has discovered that the mere unlimited possession of money is not "enough." When he is learning to be a gentleman in London with Herbert Pocket he gets further and further into debt, and his device of projecting the debt limit further and further by leaving a "margin" is an effective dramatization of the ever-receding character of his attempt to achieve peace and stability through money. Each time he runs into debt immediately "to the full extent of the margin, and sometimes, in the sense of freedom and solvency it impart[s], [gets] pretty far on into another margin" (34). The more money Pip spends, the more he needs, and the goal of satisfaction recedes further and further, like the end of the rainbow. The actual possession of the tangible evidence of his great expectations leaves him what he has always been: "restless aspiring discontented me"(14). Dickens is dramatizing here his recognition of the bankruptcy of the idea of the gentleman, who rules by inherited right, but owes protection and help to those beneath. Since society has ceased, in Dickens' view, to be an organic structure, being a gentleman means chiefly having the money to buy education and luxuries. It no more means being part of a community than does being sent to the hulks, like Magwitch, or being bound apprentice, like Pip. Pip the gentleman, spending money in London, enjoying the frivolities of his club, the Finches of the Grove, has no authentic relation to anybody. Instead of improv-[269/270]ing his condition, he has substituted for a dehumanizing relation to society no relation at all.[3]

Moreover, Pip discovers when he at last openly admits his love for Estella that she cannot at the same time be both distant judge, and possessed and enjoyed as a wife. As transcendent judge she is not really human at all, but a superhuman goddess, and as a woman she could not play the role of judge. It is not until Pip learns that Estella is not "destined" for him that he really faces the fact that she has no heart, and cannot love him. Until then he has believed, in the *hubris* of his great expectations, that she would be able to combine the two incompatible roles. Whenever she has appeared particularly cold, proud, or unfeeling, he has been able to assure himself that after all she is destined for him. It is only when he realizes that Miss Havisham does not "mean" them for one another that he can understand Estella when she says: "When you say you love me, I know what you mean, as a

---

[3] Dickens shares with other Victorian novelists a concern for the validity and meaning of the term "gentleman." In *Great Expectations*, as in the ironies of *Little Dorrit*, he tends to repudiate the term altogether. For him it is a mere expression of the impostures and injustices of society. However, as G. N. Ray has shown in *Thackeray: The Uses of Adversity, 1811–1846* (New York, 1955), Thackeray believes that the idea of the gentleman is undergoing a profound revaluation, but still is an indispensable concept, whereas the more conservative Trollope feels that right ethical actions are performed spontaneously only by those who possess by nature the unanalyzable qualities of a gentleman or lady.

form of words; but nothing more. You address nothing in my breast, you touch nothing there. I don't care for what you say at all" (44).

Finally, Pip discovers the emptiness of his hope of being given a justified place in the ruling class. He discovers that his real benefactor is not Miss Havisham, the representative of society, but the pariah Magwitch, "hunted dunghill dog." This discovery is really a discovery of the self-deception of his great expectations, his recognition that they were based on an irreconcilable contradiction. Pip has been climbing slowly toward Estella and toward the freedom and security of gentility. Now the ladder has collapsed, and he finds himself back at his origin again, back where he was at the opening of the story. Then he had received his "first most vivid and broad impression of [270/271] the identity of things," including himself, on the day he stole food from his home to feed an escaped convict. Now he has discovered that the source of his "expectations" is not Miss Havisham, but that same convict. Moreover, he has discovered that Estella, the star of his expectations and the symbol of his desire for gentility, is really the daughter of Magwitch. All that he thought was taking him further and further from his shameful beginning has only been bringing him inexorably back to his starting point. He is like a man lost in the woods who struggles for hours to find his way out, only to discover suddenly that he has returned by a circuitous route to the exact spot where he first realized that he did not know where he was.

But Pip's return is to an origin which has been transformed into its opposite. Then the tie to Magwitch was repudiated as sinful, as the guilty secret of a crime against home, as a shameful bond to the dregs of society, and as the pain of moral isolation. Now that same tie is about to be revalued. As Pip starts down the Thames on the desperate attempt to save the life of the convict who has broken parole to return to him, "a veil [seems] to be drawn from the river, and millions of sparkles burst out upon its waters," and "[f]rom [Pip], too, a veil [seems] to be drawn" (53). The mists that rose from the marshes as he started off for London (19) have been dissipated at last, and Pip stands ready to face the truth which lies at the very center of *Great Expectations*: all the claims made by wealth, social rank, and culture to endow the individual with true selfhood are absolutely false. However far he apparently travels from his origin he will still be akin to the mud and briars of the marshes and to the terrible man he met there on the day he became aware of himself as Pip, the Pip who has named himself because there is no person and no institution that cares enough for him to give him a name. And, at the same time, Pip discovers that he himself has initiated the series of events which he believed were descending on him from the outside through a mysterious grace. He it was who committed the act of aggression against his family, stole for the convict, did not give him up to the soldiers, and formed the secret "taint of prison and crime" which has stuck to him all his life. He it is who is him-[271/272]self the source of all that has happened to him, all that he has believed was not his responsibility. The appearance of Magwitch to claim the "gentleman what he has made" reveals to the horrified Pip that he has not been free, that he has been secretly manipulated as though he were a passive tool, or puppet, or a mechanical man created for Magwitch's revenge on society. But it also reminds him that he has himself been guilty of the act of kindness, outside the bounds of all socially approved morality, which formed his tie to the convict. Moreover, he has also been Miss Havisham's "tool." She has not been secretly planning to bestow on him Estella and her jewels as a reward for his intrinsic nobility of character. No, she has rather been using him as something for Estella to practice her techniques of heartbreaking on. Pip's voyage, his attempt to sustain himself above all coercion and determination, and yet not to accept any responsibility for this, has ended in utter shipwreck: "Miss Havisham's intentions toward me, all a mere dream; Estella not designed for me; I only suffered in Satis House as a convenience, a sting for the greedy relations, a model with a mechanical heart to practise on when no other practice was at hand; those were the first smarts I had. But, sharpest and deepest pain of all—it was for the convict, guilty of I knew not what crimes, and liable to be taken out of those rooms where I sat thinking, and hanged at the Old Bailey door, that I had deserted Joe" (39).

Pip's life as a gentleman turns out to have combined the worst possible aspects of both sides of the human condition: its unjustifiable freedom, and its imprisonment in a given situation. On the one hand, Pip's life as a gentleman has been a fraud practiced on society. He has in effect pushed and elbowed his way into a place in the upper class— gratuitously and under false pretenses. He must experience the bad conscience of the social climber, the parvenu. Pip is thrown back, therefore, on his initial isolation. There is nothing outside himself that judges, approves, consecrates his existence. On the other hand, Pip discovers that his life as a gentleman has been unwittingly a return to the life of a manipulated object he had so hated when he was a child being brought up "by hand." He [272/273] is returned to his alienation, and to his submission to what is imposed on him by force from the outside, and determines his actions, his place in the world, and even his nature: "The imaginary student pursued by the misshapen creature he had impiously made, was not more wretched than I, pursued by the creature who had made me, and recoiling from him with a stronger repulsion, the more he admired me and the fonder he was of me" (40). Indeed, as this passage implies, Pip is both Frankenstein's monster and Frankenstein himself. He has without knowing it been the creature of Magwitch's project of revenge, but at the same time he himself has made this possible by the initial act of pity and kindness which in- extricably linked Magwitch's life to his. Magwitch chose to make Pip a gentleman only because Pip had "kep life in [him]" when he was a "hunted dunghill dog"(39). "Look'ee here, Pip," says Magwitch. "I'm your second father. You're my son—more to me nor any son!"(39) —"more" because in this case the son has been as much maker of his father as father the maker of son. From the height of his great ex- pectations, Pip is cast down again into the depths of disinheritance. He has indeed acted freely in forming his filial bond to Magwitch, freely in the sense that he has acted outside every social law. His freedom has been horrifyingly transformed into a wholesale assault and fraud on society. He is, in fact, even more disinherited than he was at the beginning, for now he knows the full meaning of his state, and he is able to compare this realization that he is nothing except what he has made himself with the self-deceiving hope of the great expecta- tions he has so recently lost. At "the end of the second stage of [his] expectations" (39), Pip is at the deepest point of his wretchedness: "... it was not until I began to think," he says, "that I began fully to know how wrecked I was, and how the ship in which I had sailed was gone to pieces" (39).

V

The third part of "Pip's Expectations" traces the slow rise of the hero's fortunes. He comes out of the depths of despair in which he finds himself at the end of the second part. Love is [273/274] the cause of this reversal of fortune. For Dickens, as for the general tradition of ethical thought, love is the only successful escape from the unhappiness of singularity, the unhappiness of being this unique and isolated person, Pip.

For Dickens, as for generations of Christian moralists, love means sacrifice. Pip must abandon all the proud hopes which have formed the secret core of his life. He must abandon forever his project of being a gentleman, the belief that somewhere there is a place for him which he can possess by right. He must accept the fact that he can in no way transcend the gap between "the small bundle of shivers growing afraid of it all and beginning to cry" and the wind, sea, sky, and marshland, the alien universe—in no way, that is, but by willingly accepting this separation. And to accept this means to accept Magwitch, who springs up with "a terrible voice" from the marshes at the moment Pip becomes aware of his separateness.

Pip learns about love, then, not through Estella, but through the slow change in his relation to Magwitch. Only this change makes possible a transformation of his relation to Estella. Otherwise, Pip would have remained, even if he had possessed Estella, the submissive worshipper of a cold and distant authority. Just as Mrs. Joe atones for her cruelties to Pip and Joe by bowing down to Orlick, so Pip can escape from despair, from the total loss of his great expectations, only by a change in his attitude toward Magwitch. His acceptance of Magwitch is not only the relinquishment of his great expectations; it is also the replacement of these by a positive assertion that he, Pip alone, will be the source of the meaning of his own life. Pip finally accepts as the foundation of his life the guilt which has always haunted him: his secret and gratuitous act of charity to the escaped convict. Pip slowly realizes that if he betrays Magwitch, as Razumov betrays Victor Haldin in Conrad's *Under Western Eyes*, it will be to betray himself, to betray the possible foundation of himself by self-denial, by the abandonment of his egoistic expectations. And to betray Magwitch will be to plunge Magwitch back into the nothingness of the complete outcast. It is a case of the hunter hunted. Pip had been seeking in social position and in Estella a basis for his identity. Now he finds [274/275] that he himself has been sought. Just as Razumov finds that he cannot escape having *some* relation to Victor Haldin, even though he has not sought any (since Haldin has "taken" him as a revolutionary, he must be either faithful to the image of himself the other has formed, or he must betray it), so Pip has been seized, will-nilly, by Magwitch, and, whatever he does thenceforth, cannot avoid his tie to Magwitch. In Dickens' world, as in Conrad's, people exist in the exact degree that they exist in other people's eyes. And for Dickens, as for Conrad, one person can impose on another, whether he wishes it or not, the responsibility of betraying him or being faithful to him. Pip attempts all through his life, until his change, to remain neutral toward Magwitch, to "beat the dust of Newgate out of his clothes," to wipe out of existence the charitable theft for Magwitch which happened so long ago in his childhood. But he cannot erase this act from existence. He can only betray it, or reaffirm it. His whole life has been determined by that initial act. In spite of himself Pip is forced into complicity with convicts. He is forced to make a choice: either give Magwitch up to the police, or commit against society the crime of harboring an escaped felon.

Whereas Razumov betrays Haldin, Pip is faithful to Magwitch, and perhaps this marks the difference between the two novelists, and between the two centuries. But it is only slowly that Pip realizes what his faithfulness means. It means facing the fact that he and Magwitch are in the same position of isolation. If they do not help one another, no one will. It means discovering that each can help the other by offering himself as the foundation of the other's selfhood, Pip by sacrificing all his hopes, Magwitch by his change from a fierce desire to "make" a gentleman for revenge, to the desire to help Pip be a gentleman for Pip's own sake: "For now my repugnance to him had all melted away, and in the hunted wounded shackled creature who held my hand in his, I only saw a man who had meant to be my benefactor, and who had felt affectionately, gratefully, and generously, towards me with great constancy through a series of years" (54). Magwitch's handclasp, originally a symbolic appropriation of Pip as his creation and possession, now [275/276] becomes the symbol of their mutual love, and of their willingness to sacrifice all for one another. This transformation is complete after the unsuccessful attempt to get Magwitch safely out of the country. Thereafter, Magwitch thinks only of Pip, and not at all of the "society" he had so hated, and Pip thinks only of Magwitch (56).

Pip remains faithful to Magwitch, publicly manifesting his allegiance throughout Magwitch's imprisonment, trial, and death. He hides from Magwitch the fact that all his money will be forfeited to the crown, and that his hopes of leaving Pip a gentleman will fail. And just before Magwitch dies Pip tells him that Estella, his child, is still alive, "is a lady and very beautiful. And I love her!" (56). This is in a way his greatest sacrifice. He admits that he even owes Estella to Magwitch, and brings all the hope and dreams which had centered on Estella completely into the orbit of his relation to Magwitch. Magwitch is the source of everything he has and is.

By choosing his servitude to Magwitch, Pip transforms it into freedom. The dialectic of love in Dickens is more like the Kierkegaardian choice of oneself than like Sartre's endlessly frustrated conflict between two freedoms striving to be both free and secure at the same time. In place of the self-assertive love which requires the other to make himself the basis of one's selfhood, there is substituted by Magwitch and Pip the mutual sacrifice of their dearest claims to selfhood. For Dickens, as for Kierkegaard, the self can only affirm itself through self-sacrifice. But what was for Kierkegaard the relation of man to God becomes in Dickens the relation of man to man. No character in Dickens finally achieves authentic selfhood by establishing direct relation to God. Only the mutually self-denying, self-creating relationship of love succeeds, whereas the active assertion of will and the passive hope of great expectations both fail.

The divine power functions in *Great Expectations* primarily as the supreme judge before whom all social distinctions are as nothing: "The sun was striking in at the great windows of the court, through the glittering drops of rain upon the glass, and it made a broad shaft of light between the two-and-thirty [crim-[276/277]inals] and the Judge, linking both together, and perhaps reminding some among the audience, how both were passing on, with absolute equality, to the greater Judgment that knoweth all things and cannot err" (56). There is a true religious motif here. The light is God's judgment before which earthly judge and earthly judged, gentleman and common thief, are equal. But the meaning of the passage is as much social as religious. It is a final dramatization of the fact that social eminence such as Pip had sought and social judgments such as have hounded Magwitch all his life are altogether unimportant as sources of selfhood. At the center of Dickens' novels is a recognition of the bankruptcy of the relation of the individual to society as it now exists, the objective structure of given institutions and values. Only what an individual makes of himself, in charitable relations to others, counts. And this self-creation tends to require open revolt against the pressures of society. Human beings are themselves the source of the transcendence of their isolation.

Once Pip has established his new relationship to Magwitch he is able at last to win Estella. Pip's final love for Estella is a single complex relation which is both identification with the loved person (he is no longer conscious of a lack, a void of unfulfilled desire), and separation (he is still aware of himself as a self, as a separate identity; he does not melt into the loved person, and lose himself altogether). As in *Little Dorrit* and *A Tale of Two Cities*, the irreducible otherness, the permanent area of mystery in the loved one, is recognized and maintained.

Pip and Estella have experienced before their union their most complete separation, Pip in the agony of his discovery that Estella is not destined for him and that Magwitch is his real benefactor, and Estella in her unhappy marriage to Bentley Drummle, who has "used her with great cruelty," just as Pip has been "used" by Estella. These experiences have transformed them both. It is only when Estella has been tamed by the cruelty of her bad husband that she and Pip can enter into a wholy different relationship. Only when Estella's proud, cold glance is transformed into "the saddened softened light of the once proud eyes" (59) can she and Pip transform the fettering of slave by master into the handclasp of love. Estella too must [277/278] suffer the slave's loss of selfhood in order to be herself transformed. Both have come back from a kind of death to meet and join in the moonlight in Miss Havisham's ruined garden. The second ending is, in my opinion, the best. Not only was it, after all, the one Dickens published (would he really have acceded to Mrs. Grundy in the mask of Bulwer-Lytton without reasons of his own ?), but, it seems to me, the second ending, in joining Pip and Estella, is much truer to the real direction of the story. The paragraphs which, in the second version of the ending, close the novel remind us, in their echo of Milton, that Estella and Pip are accepting their exile from the garden of false hopes. Now that the mists of infatuation have cleared away Pip and Estella are different persons. They go forth from the ruined garden into a fallen world. In this world their lives will be given meaning only by their own acts and by their dependence on one another. Pip now has all that he wanted, Estella and her jewels, but what he has is altogether different from what he expected. Rather than possessing the impossible recon-ciliation of freedom and security he had sought in Estella and in gentility, he now loves and is loved by another fallible and imperfect being like himself:

The silvery mist was touched with the first rays of the moonlight, and the same rays touched the tears that dropped from her eyes. . . .

I took her hand in mine, and we went out of the ruined place; and, as the morning mists had risen long ago when I first left the forge, so, the evening mists were rising now, and in all the broad expanse of tranquil light they showed to me, I saw no shadow of another parting from her. (59)   [end on 278]

PROBLEMS: J. Hillis Miller

1. What is "poetic compression" [p. 250]? How does Dickens achieve it in the early pages of *Great Expectations*?

2. Miller says that the typical Dickensian hero "will be totally responsible, himself, for any identity he achieves" [pp. 252–253]. Apply
   this statement to Pip.

3. Look for characters in *Great Expectations* who attempt to be neither
   oppressors nor the oppressed, and determine the extent to which
   they succeed. The comments of the other critics should help you.

4. Miller says that the attempt to dominate those beneath one on the
   social scale is an inadequate expedient for satisfaction. To which
   characters in *Great Expectations* is this statement applicable? To
   which is it not applicable? Are the "good" characters all in one
   group, and the "bad" all in the other? What are your conclusions
   about the effects of attempts to dominate on the characters in this
   novel?

5. What has Miller added to your understanding of Estella's role?
   Are his ideas in conflict with, or do they extend or repeat, the
   opinions of other critics concerning Estella?

6. Review what other critics have to say about the father-son relationship between Magwitch and Pip. Which critics besides Miller also
   suggest that this relationship may in some sense be reversed, so that
   Magwitch becomes the son, and Pip the father? What basis for this
   suggestion can be found in the novel?

7. To what extent do you accept the statement that Magwitch is the
   source of everything Pip is [p. 276]?

8. Engel has called *Great Expectations* "subversive." What does Miller
   say that helps to support this assertion?

9. Discuss the conclusion of *Great Expectations* in the light of Miller's
   comments. Take into consideration the original ending which
   Dickens wrote for the novel.

The Hero's Guilt:
The Case of *Great Expectations**

by Julian Moynahan

Two recent essays on *Great Expectations* have stressed guilt as the dominant theme. They are Dorothy Van Ghent's 'On Great Expectations' (*The English Novel: Form and Function*, New York, 1953) and G. R. Stange's 'Dickens's Fable for his Time' (*College English*, XVI, October 1954). Mr. Stange remarks *inter alia* that 'profound and suggestive as is Dickens's treatment of guilt and expiation in this novel, to trace its remoter implications is to find something excessive and idiosyncratic; and he has concluded that 'compared to most of the writers of his time the Dickens of the later novels seems to be obsessed with guilt'. He does not develop this criticism, if it is a criticism, but one might guess he is disturbed by a certain discrepancy appearing in the narrative between the hero's sense of guilt and the actual amount of wrong-doing for which he may be said to be responsible. Pip has certainly one of the guiltiest consciences in literature. He not only suffers *agenbite of inwit* for his sin of snobbish ingratitude toward Joe and Biddy, but also suffers through much of the novel from what can only be called a conviction of criminal guilt. Whereas he expiates his sins of snobbery and ingratitude by ultimately accepting the convict Magwitch's unspoken claim for his protection and help, by willingly renouncing his great expectations, and by returning in a chastened mood to Joe and Biddy, he cannot expiate—or exorcise—his conviction of criminality, because it does not seem to correspond with any real criminal acts or intentions.

* Reprinted from *Essays in Criticism*, X, 1 (January 1960), pp. 60-79.

Snobbery is not a crime. Why should Pip feel like a criminal? Perhaps the novel is saying that snobbery of the sort practiced by Pip in the second stage of his career is not very different from certain types of criminal behaviour. For instance, a severe moralist might point out that snobbery and murder are alike in [60/61] that they are both offences against persons rather than property, and both involve the culpable wish to repudiate or deny the existence of other human beings. On this view, Pip reaches the height of moral insight at the start of the trip down the river, when he looks at Magwitch and sees in him only 'a much better man than I had been to Joe'. By changing places with the convict here, he apparently defines his neglectful behaviour toward Joe as criminal. Does this moment of vision objectify Pip's sense of criminality and prepare the way for expiation? Perhaps, but if so, then Pip's pharisaic rewording of the publican's speech, which occurs a few pages later while he is describing Magwitch's death in the prison, must somehow be explained away:

Mindful, then, of what we had read together, I thought of the two men who went up into the Temple to pray, and I thought I knew there were no better words that I could say beside his bed, than 'O Lord, be merciful to him, a sinner!'

Even Homer nods, and Dickens is not, morally speaking, at his keenest in deathbed scenes, where his love of the swelling organ tone is apt to make him forget where he is going. Still, we ought not to explain anything away before the entire problem of Pip's guilt has been explored at further length.

Others answers to the question I have raised are possible. Consider the following passage, wherein Pip most fully expresses his sense of a criminal 'taint'. He has just strolled through Newgate prison with Wemmick and is waiting near a London coach office for the arrival of Estella from Miss Havisham's:

I consumed the whole time in thinking how strange it was that I should be encompassed by all this taint of prison and crime; that, in my childhood out on our lonely marshes on a winter evening I should have first encountered it; that, it should have reappeared on two occasions, starting out like a stain that was faded but not gone; that, it should in this new way pervade my fortune and advancement. While my mind was thus engaged, I thought of the beautiful [61/62] young Estella, proud and refined, coming toward me, and I thought with absolute abhorrence of the contrast between the jail and her. I wished that Wemmick had not met me, or that I had not yielded to him and gone with him, so that, of all days in the year, on this day I might not have had Newgate in my breath and on my clothes. I beat the prison dust off my clothes as I sauntered to and fro, and I shook it out of my dress, and I exhaled its air from my lungs. So contaminated did I feel, remembering who was coming, that the coach came quickly after all, and I was not yet free from the soiling consciousness of Mr. Wemmick's conservatory, when I saw her face at the coach window and her hand waving at me.

Without question, Pip here interprets the frequent manifestations in his experience of criminal elements—the runaway prisoner on the marshes, the man with the two pound notes, the reappearance of the same man in chains on the coach going down into the marsh country, the reappearance of Magwitch's leg iron as the weapon which fells Mrs. Joe, the accident making the criminal lawyer Jaggers, whose office is beside Newgate prison, the financial agent of his unknown patron—as signs that indicate some deep affinity between him and a world of criminal violence. But a question that the reader must face here and elsewhere in the novel is whether to accept Pip's interpretation. If we conclude that Pip is in fact tainted with criminality, we must rest our conclusion on a kind of symbolic reading of the coincidences of the plot. Through these coincidences and recurrences, which violate all ordinary notions of probability, Dickens, so this argument must go, weaves together a net in whose meshes his hero is entrapped. Regardless of the fact that Pip's association with crimes and criminals is purely adventitious and that he evidently bears no responsibility for any act or intention of criminal violence, he must be condemned on the principle of guilt by association.

Nevertheless, if the reader is himself not to appear a bit of a pharisee, he must be able to show good reason for accepting the principle of guilt by association in settling the question of the hero's criminality. Both Mr. Stange and Miss Van Ghent [62/63] present readings of the guilt theme which are an attempt to validate this principle. Mr. Stange decides that 'the last stage of Pip's progression is reached when he learns to love the criminal and to accept his own implication in the common guilt'. He believes that one of Dickens's major points is that 'criminality is the condition of life'. Pip, therefore, feels criminal guilt because he is criminal as we are all criminal. Along similar lines, Miss Van Ghent remarks, 'Pip . . . carries the convict inside him, as the negative potential of his 'great expectations'—Magwitch is the concretion of his potential guilt.' The appearance of Magwitch at Pip's apartment in the Temple is 'from a metaphysical point of view . . . that of Pip's own unwrought deeds'. Finally, she maintains that Pip bows down before Magwitch, who has been guilty towards him, instead of bowing down before Joe, toward whom Pip has been guilty. In so doing Pip reveals by a symbolic act that he takes the guilt of the world on his shoulders—rather in the style of Father Zossima in *The Brothers Karamazov*. This is shown particularly by the fact that Pip assumes culpability in a relationship where he is, in fact, the innocent party.

Objections to these metaphysical readings can be raised. If criminality is the condition of life, and if guilt is universal in the world of the novel, what world may Joe Gargery, Biddy, and Herbert Pocket be said to inhabit? Miss Van Ghent's theory of Pip's guilt as the negative potential of his great expectations is more promising, because it seems to exempt humble people from the guilt attaching itself to a society of wealth and power which thrives on the expropriation of the fruits of labour of its weaker members. But in her description of Pip's redemptory act, Miss Van Ghent insists upon the pervasiveness of guilt throughout the Dickens world. Less disturbing than this contradiction but still questionable is her assumption that Magwitch has been guilty of great wrong-doing towards Pip. Metaphysics aside, how badly has he treated Pip? Does his wrongdoing stand comparison with the vicious practices of an Orlick or even a Miss Havisham? Who, in the light of the virtues of faithfulness and love, virtues which the novel surely holds up for admiration, is the better, Magwitch or his daughter Estella?

My final objection to these interpretations is Pip's language [63/64] at Magwitch's deathbed. Pip, after all, tells his own story. Evidence that he has attained an unflawed moral grasp of experience in which the distinction between criminal and noncriminal forms of evil is transcended through the confession *mea culpa* must come, at least partly, from Pip himself. On the strength—on the weakness rather—of his biblical flight, this reader is not convinced that the evidence is clear.

Miss Van Ghent's and Mr. Stange's efforts to demonstrate Pip's metaphysical involvement in the criminal milieu of *Great Expectations* are dictated, rightly enough, by their concern for the unifying and inclusive significance of the guilt theme. Their readings provide a means of bridging the gulf between Pip's social sins and the more drastic phenomena of criminality presented in the novel—attempts to moralise the melodrama, as it were, attempts to make the complete narrative presentation revolve around the crucial question of Pip's moral nature. Sensitive readers of the novel will sympathise with this effort, but I do not believe they will agree that the gulf *is* bridged by making criminal guilt a universal condition and by insisting that this is what Pip comes to understand by the time his story is told.

II

In my opinion, Pip's relation to the criminal milieu of *Great Expectations* is not that of an Everyman to a universal condition. It is rather a more concrete and particularised relation than the metaphysical approach would indicate, although the novel defines that relation obliquely and associatively, not through discursive analysis. Miss Van Ghent has suggested a metaphoric connection between Magwitch and Pip. Her proposal of such implicit relations between character and character, even though they do not become rationalised anywhere, is an illuminating insight into the artistic method of the mature Dickens. But her principle can be applied differently and yield rather different results.

I would suggest that Orlick rather than Magwitch is the figure from the criminal milieu of the novel whose relations to him come to define Pip's implicit participation in the acts of violence with which the novel abounds. Considered by himself, [64/65] Orlick is a figure of melodrama. He is unmotivated, his origins are shrouded in mystery, his violence is unqualified by regret. In this last respect he is the exact opposite of Pip, who is, of course, filled with regret whenever he remembers how he has neglected his old friends at the forge.

On the other hand, if we consider Orlick in his connections with Pip, some rather different observations can be made. In the first place, there is a peculiar parallel between the careers of the two characters. We first encounter Orlick as he works side by side with Pip at the forge. Circumstances also cause them to be associated in the assault on Mrs. Joe. Orlick strikes the blow, but Pip feels, with some justification, that he supplied the assault weapon. Pip begins to develop his sense of alienation from the village after he has been employed by Miss Havisham to entertain her in her house. But Orlick too turns up later on working for Miss Havisham as gatekeeper. Finally, after Pip has become a partisan of the convict, it turns out that Orlick also has become a partisan of an ex-convict, Compeyson, who is Magwitch's bitter enemy.

Up to a point, Orlick seems not only to dog Pip's footsteps, but also to present a parody of Pip's upward progress through the novel, as though he were in competitive pursuit of some obscene great expectations of his own. Just as Pip centres his hopes successively on the forge, Satis House, and London, so Orlick moves his base of operations successively from the forge, to Satis House, and to London. From Pip's point of view, Orlick has no right to interest himself in any of the people with whom Pip has developed close ties. For instance, he is appalled when he discovers that his tender feeling for Biddy is given a distorted echo by Orlick's obviously lecherous interest in the same girl. And when he discovers that Orlick has the right of entry into Satis House he warns Jaggers to advise Miss Havisham to get rid of him. But somehow he cannot keep Orlick out of his affairs. When Magwitch appears at Pip's London lodging half-way through the novel, Orlick is crouching in darkness on the landing below Pip's apartment. And when Pip is about to launch the escape attempt down the Thames, his plans are frustrated by the trick which brings him down to the marshes to face Orlick in the hut by the limekiln. Its lurid [65/66] melodrama and the awkwardness of its integration with the surrounding narrative has made many readers dismiss this scene as a piece of popular writing aimed at the less intelligent members of Dickens's audience. But the confrontation of Orlick and Pip on the marshes is crucial for an understanding of the problem I am discussing, because it is the scene in which Dickens comes closest to making explicit the analogy between the hero and the novel's principal villain and criminal.

Orlick inveigles Pip to the limepit not only to kill him but to overwhelm him with accusations. Addressing Pip over and over again as 'Wolf', an epithet he might more readily apply to himself, he complains that Pip has cost him his place, come between him and a young woman in whom he was interested, tried to drive him out of the country, and been a perpetual obstacle in the path of his own uncouth ambitions. But the charge he makes with the greatest force and conviction is that Pip bears the final responsibility for the assault on Mrs. Joe:

'I tell you it was your doing—I tell you it was done through you,' he retorted, catching up the gun and making a blow with the stock at the vacant air between us. 'I come upon her from behind, as I come upon you to-night. I giv' it to her! I left her for dead, and if there had been a limekiln as nigh her as there is now nigh you, she shouldn't have come to life again. But it warn't old Orlick as did it; it was you. You was favoured, and he was bullied and beat. Old Orlick bullied and beat, eh? Now you pays for it. You done it; now you pays for it.'

The entire scene was a nightmare quality. This is at least partly due to the weird reversal of rôles, by which the innocent figure is made the accused and the guilty one the accuser. As in a dream the situation is absurd, yet like a dream it may contain hidden truth. On the one hand Orlick, in interpreting Pip's character, seems only to succeed in describing himself—ambitious, treacherous, murderous, and without compunction. On the other hand, several of Orlick's charges are justified, and it is only in the assumption that Pip's motives are as black as his own that he goes wrong. We know, after all, that Pip is ambitious, and that he has repudiated his early associates as [66/67] obstacles to the fulfilment of his genteel aspirations. Another interesting observation can be made about Orlick's charge that 'it was you as did for your shrew sister'. Here Orlick presents Pip as the responsible agent, himself merely as the weapon. But this is an exact reversal of Pip's former assumptions about the affair. All in all, Orlick confronts the hero in this scene, not merely as would-be murderer, but also as a distorted and darkened mirror-image. In fact, he presents himself as a monstrous caricature of the tender-minded hero, insisting that they are two of a kind with the same ends, pursued through similarly predatory and criminal means. This is what his wild accusations come down to.

III

Is Orlick mistaken in representing himself in this scene as a sort of double, *alter ego*, or shadow of Pip? Is he merely projecting his own qualities upon him, or do Orlick's accusations, in any sense, constitute a partially or wholly valid comment on Pip's actions? In order to answer these questions we shall have to begin by analysing the fantasy of great expectations which gives the book so much of its universal appeal. This fantasy, so the psychologists tell us, is a well-nigh universal imaginative flight of childhood. By creating for himself a fiction wherein the world is made to conform to his desire and will, the child succeeds in compensating himself for the fact that his real position is without power and that the quantity of love and nurture to which he believes himself entitled is greatly in excess of the amount he actually receives. Out of this unbalance between an unbounded demand and a limited supply of love and power proceed the fairy godmothers as well as the vicious step-parents and bad giants in which world legend abounds. The fantasy element *Great Expectations* shares with such stories as *Cinderella* and *Jack and the Beanstalk* contains, then, two implicit motives: the drive for power and the drive for more mother-love. However, of the two, the power motive, since it involves the aggressive wish to push beyond the authoritarian figures who hold the child powerless, is apt to be more productive of guilt and, consequently, is likely to be expressed with a certain amount of concealment. Thus, Jack in the folk tale [67/68] conquers authority in the fictional guise of killing the wicked giant. But there is no attempt to disguise the fact that he steals from the giant in order to live in affluence with his widowed mother, enjoying her undivided love and admiration. We might add that the type of love sought in this fantasy is a childish version of mature love. It is largely passive. It is associated with a super-abundance of the good things of life, often with the enjoyment of great wealth.

In *Great Expectations*, the second motive is clearly represented in the early stages of Pip's career. His early experiences follow the fairy-tale pattern. Circumstances magically conspire to rescue him from the spartan rigours of Mrs. Joe. In taking him up, Miss Havisham plays the rôle of fairy godmother, and later permits him to continue in his belief that she is also the sponsor of his luxury in London—until he is brought up short by the rough figure of Magwitch. Until the real world breaks in on him, Pip allows himself to be pushed along, never challenging the requirement that he must not look too closely into the sources of his good fortune. Likewise, he is passive in his longing for Estella, who, in her metaphoric associations with precious jewels and lofty stars, comes to symbolise to him the final goal of his dreams of love, luxury, and high position. Instead of trying to capture her through an aggressive courtship he simply pines, assuming on very little evidence that one day she will be bestowed upon him by Miss Havisham as everything else has been.

Upon the return of Magwitch, Pip is forced to wake up and recognise that life is not, after all, a fairy tale. He learns that his own wealth comes from a criminal, that even the magical figures of Satis House, Miss Havisham and Estella have criminal connections, and, as we have seen, that his callous treatment of Joe Gargery was essentially criminal. This linking up of the criminal milieu and the milieu of wealth and high position is a way of drawing the strongest possible contrast between Pip's regressive fantasy-world, where wealth and good luck have seemed unremitting and uncompromised, and a real world where the dominant moral colouring is at best a dirty grey.

In terms of what we have called the love-motive, then, Dickens has shown fantasy in collision with reality. Pip learns [68/69] that the world is not a vast mammary gland from which he can draw rich nourishment with moral impunity. He finds that he must hunger and struggle like all the rest. Furthermore, he must accept the unhappy fact that his participation in the old dream of great expectations has hurt real people. With his awakening to reality he develops a capacity for active, self-bestowing love. But the mature tough-minded perspective from which the hero's development is viewed does not permit him to move on into happiness and fulfilment. In the final chapters of *Great Expectations* Pip wants to give himself, but there is no longer anyone in a position to accept his gift. Magwitch's fate is upon him; the circumstance of marriage has carried both Biddy and Estella beyond his reach. In bestowing himself upon the family of Herbert Pocket, Pip comes to rest in a kind of limbo. The book seems to imply that Pip is doomed to a lifetime of vicarious experience, because he lingered too long in his condition of alienation from the real.

This is not a complete account of Dickens's critique of the great expectations fantasy, that dream of huge and easy success which has always haunted the imagination of children and also haunted the imaginations of adults in the increasingly commercial and industrial society of nineteenth-century England. In *Great Expectations*, as in its legendary prototypes, the theme of ambition is treated under the two aspects of desire and will, the search for a superabundance of love and the drive for power. And it is in his presentation of the theme in the latter aspect that Dickens makes the more profound analysis of the immoral and criminal elements in his hero's (and the century's) favourite dream.

But Pip's ambition is passive. He only becomes active and aggressive after he has ceased to be ambitious. How then does *Great Expectations* treat the theme of ambition in terms that are relevant to the total action of which Pip is the centre? I have already begun to suggest an answer to the question. Ambition as the instinct of aggression, as the pitiless drive for power directed against what we have called authority-figures is both coalesced and disguised in the figure of Orlick. And Orlick is bound to be the hero by ties of analogy as double, *alter ego* and dark mirror-image. We are dealing here with an art which [69/70] simultaneously disguises and reveals its deepest implications of meaning, with a method which apparently dissociates its thematic materials and its subject matter into moral fable-*cum*-melodramatic accompaniment, yet simultaneously presents through patterns of analogy a dramatic perspective in which the apparent opposites are unified. In *Great Expectations* criminality is displaced from the hero on to a melodramatic villain. But on closer inspection that villain becomes part of a complex unity—we might call it Pip-Orlick—in which all aspects of the problem of guilt become interpenetrant and co-operative. The only clue to this unity which is given at the surface level of the narrative is Pip's obsession of criminal guilt. Pip tells us over and over again that he feels contaminated by crime. But we do not find the objective correlative of that conviction until we recognise in the insensate and compunctionless Orlick a shadow image of the tender-minded and yet monstrously ambitious young hero.

What is the rationale of this elusive method? In my opinion it enabled Dickens to project a radical moral insight which anticipated the more sophisticated probings of novelists like Dostoievsky and Gide without abandoning the old-fashioned traditions of melodrama and characterisation in which he had worked for more than quarter of a century before *Great Expectations* was published. Pip, by comparison with Raskolnikov, is a simple young man. But through the analogy Pip-Orlick, *Great Expectations* makes the same point about ambition as *Crime and Punishment*, and it is a very penetrating point indeed. In the *Brothers Karamazov* Ivan comes to recognise during the course of three tense interviews with his half-brother, Smerdyakov, how he shares with that brother a criminal responsibility for the murder of their father, although Smerdyakov alone wielded the weapon. The comparable scene in *Great Expectations* is the limekiln scene. Orlick even adopts the tone of a jealous sibling during the interview, as in the remark, 'You was favoured, and he was bullied and beat.' But Dickens is not a Dostoievsky. Pip does not recognise Orlick as a blood-relation, so to speak. The meaning remains submerged and is communicated to the reader through other channels than the agonised confession of a first-person narrator. Indeed, the [70/71] profoundest irony of the novel is not reached until the reader realises he must see Pip in a much harsher moral perspective than Pip ever saw himself.

IV

Recognition that Pip's ambition is definable under the aspect of aggression as well as in terms of the regressive desire for passive enjoyment of life's bounty depends upon the reader's willingness to work his way into the narrative from a different angle than the narrator's. The evidence for the hero's power-drive against the authority-figures, the evidence of his 'viciousness' if you will, is embodied in the story in a number of ways, but a clear pattern of meaning only emerges after the reader has correlated materials which are dispersed and nominally unrelated in the story *as told*. Orlick, thus far, has been the figure whose implicit relations to the hero have constituted the chief clue to the darker meaning of Pip's career. He continues to be important in any attempt to set forth the complete case, but there are also some significant correlations to be made in which he does not figure. This is fortunate, if only to forestal the objection that the whole case depends upon an imputed resemblance between two characters whom generations of devoted readers have not, after all, found very much alike. Let us, then, present the rest of the evidence, and see whether Pip, in any sense, stands self-indicted as well as indicted for the bad company he occasionally—and most reluctantly—keeps.

We might begin with the apparently cynical remark that Pip, judged on the basis of what happens to many of the characters closely associated with him, is a very dangerous young man. He is not accident-prone, but a great number of people who move into his orbit decidedly are. Mrs. Joe is bludgeoned, Miss Havisham goes up in flames, Estella is exposed through her rash marriage to vaguely specified tortures at the hands of her brutal husband, Drummle. Pumblechook has his house looted and his mouth stuffed with flowering annuals by a gang of thieves led by Orlick. All of these characters, with the exception of Estella, stand at one time or another in the relation of patron, patroness, or authority-figure to Pip the boy or Pip the man. (Pumblechook is, of course, a parody patron, and his [71/72] comic chastisement is one of the most satisfying things in the book.) Furthermore, all of these characters, including Estella, have hurt, humiliated, or thwarted Pip in some important way. All in some way have stood between him and the attainment of the full measure of his desires. All are punished.

Let us group these individual instances. Mrs. Joe, the cruel foster-mother, and Pumblechook, her approving and hypocritical relation by marriage, receive their punishment from the hands of Orlick. Mrs. Joe hurts Pip and is hurt in turn by Orlick. Pip has the motive of revenge—a lifetime of brutal beatings and scrubbings inflicted by his sister—but Orlick, a journeyman who does not even lodge with the Gargerys, bludgeons Mrs. Joe after she has provoked a quarrel between him and his master. If we put together his relative lack of motive with his previously quoted remarks at the limekiln and add to these Pip's report of his own extraordinary reaction upon first hearing of the attack—

With my head full of George Barnwell, I was at first disposed to believe that I must have had some hand in the attack upon my sister, or at all events that as her near relation, popularly known to be under obligations to her, I was a more legitimate object of suspicion than anyone else—

we arrive at an anomalous situation which can best be resolved on the assumption that Orlick acts merely as Pip's punitive instrument or weapon.

With regard to Pumblechook's chastisement, the most striking feature is not that Orlick should break into a house, but that he should break into Pumblechook's house. Why not Trabb's? One answer might be that Trabb has never stood in Pip's light. Pumblechook's punishment is nicely proportioned to his nuisance value for Pip. Since he has never succeeded in doing him any great harm with his petty slanders, he escapes with a relatively light wound. Although we are told near the end of the novel that Orlick was caught and jailed after the burglary, we are never told that Pip reported Orlick's murderous assault on him or his confessions of his assault on Mrs. Joe to the police. Despite the fact that there is enough accumulated [72/73] evidence to hang him, Orlick's end is missing from the book. Actually, it seems that Orlick simply evaporates into thin air after his punitive rôle has been performed. His case needs no final disposition because he has only existed, essentially, as an aspect of the hero's own far more problematic case.

Estella receives her chastisement at the hands of Bentley Drummle.

How does this fit into the pattern we have been exploring? In the first place, it can be shown that Drummle stands in precisely the same analogical relationship to Pip as Orlick does. Drummle is a reduplication of Orlick at a point higher on the social-economic scale up which Pip moves with such rapidity through the first three-quarters of the novel. Drummle, like Orlick, is a criminal psychopath. At Jaggers's dinner party the host, a connoisseur of criminal types, treats Drummle as 'one of the true sort', and Drummle demonstrates how deserving he is of this distinction when he tries to brain the harmless Startop with a heavy tumbler.

But the most impressive evidence that Orlick and Drummle are functional equivalents is supplied by the concrete particulars of their description. To an extraordinary degree, these two physically power-ful, inarticulate, and dark-complexioned villains are presented to the reader in terms more often identical than similar. Orlick, again and again, is one who lurks and lounges, Drummle is one who lolls and lurks. When Pip, Startop, and Drummle go out rowing, the last 'would always creep in-shore like some uncomfortable amphibious creature, even when the tide would have sent him fast on his way; and I always think of him as coming after us in the dark or by the back-water, when our own two boats were breaking the sunset or the moonlight in mid-stream'. When Startop walks home after Jaggers's party, he is followed by Drummle but on the opposite side of the street, 'in the shadow of the houses, much as he was wont to follow in his boat'. The other creeper, follower and amphibian of *Great Expecta-tions* is Orlick, whose natural habitat is the salt marsh, who creeps his way to the dark landing below Pip's apartment to witness the return of Magwitch from abroad, who creeps behind Biddy and Pip as they walk conversing on the marshes and overhears Pip say he will do anything to drive Orlick from the neighbourhood, who [73/74] appears out of the darkness near the turnpike house on the night Pip returns from Pumblechook's to discover that his sister has been assaulted, and who, finally, creeps his way so far into Pip's private business that he ends by acting as agent for Compeyson, Magwitch's—and Pip's—shadowy antagonist.

Like Orlick, Drummle is removed from the action suddenly; Pip is given no opportunity to settle old and bitter scores with him. In the last chapter we hear that he is dead 'from an accident consequent on ill-treating a horse'. This is the appropriate end for a sadist whose crimes obviously included wife-beating. But more important to the present argument is our recognition that Drummle has been employed to break a woman who had, in the trite phrase, broken Pip's heart. Once he has performed his function as Pip's vengeful surrogate he can be assigned to the fate he so richly deserves.

Mrs. Joe beats and scrubs Pip until she is struck down by heavy blows on the head and spine. Pumblechook speaks his lies about him until his mouth is stuffed with flowers. Estella treats his affections with cold contempt until her icy pride is broken by a brutal husband. In this series Orlick and Drummle behave far more like instruments of vengeance than like three-dimensional characters with understandable grudges of their own. In terms of my complete argument, they enact an aggressive potential that the novel defines, through patterns of analogy and linked resemblances, as belonging in the end to Pip and to his unconscionably ambitious hopes.

When Miss Havisham bursts into flames, there is no Orlick or Drummle in the vicinity to be accused of having set a match to her. In the long series of violence which runs through *Great Expectations* from the beginning to end, this is one climax of violence that can be construed as nothing more than accidental. And yet it is an accident which Pip, on two occasions, has foreseen. Before Miss Havisham burns under the eye of the horror-struck hero, she has already come to a violent end twice in his hallucinated fantasies—in Pip's visionary experiences in the abandoned brewery, where he sees Miss Havisham hanging by the neck from a beam. He has this vision once as a child, on the occasion of his first visit to Satis House, and once as an adult, on the occasion on his last visit, just a few minutes before [74/75] Miss Havisham's accident occurs. What are we to make, if anything, of these peculiar hallucinatory presentiments and of the coincidence by which they come true?

The child first sees his patroness hanging from a beam after his first hour of service with her. At this point the novel dwells at length on his keen awareness that he has been cruelly treated, generalises on the extreme sensitiveness of children to injustice, and describes how Pip in utter frustration vents his injured feelings by kicking a wall and twisting his own hair. In these passages it seems to me that the reader is being prepared to interpret Pip's immediately ensuing hallucination as the child's further attempt to discharge his anger and grief against his adult tormenter. In fantasy Pip punishes a woman whom in fact he cannot disturb in any way, and, by hanging her, attempts to destroy the threat to his peace and security which she represents. This interpretation excludes the possibility of a supernatural element in the experience; the novel provides abundant evidence that the imagination of a child operating under a great stress of emotion is possessed of a hallucinatory power. When Pip carries stolen provisions to Magwitch on the marshes, his guilt-ridden imagination effects a transformation of the countryside through which he passes, until even gates, dykes, banks, cattle and a signpost seem to him to be pursuing him and crying out his guilt. Pip's hallucination, then, is an imaginative fantasy which both projects and disguises the boy's desire to punish his employer and to destroy her baleful power over him.

Pip experiences no recurrence of the hallucination during the long years of an association with Miss Havisham based on his mistaken assumption that she is the sole author of his good fortunes. The fantasy returns only after his eyes have been opened to the fact that nothing has come to him from Miss Havisham except unhappiness. On that last visit to Satis House he learns definitely of Estella's marriage. With this information the last link between him and his former employer snaps. The false fairy godmother kneels to ask forgiveness for her crimes against him, and the duped hero offers forgiveness sincerely, if sadly. Nevertheless, as Pip strolls through the ruins of the estate he is not able to refrain from brooding over Miss Havisham's 'profound unfitness for this earth', and when he walks into the [75/76] chilly, twilit brewery building he is not able to prevent the return of the old hallucination of Miss Havisham hanging from the beam. We are told that this was owing to the revival of a childish association. But surely the episode represents more than a curious psychological detail. It is profoundly right that the fantasy should return at a time when he can see in complete clarity and detail how his connection with Miss Havisham has hurt him. It is profoundly right that he should forgive the false patroness and yet not forgive her, behave generously toward her and yet feel deeply that she has no right to live, treat her with some degree of melancholy affection, yet hate her also in the depths of his being.

We need not deny Dickens the insight necessary to the imagining of so ambivalent a response in the hero of his great novel. And we should not commit the anachronism of demanding that this response be defined in the novel analytically and self-consciously—that the hero should tell us, 'I forgave Miss Havisham as fully as I could, but continued to think how well it would have been for me if she had never set foot on this earth.' Pip's ambivalence is embodied dramatically. It must be known not as it is talked about, but as enacted. A man forgives a woman, then hallucinates her death by hanging. A man watches a woman burst into flames, then leaps bravely to her rescue, but in the course of describing this rescue is forced to remark, 'We were on the ground struggling like desperate enemies.'

How do these hallucinations, the second followed immediately by Miss Havisham's fatal accident, add to the burden of the hero's guilt? The answer is obvious. Because Pip's destructive fantasy comes true in reality, he experiences the equivalent of a murderer's guilt. As though he had the evil eye, or as though there were more than a psychological truth in the old cliché, 'if looks could kill', Pip moves from the brewery, where he has seen Miss Havisham hanging, to the door of her room, where he gives her one long, last look—until she is consumed by fire. But here the psychological truth suffices to establish imaginative proof that Pip can no more escape untainted from his relationship to the former patroness than he can escape untainted from any of his relationships to characters who have [76/77] held and used the power to destroy or hamper his ambitious struggles. In all these relationships the hero becomes implicated in violence. With Estella, Pumblechook, and Mrs. Joe, the aggressive drive is enacted by surrogates linked to the hero himself by ties of analogy. With Miss Havisham the surrogate is missing. Miss Havisham falls victim to the purely accidental. But the 'impurity' of Pip's motivation, as it is revealed through the device of the recurrent hallucination, suggests an analogy between that part of Pip which wants Miss Havisham at least punished, at most removed from this earth for which she is so profoundly unfit, and the destroying fire itself.

V

In this essay I have argued that Dickens's novel defines its hero's dream of great expectations and the consequences stemming from indulgence in that dream under the two aspects of desire and will, of regressive longing for an excess of love and of violent aggressiveness. In the unfolding of the action these two dramas are not presented separately. Instead they are combined into Dickens's most complex representation of character in action. Pip is Dickens's most complicated hero, demonstrating at once the traits of criminal and gull, of victimiser and victim. He is victimised by his dream and the dream itself, by virtue of its profoundly anti-social and unethical nature, forces him into relation with a world in which other human beings fall victim to his drive for power. He is, in short, a hero sinned against and sinning: sinned against because in the first place the dream was thrust upon the helpless child by powerful and corrupt figures from the adult world; a sinner because in accepting for himself a goal in life based upon unbridled individualism and indifference to others he takes up a career which *Great Expectations* repeatedly, through a variety of artistic means, portrays as essentially criminal.

After Magwitch's death, Pip falls a prey to brain fever. During his weeks of delirium it seems to me that his hallucinations articulate the division in his character between helpless passivity and demonic aggressiveness. Pip tells us he dreamed   [77/78]

that I was a brick in the house wall, and yet entreating to be released from the giddy place where the builders had set me; that I was a steel beam of a vast engine clashing and whirling over a great gulf, yet that I implored in my own person to have the engine stopped, and my part in it hammered off.

It is tempting to read these images as dream logic. The hero-victim cries for release from his unsought position of height and power, but cannot help himself from functioning as a moving part of a monstrous apparatus which seems to sustain itself from a plunge into the abyss only through the continuous expenditure of destructive force. In the narrative's full context this vast engine can be taken to represent at one and the same time the demonic side of the hero's career and a society that maintains its power intact by the continuous destruction of the hopes and lives of its weaker members. In the latter connection we can think of Magwitch's account of his childhood and youth, and of the judge who passed a death sentence on thirty-two men and women, while the sun struck in through the courtroom windows making a 'broad shaft of light between the two-and-thirty and the judge, linking them both together'. But to think of the engine as a symbol of society is still to think of Pip. For Pip's career enacts his society's condition of being—its guilt, its sinfulness, and in the end, its helplessness to cleanse itself of a taint 'of prison and crime'.

When Pip wakes up from his delirium he finds himself a child again, safe in the arms of the angelic Joe Gargery. But the guilt of great expectations remains inexpiable, and the cruelly beautiful original ending of the novel remains the only possible 'true' ending. Estella and Pip face each other across the insurmountable barrier of lost innocence. The novel dramatises the loss of innocence, and does not glibly present the hope of a redemptory second birth for either its guilty hero or the guilty society which shaped him. I have already said that Pip's fantasy of superabundant love brings him at last to a point of alienation from the real world. And similarly Pip's fantasy of power brings him finally to a point where withdrawal is the only positive moral response left to him.   [78/79]

The brick is taken down from its giddy place, a part of the engine is hammered off. Pip cannot redeem his world. In no conceivable sense a leader, he can only lead himself into a sort of exile from his society's power centres. Living abroad as the partner of a small, unambitious firm, he is to devote his remaining life to doing the least possible harm to the smallest number of people, so earning a visitor's privileges in the lost paradise where Biddy and Joe, the genuine innocents of the novel, flourish in thoughtless content. [end on 79]

PROBLEMS: Julian Moynahan

1. What is Mr. Moynahan's quarrel with G. R. Stange's article?

2. What do you find wrong with Magwitch's deathbed scene? How does this scene reflect Dickens's attitude toward death?

3. What does Moynahan mean by "criminal 'taint'"? How pervasive is this "taint" in the novel?

4. Moynahan calls Mr. Stange's and Mrs. Van Ghent's readings of *Great Expectations* "metaphysical" [p. 63]. What does he mean?

5. What is Moynahan's quarrel with Dorothy Van Ghent's article? With which critic do you agree?

6. Why does Moynahan say Orlick is a figure of melodrama? This term is often used disparagingly; is it so used here?

7. Moynahan suggests replacing Magwitch with Orlick as the character who defines Pip's connection with criminality. Which character do you prefer in this capacity? Does the acceptance of one necessarily mean the rejection of the other, in your opinion?

8. Hagan proposes Compeyson as the principal villain of *Great Expectations*, but Moynahan prefers Orlick. Upon what grounds do these two critics base their preferences?

9. Are critics in general agreement with Moynahan's assertion about the role of Orlick? If so, what is the consensus on Orlick's function in the novel? If not, in what respects do other critics disagree with Moynahan's analysis of Orlick's function? Are there flaws in Moynahan's case for Orlick's being the principal villain?

10. Answer the questions Moynahan asks at the beginning of his third section [p. 67].

11. What is the connection between *Great Expectations* and such stories as *Cinderella* and *Jack and the Beanstalk*? In showing this connection, what does Moynahan say about the mythic background of *Great Expectations*?

12. How does Moynahan use the word "fantasy" in relation to *Great Expectations* [pp. 68 and 69]?

13. What does "mother love" have to do with *Great Expectations*?

14. What does the term "objective correlative" [p. 70] mean? How is it related to *Great Expectations*?

15. How well unified, according to Moynahan, is the novel?

16. Does Hagan's article present a satisfactory answer to the question of Pip's association with the taint of guilt which Moynahan raises? Evaluate one of these articles in terms of the other, using any views of other critics which may be helpful.

Patterns of Communication in
*Great Expectations**

by Ruth M. Vande Kieft

Much has been made of the theme of isolation and lack of communication in Dickens's novels. V. S. Prichett says of Dickens's people,

[Their] distinguishing quality . . . is that they are solitaries. They are people caught living in a world of their own. They soliloquize in it. They do not talk to one another; they talk to themselves . . . The people and the things of Dickens are all out of touch and out of hearing of each other, each conducting its own inner monologue, grandiloquent or dismaying [*The Living Novel*, p. 88].

Dorothy Van Ghent supports this proposition by attempting to show exactly how the characters in *Great Expectations* soliloquize, how their communication fails and occasionally lapses into "the frenzied rotary unintelligibility of an idiot's obsession." Each soul is solitary, an integer, and

you cannot make "order" with an integer, one thing alone, for order is definitely a relationship among things. Absolute noncommunication is an unthinkable madness for it negates all relationship and therefore all order, and even an ordinary madman has to create a kind of order for himself by illusions of communication. Dickens' soliloquizing characters, for all their funniness, . . . suggest a world of isolated integers, terrifyingly alone and unrelated. . . . Technique is vision. Dickens' technique is an index of a vision of life that sees human separatedness as the ordinary condition, where speech is speech *to* nobody and where human encounter is mere collision (*The English Novel*, pp. 125–127).

The sources of these critical judgments are elusive, unless they spring

* Reprinted from *Nineteenth-Century Fiction*, XV, 4 (March 1961), pp. 325–334. Copyright © 1961 by The Regents of the University of California.

from the assumption that to be successful or meaningful, relationships and ties between humans must be strictly logical, and always accompanied with or expressed by a completely rational process of articulation. The fact is that not only does each character in *Great Expectations* have a "language" sensitive and adaptable to human intercourse, but also the characters are [325/326] bound together in a highly intricate pattern of relationships which provide for their interaction, communication, and final union with each other. This pattern, both in its comic and tragic effects, is the organizing principle of the novel, is Dickens's "vision" as well as his "technique" in *Great Expectations*.

It is possible first of all to demonstrate that language is not a problem in this novel. One piece of evidence Mrs. Van Ghent uses to illustrate the failure of language is the interview in which Mr. Jaggers discloses to Pip his great expectations, and Joe is offered a compensation for the loss of his apprentice. Shortly before the close of the interview, Joe "swings on [Jaggers]," Mrs. Van Ghent claims, "with unintelligible pugilistic jargon": " 'Which I meantersay . . . that if you come into my place bull-baiting and badgering me, come out! Which I meantersay as sech if you're a man, come on! Which I meantersay, that what I say, I meantersay and stand or fall by!' "

In context, however, this speech seems to me not only completely intelligible, but solidly motivated. Joe has been grossly insulted by Jaggers's implication that he does not keep his word, and is simply challenging Jaggers to a fight involving his honor. Repeatedly, both before and after the great disclosure, Jaggers has pressed Joe about his desire for compensation at the loss of Pip's services. Joe has refused it several times clearly and unequivocally, finally breaking down to the point of saying, " 'If you think as money can make compensation to me for the loss of the little child—what come to the forge—and ever the best of friends!—' " When Jaggers persists in questioning Joe's sincerity, it is too much, and the challenge bursts out of a heart charged with offended love and honor.

Mrs. Van Ghent cites as further evidence the scene in which Joe asserts pleasure in the art of reading when he can find *j*'s and *o*'s, of which he says, "there is no purer expression of solipsism in literature."

But when has literacy ever been considered the *sine qua non* of human communication? (By the end of the novel Joe has become more or less literate, but that is irrelevant.) Mrs. Van Ghent says further that in the scene in which Magwitch enjoys hearing Pip read in a foreign language, "the cultivation of the peculiar Dickensian values of language reaches its apogee." This again seems to me a misinterpretation of the context. Mag-[326/327]witch's pleasure is so clearly motivated by his sense of the "prestige value" of knowing foreign languages, that intelligibility is beside the point. Pip's reading would be far less impressive, because far less a sign of accomplishment, if Magwitch *could* understand him. If he wants to speak to "his boy" he can, well enough, and often does at great length. His own language is quite adequate to what he has to express; in fact, at the scene of his sentence in court, it is almost unrealistically noble and profound.

Nor are the verbal "signatures" Dickens supplies for his characters meaningless: such phrases as Mrs. Joe's " 'Be grateful to them which brought you up by hand,' " Pumblechook's mincing " 'May I?— May I?' " and Wemmick's " 'It's portable property' " do not assume, as Mrs. Van Ghent suggests, "the frenzied rotary unintelligibility of an idiot's obsession": they are rather the clichés which serve as touchstones to the natures and motivations of their characters; meaningful, though not always logically or rationally so, both to those who utter and those who hear them.

Another of the passages Mrs. Van Ghent selects as an illustration of "fantastic private language" is significant as an example of oblique discourse. It is the interview Miss Havisham holds with Joe before Pip leaves her to be apprenticed to Joe as a blacksmith. Of this scene Mrs. Van Ghent says, "for each question she asks him, Joe persists in addressing his reply to Pip rather than herself, and his replies have not the remotest relation to the questions." It is certainly true that Joe addresses himself to Pip, but it is patently untrue that his replies are irrelevant to the questions Miss Havisham is asking. Each of his statements answers her question exactly, though he talks to her obliquely, through Pip. The conversation goes like this (in brackets I provide dull commonsense paraphrases for Joe's delightfully baroque replies):

MISS HAVISHAM: You are the husband of the sister of this boy?

JOE: Which I meantersay, Pip, as I hup and married your sister, and I were at the time what you might call (if you was any ways inclined) a single man. [Yes, Pip's sister has been my first and only wife.]

MISS H.: And you have reared the boy, with the intention of taking him for your apprentice?

JOE: You know, Pip, as you and me were ever friends, and it were looked for'ard to betwixt us, as being calc'lated to lead to larks. Not but what, Pip, if you had ever made objections to the business—such as its being open to black and sut, or such-like—not but what they would [327/328] have been attended to. [It wasn't so much that I reared him with the intention of making him my apprentice, as that the two of us have always looked forward to the joy of working together. Of course if Pip had had objections to the trade because of the filth involved, or for other reasons, I shouldn't have tried to force him into it.]

MISS H.: Has the boy ever made any objections? Does he like the trade?

JOE: Which it is well beknown to yourself, Pip, that it were the wish of your own hart. . . . And there weren't no objections on your part, and, Pip, it were the great wish of your hart! [No, he has always seemed to me very eager to do this.]

MISS H.: Have you brought your indentures with you?

JOE: Well, Pip, you know, you yourself see me put 'em in my 'at, and therefore you know as they are here. (*Joe produces the indentures and gives them to Pip, who gives them to Miss H., who inspects them.*)

MISS H.: You expected no premium with the boy? (*Joe is dumbstruck for an instant, obviously insulted and hurt at the suggestion. Pip remonstrates with Joe, is cut off by—*)

JOE: Pip, which I meantersay that were not a question requiring an answer betwixt yourself and me, and which you know the answer to be full well No. You know it to be No, Pip, and wherefore should I say It? [No, I expected no premium whatever—the idea is preposterous and insulting.] (*At this point the narrator asserts that "Miss Havisham glanced at him as if she understood what he really was, better than I had thought possible, seeing what he was there." She then takes up a small bag from the table beside her, and falling gracefully into the oblique pattern of communication established by Joe, presents the bag to Pip.*)

MISS H.: Pip has earned a premium here, and here it is. There are five-and-twenty guineas in this bag. Give it to your master, Pip.

JOE: This is very liberal on your part, Pip, and it is as such received and grateful welcome, though never looked for, far nor near nowheres. And now, old chap, may we do our duty! May you and me do our duty, both on us by one another, and by them which your liberal present—have—conweyed—to be—for the satisfaction of mind of them as never—(*Here Joe shows he has fallen into frightful difficulties, but he rescues himself triumphantly with the words—*) and from myself far be it! [Thank you for the gift, and you, Pip, for making it possible through your service of Miss Havisham. I certainly never expected it. I hope Pip and I will be worthy of each other, and of your generous interest as evidenced in this gift, which I must again say quite overwhelms me.]

After a final injunction from Miss Havisham that Joe is to expect no further reward but that of a good boy, the interview is terminated.

It is surely evident that there is genuine communication in this scene, that speech is speech *to* somebody, but one may well ask [328/329] why it should be so circular—or more accurately, in this case, triangular. There is again a quite valid psychological motivation: Joe is in an agony of terror and wonder at this strange and formidable creature in her bizarre setting, and small wonder, considering what she is. What is more natural and human than to approach the unknown and frightening through the known and loved? In this indirect discourse Joe finds a delightfully spontaneous way out of his social and verbal difficulties, saves his dignity, and communicates successfully with Miss Havisham. But there is a further beautiful propriety in this indirect discourse, in that what transpires is essentially a ritual or ceremony, in which the chief participants are Pip and Joe, man and boy already held together by strong bonds of love, now being bound as master and apprentice in fulfillment of their long-cherished desire (though Joe at this point does not know of Pip's growing infidelity). Miss Havisham has a function only comparable to that of the justice of the peace or clergyman in a marriage ceremony: the lovers must make their vows to each other (and to God, in a religious ceremony), not the presiding official. Joe turns this potentially disagreeable business interview into a ceremony of love; he makes vows of duty and affection. It is no wonder he is distressed at the cold suggestion that he has been looking for money to come with the boy: it would be like asking an ardent groom, in the middle of the wedding ceremony, whether he expects his wife to bring him a fortune. He can accept Miss Havisham's money only as a groom might accept a wedding gift, and promptly gives it all to Pip's sister, who spends it on a general celebration.

Beautiful as is Joe's oblique expression, the scene as a whole strikes the reader as comic. This is because obliquity may be related to incongruity, one of the chief sources of comic effect, and there are many incongruities in the scene. Pip is aware of Joe's looking like "an extraordinary bird . . . with his tuft of feathers ruffled." He is standing in the presence of Miss Havisham, herself something grotesque in her fantastic surroundings; his speech seems, to the sniggering Estella, comically misdirected, and Pip is in a sweat of embarrassment. But though among the characters there may be some failure of sympathy, there is surely no failure of language to communicate effectively.

This is one instance of obliquity of discourse, and there are [329/330] several others in the novel. It is a favorite device of Joe, who frequently speaks of himself or others in the third person, sometimes with a rhetorical flourish, sometimes out of delicacy (as in the scene in chapter lvii in which he prevents Pip from speaking out the painful truth about the history of Magwitch, to save Pip from humiliation). Indirect discourse, evasiveness, or deviation from directness in speech, is also used by Jaggers in relating to Pip the story of Estella and her mother, by Wemmick in his warnings to Pip concerning the safety of Magwitch, and again by Wemmick in his delightfully evasive wedding arrangements with Pip—in each case from a need, real or imaginary, for self-protection. In none of these instances, however, is obliquity of discourse any hindrance to finally successful communication.

If language is an effective agent of communication, the implication is that the persons speaking are in some way related to each other, that individual motives are at least perceived, if not shared, that meanings and assumptions are common, and hence understood. In *Great Expectations* much of this interrelation of the main characters in the novel comes from a common implication in guilt, a common process of suffering because of violation of the moral order, a common process of repentance and regeneration. The sins of parents against children and children against parents, and the sins of social snobbery, are elaborated throughout the novel: not only in the relationships among the principal characters, Joe, Pip, Magwitch, Miss Havisham, and Estella, but tangentially in the aristocratic pretensions of Mrs. Pocket and her abysmal failure as a mother; the false "adoption" of Pip by Pumblechook, and the reactions of the whole town to Pip during the three major stages of his career. And in this guilt, as Edmund Wilson has pointed out, "the highest and the lowest in that English society of shocking contrasts are inextricably tied together" (*The Wound and the Bow*, p. 42). There is a reason why, in Pip's fantasies, the glamorous images of Estella and Miss Havisham are so often strangely blended with the horrible images of convicts and Newgate prison.

The characters are related, then, in their state of shared guilt which is compounded when the victims of these personal and social crimes take their revenge. But according to the Christian ethical pattern which Dickens follows in the novel, sin must be [330/331] followed by punishment and repentance, which in turn must be followed by pleas for pardon. The first of the major reconciliation scenes in the novel is that in which Mrs. Joe asks forgiveness of Joe and Pip. Biddy describes the scene as follows:

"She had been in one of her bad states . . . for four days, when she came out of it in the evening, just at tea-time, and said quite plainly, 'Joe.' As she had never said any word for a long while, I ran and fetched in Mr. Gargery from the forge. She made signs to me that she wanted him to sit down close to her, and wanted me to put her arms round his neck. So I put them round his neck, and she laid her head down on his shoulder quite content and satisfied. And so she presently said 'Joe' again, and once 'Pardon,' and once 'Pip.' And so she never lifted her head up any more. . . ."

Her plea for pardon is echoed through the novel: Pip asks it of Joe and Biddy; Miss Havisham asks it of Pip (" 'Take the pencil and write under my name, "I forgive her" ' "); Estelle asks it of Pip. But Pip recognizes a still higher point of reference than human forgiveness. Threatened with death at Orlick's hand, he "humbly beseeches pardon . . . of Heaven"; to Estella he says, " 'Oh God bless you, God forgive you' "; and at Magwitch's deathbed he prays, " 'O Lord, be merciful to him, a sinner!' "

Among persons so deeply involved with each other morally, so wise with the knowledge of evil and so chastened by suffering, it is not relevant to speak of problems of communication. The characters who share this understanding cannot be considered solitudes. Their language is adequate, and sometimes more than adequate. This final illustration, from Magwitch, riding out on the river toward the sea to meet—he knows not what: freedom, or another, and final, capture:

"We'd be puzzled to be more quiet and easy-going than we are at present. But—it's a-flowing so soft and pleasant through the water, p'raps, as makes me think it—I was a-thinking through my smoke just then, that we can no more see to the bottom of the next few hours, than we can see to the bottom of this river what I catches hold of. Nor yet we can't no more hold their tide than I can hold this. And it's run through my fingers and gone, you see!" holding up his dripping hand.

"But for your face, I should think you were a little despondent," said I.

"Not a bit on it, dear boy! It comes of flowing on so quiet, and of that there rippling at the boat's head making a sort of Sunday tune. Maybe I'm a-growing a trifle old besides."   [331/332]

This seems to me sensitive use of language, a clear sign that the persons communicating are closely in touch with each other's deepest feelings. By his words and his tone Magwitch has told Pip of his resignation, his realistic awareness of what dangers may follow; by the look on his face he has communicated his peace, and even, apparently, a mild hope and cheerfulness.

But though they use language, these two scarcely need it. "The old sound in his throat—softened now, like the rest of him" (Magwitch's inarticulate response to the unfamiliar and strangely moving human pity which first sparked his love for Pip), the pressure of Pip's hand— these are signs of a kind of love and mutual responsiveness which obviate the need for language.

There are in the novel at least two dramatic examples of the fact that language is not indispensable to human communication. One already alluded to is that of Pip's sister after she is struck dumb. Here communication is starkly basic and simple, but it is satisfactory: it is the inarticulate expression of the spirit of penitence and forgiveness. The other example is the case, half-tenderly, half-comically described, of the

Aged P., Wemmick's father. He is shut off from human discourse by his deafness, and symbolically, from society, by his position in the little fortress surrounded by the little moat ("'After I have crossed the bridge,'" says Wemmick, "'I hoist it up—so—and cut off communication'"). Yet he is in no way really or essentially isolated, simply because he loves and is loved, and out of this wholeness of his being he reaches warmly to the outside world. There is something enormously satisfied and satisfying about this old man: "clean, comfortable, and well cared for." Language is useless, but rituals are important and effective as means of communication in his life: the nightly flag and gun ceremony, the vigorous nodding, the reading of the paper, the little wooden flap which announces names, and above all, the drinking of tea, an occasion at which everybody gets delightfully warm and greasy, and "the Aged especially, might have passed for some clean old chief of a savage tribe, just oiled."

It seems clear that in this novel Dickens does not present human isolation and the failure of communication: rather, his assumption closely resembles that famous one of Donne's, "No man is an island." Yet, though communication among the characters is generally and sometimes even beautifully successful, it has distinct [332/333] limitations. It is primitive and basic rather than full, complex, or rich in nuance. Its boundaries are determined by the fact that all the characters, with the exception of Pip, are monolithic. Their characters are not really flexible and changing; the large movements of their souls, from sin and hatred to sorrow and repentance, do not serve to make them more complex and subtle in their dealings with others, do not equip them to enter with deep imaginative intelligence into each other's worlds. At the end Pip, who has grown more complex psychologically as well as morally, still seems to be left alone (at least in the first version of the ending), without promise of bliss; and the tone of the book is predominantly melancholy. This is because the narrator is so keenly aware of how life defeats personal happiness, and because he does not, despite the inclusion of Pip's prayers, really know or see beyond this life. Happiness which comes obliquely, through the joy of seeing others happy, is not really enough; the softened heart is left unfulfilled and hungry. Hence, though the ethical pattern of the novel is Christian, the vision is not, finally, religious: there is no real communication between God and man. There is only the basic communion of men who are related in guilt and sorrow, in forgiveness and in love.

It is this kind of communion, and communication, which some of Dickens's modern critics have apparently overlooked. It seems to me that they have rather superimposed a specifically modern problem on 'this novel of Dickens. It is the problem suggested by T. S. Eliot's description of "the intolerable wrestle with words and meanings": the burdening sense of isolation which comes out of a period in which the conventions of meaning and expression are questioned, because none are widely assumed; a period in which there are no contexts for unity and order. The process of social dissolution had, doubtless, begun by Dickens's time, but Dickens seems to have assumed he knew what "order" was, or ought to be. The narrator of *Great Expectations* states this clearly, though in terms largely negative, in his response to Miss Havisham's agonized cry of epiphany: " 'What have I done? What have I done?' " His response to her outburst is one of pity and tolerance for the sinner, but absolute condemnation of the sin, an attitude he has achieved through his own implication in guilt:

I knew not how to answer, or how to comfort her. That she had done [333/334] a grievous thing in taking an impressionable child to mold it into the form that her wild resentment, spurned affection, and wounded pride, found vengeance in, I knew full well. But that, in shutting out the light of day, she had shut out infinitely more; that, in seclusion, she had secluded herself from a thousand natural and healing influences; that, her mind, brooding solitary, had grown diseased, as all minds do and must that reverse the appointed order of their Maker; I knew equally well. And could I look upon her without compassion, seeing her punishment in the ruin she was, in her profound unfitness for this earth on which she was placed, in the vanity of sorrow which had become a master mania, like the vanity of penitence, the vanity of remorse, the vanity of unworthiness, and other monstrous vanities that have been curses in this world?

"The appointed order of their Maker" is assumed as the norm in this novel, and the terms of that moral order are defined, both negatively and positively, in the lives of the characters. It may be called the metaphysical basis for the communication in this novel.

The kind of communication which Dickens presents in *Great Expectations* is free either to use or dispense with language: if to use it, to do so directly or obliquely, rationally or irrationally: if to be inarticulate, to employ symbolic actions which convey meaning through gesture, ceremony, or ritual. But it is always a kind of communication in which the deepest and most basic moral needs and intents of the human heart have been received by and conveyed to others.

[end on 334]

PROBLEMS: Ruth M. Vande Kieft

1. Do you agree with Ruth Vande Kieft on the organizing principle of *Great Expectations?* If so, elaborate on her thesis through a detailed presentation of your reading of the novel. If not, show where you believe she is in error.

2. Sketch the basic differences between Miss Vande Kieft's and Mrs. Van Ghent's articles and decide which one is closer to your own views.

3. What is the "violation of moral order" that Miss Vande Kieft mentions [page 330]? To what extent are the characters aware of this violation?

4. Part of Moynahan's article is built around the difficulty of understanding Pip's prayer at Magwitch's deathbed. Miss Vande Kieft attempts [p. 331] to fit this prayer into a series of speeches of forgiveness in the novel. Does she provide an answer that helps, hurts, or destroys Moynahan's point?

5. How are John Donne's words, "No man is an island" (from his *Devotions upon Emergent Occasions*) relevant to *Great Expectations* [p. 332]?

6. What does Miss Vande Kieft mean by saying that all the characters, except Pip, are monolithic [p. 333]? Do you agree with her?

7. Miss Vande Kieft finds that "the tone of the book is predominantly melancholy" [p. 333] while Edgar Johnson says that it "is not in its pervading atmosphere a melancholy book." Which opinion seems more nearly correct to you?

8. What are the limits of *Great Expectations* as Miss Vande Kieft sees them? Do you agree?

9. Explain in detail why Miss Vande Kieft believes that while the ethical pattern of *Great Expectations* is Christian, the novel's vision is not religious.

The Change of Heart
in Dickens' Novels*

by Barbara Hardy

Pip's progress in *Great Expectations* is probably the only instance of a moral action where the events precipitate change and growth as they do in George Eliot or Henry James. Pip is marked by a dominant flaw like Scrooge, but the flaw does not absorb the whole vitality of the character. He is a more realistic and analytical Martin Chuzzlewit and he is shown subjected to the influences of accident and environment, and hardening in his pride and ingratitude, though never without some measure of shame. The main converting event is his discovery of the source of his expectations, but this is a fairly complex business, involving the delicately handled shifting relationship with Magwitch. This is certainly not only a symbolic delineation of the criminal basis of wealth, though at times it carries that implication. Magwitch is also an important agent in the conversion of Pip. He first exacerbates and then exorcises pride and ingratitude.

Pip's view of this nemesis is still steeped in his twin failings: "But, sharpest and deepest pain of all—it was for the convict, guilty of I knew not what crimes, and liable to be taken out of those rooms where I sat thinking, and hanged at the Old Bailey door, that I had deserted Joe" (ch. xxxix). Here he is merely revaluing one particular instance of pride and ingratitude, and what he has to learn, like all unimaginative men, is a generalized and renewable morality. He has to revalue his defects, not an isolated example of them. Magwitch plays a role in this

* From *Victorian Studies*, V, 1 (September 1961), pp. 61–67. Reprinted by permission of the author and the publisher.

Morality rather like that of King Grizzlybeard in the fairy tale, who degrades pride and gives it a real cause and a fitting punishment. Pip, like a spoilt child, is really given something to cry about. Pip has winced at Joe's illiteracy and manners, and so he is forced into the gross parody and ordeal of stomaching Magwitch, who has paid for Pip's education and fastidiousness. Then Pip becomes involved in Magwitch's past and future, and Magwitch himself is given dignity and sympathy. Both he and Pip move out of aggressive pride into trust and love. Magwitch then provokes a further revaluation in Pip, based now on an appraisal of the convict's gratitude, and an acknowledgement of his own debt: [61/62]

When I took my place by Magwitch's side, I felt that that was my place henceforth while he lived.

    For now my repugnance to him had all melted away, and in the hunted wounded shackled creature who held my hand in his, I only saw a man who had meant to be my benefactor, and who had felt affectionately, gratefully, and generously, towards me with great constancy through a series of years. I only saw in him a much better man that I had been to Joe.   (ch. liv)

Magwitch draws out and punishes Pip's pride and ingratitude,[6] then delineates Pip for himself and the reader in his role as moral opposite. Finally, he provides the final ordeal which proves Pip's conversion. Pip holds Magwitch's hand during the trial, and the spectators "pointed down at this criminal or at that, and most of all at him and me" (ch. lvi).

    Although Estella's relations with her benefactor largely parallel Pip's, her moral change takes place offstage, and it is Miss Havisham's conversion which corresponds to Pip's. She is like Miss Wade in strengthening her own ruling passion by encouraging it in someone else—a subtle form of self-justification and revenge. She of course propagates her lovelessness in her education of Estella, and like Gradgrind she is punished at the hands of the pupil who has learnt only too well. Estella hear's Pip's declaration of love unmoved, and explains,

---

    [6] Although I cannot entirely accept Dorothy Van Ghent's view of this relationship (*The English Novel: Form and Function* [New York, 1953]), this account is not irreconcilable with her intepretation.

"It is in the nature formed within me." When Miss Havisham demands the one thing she has trained Estella not to give—"Would it be weakness to return my love?"—Estella can only ask:

If you had taught her, from the dawn of her intelligence, with your utmost energy and might, that there was such a thing as daylight but that it was made to be her enemy and destroyer, and she must always turn against it, for it had blighted you and would else blight her;—if you had done this, and then, for a purpose, had wanted her to take naturally to the daylight and she could not do it, you would have been disappointed and angry?   (ch. xxxviii)

Miss Havisham is taught by her self-created double, but the encounter shows her that she is in fact teaching lovelessness while desperately needing love. She sees her error in this distorting mirror. Then, like Scrooge, she sees her old self in the image of Pip. He provides this image of love just after she has been rebuffed by the image of lovelessness, and she tells Pip, after his rejection by Estella, "Until you spoke to her the other day, and until I saw in you a looking-glass that showed [62/63] me what I once felt myself, I did not know what I had done" (ch. xlix). There is no action left for her, but she admits responsibility, and knows that she has shut Estella, like herself, away from the influences that form "the natural heart," that "with this figure of myself always before her, a warning to back and point my lesson, I stole her heart away and put ice in its place." Estella comes to find that suffering is "stronger than all other teaching" but that is a process not demonstrated in the novel.   [end on 63]

PROBLEMS: Barbara Hardy

1. What does Miss Hardy mean by saying that Pip's "flaw does not absorb the whole vitality of the character" [p. 61]?
2. Why is the relationship between Pip and Magwitch a "delicately handled shifting relationship" [p. 61]?
3. Why and in what way must Pip revalue his defects?
4. Write an essay explaining Miss Hardy's statement in footnote six [p. 62].
5. Does Miss Hardy mean that Magwitch is Pip's alter ego? If so, is

she justified in her belief? If not, what is she saying about their relationship?

6. Delineate the parallelism between Estella's and Pip's relationships with their benefactors which Miss Hardy notes.

7. Miss Hardy says Estella's moral change takes place offstage. Do other moral changes, then, take place onstage? Discuss moral change in *Great Expectations* in terms of dramatic technique.

Individual Conscience and Social Injustice in *Great Expectations**

by John Lindberg

"Oh! To hear him!... To hear the names he's giving me! That Orlick! In my own house! Me, a married woman! With my husband standing by! Oh! Oh!" With these words, Mrs. Joe Gargery reaches the climax of her hysterical fit and Dickens begins a series of violent incidents that seem to bear but an obscure relevance to the plot of *Great Expectations*. A unified reading of the subsequent episodes that develop Mrs. Joe's character might treat her as an extended metaphor or allegory among the many others expressing the theme of the novel. Mrs. Joe's passion for respectability is central to the main theme of *Great Expectations*, because more than any other person she has had the shaping of Pip's conscience, his infantile and perdurable sense of right and wrong. The novel as a whole treats of social injustice, and that theme too may also explicate Mrs. Joe's private struggle with her own conscience, for Dickens is apparently very concerned with the conflict between respectable prosperity and shameful poverty in the public scene and with the individual attempt to adapt private values to the status quo.

Mrs. Joe is a hysterical, passionate woman, barely in control of herself. Her sweetness to Pumblechook, even her struggle to keep herself and Pip off the parish before Joe took pity on them, betray the specious piety of a barbarous egotism seeking status in conventional respectability. She is fiercely respectable, with a suspect carefulness in

* From *College English*, XXIII, 2 (November 1961), pp. 118–122. Reprinted with permission of the National Council of Teachers of English.

minutiae of conduct. She makes a point of pride in the fact that she never doffs her apron, an offensively ugly, coarse apron with a large bib like a breastplate of righteousness, stuck full of pins and needles which often come off in the bread that she cuts against her breast for Pip and Joe and butters with a curiously belligerent thoroughness. She scorns Joe, perhaps because he had the weakness to pity her [118/119] in her struggle to keep her respectability after the decease of Philip Pirrip and Also Georgiana, but certainly because he has not the character and ambition to rise above his lowly occupation. And with maddening hypocrisy, she uses good deeds to satisfy her own bad nature. Let Pip display the least deviation in appetite, he is doused with tar water; let him display the least development of curiosity, he is dratted and condescended into silence (her hard-wrung answer about the Hulks is Pip's first intimation that his monster on the marsh was human, and criminal); let Pip and Joe between them fall unluckily into a social recognition that does not extend to her, they are forced to stand in the cold while Mrs. Joe scrubs the house, as if expunging her own vile temper from the walls that immure her soul. She laughs once, upon the occasion of Miss Havisham's generous premium for Pip's apprenticeship, in delighted surprise at the rare event of the world being as she wills it.

Her respectability is hysterical because she partly knows that it comes hard to her, that she is ill at ease in Zion. The quarrel with Orlick is the climax of her hysterical nature, for the quarrel is sought: "it is undeniable that instead of lapsing into passion, she consciously and deliberately took extraordinary pains to force herself into it, and became blindly furious by regular stages; 'what was the name that he gave me before the base man who swore to defend me? Oh! Hold me! Oh!'" The worst of the offense is its insult to her status as a respectable married woman. This is her masterpiece in a hypocrisy that fully indulges emotions unacceptable in pious life, but expresses them through conventional respectable channels. She finds in Orlick a match to her own nature, and admires him furtively for his ill-suppressed badness. She is so sure of her similarity to Orlick that even though her back is turned when Orlick strikes her down with the manacle, she knows intuitively that it was he who struck her, and her subsequent desire to propitiate him, though developing into genuine repentance, may very possibly have begun in the emotional excitement of receiving the brutal attentions of a man who recognizes her own nature rather than pities her position in life.

She descended to her worst nature and was there surprised by it when it called up Orlick; the violence of the assault is but a physical version of her loss of the personality upon which she depended for security and direction in ordinary life. That personality was a formidably self-righteous image of herself as a conscientious housewife much plagued by an unruly boy and a worthless husband. On this image she relies for protection from her worst nature, but she can free herself from the image in her bursts of fury. After a hysterical fit, she is calm; she has taken a vacation from her conscience. By a physical extension of her moral state, Dickens also absolves her from active participation in life when the blow from the manacle brings on aphasia and paralysis. She can relax from her struggle toward respectability. Her aphasia is truly moral, a symbolic cessation from action, because it would be impossible for her to live a normal life without her conscientious image of herself.

It is at this point that her regeneration begins. She can only remain on her lowest moral level, or rise from it with a new knowledge of herself. The formidably self-righteous image has been discarded, not to be replaced by any other incomplete mask. Her identity is now becoming lost in calm love rather than in frenzied hate. She is much gentler, more placid, more anxious to please, to cause no trouble or pain. She is grateful to Orlick for his help in her self-recognition and wishes that he might follow the same path of regeneration that he has unconsciously pointed out to her. At her death, she mutters a pathetic request [119/120] for forgiveness, because she has come to understand that her discarded protective image, formed to satisfy conventional mores, was a cruel imposition on her household.

Of course, this analysis of her motives is highly interpretive, depending on the fragmentary actions by which alone Mrs. Joe can indicate her feelings after her paralysis, but it seems that the great contrast in her behavior before and after the assault bespeaks a deep inner reform.

If in hysteria she found fugitive freedom from the force of conventional conscience, in aphasia she found a higher liberation, in which her newly educated soul rose beyond the imperatives of everyday morality.

Ripped from context, the episode of Mrs. Joe and Orlick may seem too slight to bear an interpretation which must affect the meaning of the whole novel, but many other episodes also support Mrs. Joe's allegory, for her private conscience is but one expression of the Victorian ambition to rise. Separate aspects of the private moral tangle involving her, Orlick, and Pip seem to be parallel to more public attitudes towards respectability, success, and good conduct.

The convicts in *Great Expectations* are the bad conscience of Victorian England. Orlick is a criminal type, at the opposite pole in the novel from the simple goodness of Joe. For his weapon against Mrs. Joe, there lies easy to hand a discarded manacle, part of the impedimenta with which respectable people hope to protect themselves from the untamed elements among them. Orlick hates Pip with a quite understandable passion because Pip has always frustrated his attempts to improve his condition. Criminals lurk and prowl through the novel. They dominate the horizon of Pip's childhood world from the black threat of the Hulks. Pip's first impression of London is the ironic contrast of Smithfield and Newgate close by the symbolically named Little Britain, while golden St. Paul's is visible far off and above it all; his last impression of his first day in London is of a staggering porter loitering about Barnard's Inn for whatever he can pick up. On a visit to Miss Havisham, he is painfully aware of the convict breathing down his neck on the stage, the same convict who had leered at him in the pub at home. When Magwitch returns, there is an unknown informer on the stairs; and when Magwitch (now Provis) is safe at Chink's Basin and Pip relaxes at the play, then Compeyson is closest to him. Hiding at the Hummums from his quickly encroaching enemies, Pip seems to see the walls of his cuddy splotched with disease from the very light of his candle, and at last facing his enemy at the lime kiln with its sinister haze of fumes snaking along the ground, Pip finds all of his unworthy deeds embodied in the drunken brute who proposes to beat him to a pulp and burn the pulp to dust.

Mrs. Joe was taken quite by surprise when she challenged Orlick, inspiring motives which rapidly passed beyond her control. Similarly, society prepares its own downfall when most attempting to secure itself against its own worst nature. Miss Havisham unwittingly offered an object to criminal cupidity because her wealth developed a false sense of her own worth; her pride insured her deception. Now her brewery is full of hollow casks and weeds, and Pip has an appropriate vision of her hanging among the ruins. Discussing the fate of Compeyson and of Arthur Havisham, Herbert Pocket quite naturally speaks of their descending into ever lower depths of criminality, going from bad to worse by a necessary progression. The incompetent, weak, and ill-natured find no purchase on the smooth slope of the social pyramid; nowhere is there a niche provided for them: society rests on a base of unused human beings, who must be violent and criminal to express them-[120/121]selves at all, and for whom to exist is to do wrong. Pip should never have given Magwitch that pork pie. The practice of deportation to the colonies is the last absurdity of a conscientious public, who assume that criminals will be grateful for the opportunity to build a new life which they are unprepared to begin. The final irony in the novel is that the authorities view Provis as confirmed in evil when he returns out of love; and the final stage in Pip's maturity is that, seeing Provis refuse "to bend the past out of its eternal shape," he strives to arrange his relations with Joe and Herbert so that his present also shall redeem the past.

If the underworld viewed as the bad conscience of society is a thematic extension of Mrs. Joe's attempts to master her worst nature in a desire to rise, it is even more an extension of Pip's compunctions. Pip finds himself in a suggestive situation on the night of the attack; he is reading *The London Merchant* with Wopsle and Pumblechook at the very time when Mrs. Joe is struck down. The play has reminded him, and Pumblechook has jogged his memory, that Mrs. Joe and Pumblechook are not entirely preposterous in their claims to have found Pip a station in life. Mrs. Joe raised him up by hand, and Pumblechook told him of the position at Satis House when he might have recommended another boy. Under the influence of the play, Pip's dissatisfaction with his lot assumes a color of ingratitude and selfishness, which darkens to irrational guilt when he learns that the weapon was of his own providing. The very inadvertency of the manacle's offering itself is a proof of the persistent influence of bad deeds. Pip writhes once again at his evil ways, his weakness that allowed him to succor a convict rather than report him, his unwelcome two pounds from the convict who brought him down with an invisible gun, his sly colloguing with the lowest kind of man.

Pip's earliest associations have borne his moral depravity in upon him. Despite his contempt of coarseness and dirt, he is even more ashamed of his innermost thoughts than he is of his outward circumstances. It is no help that he never did what he knew to be wrong except when in mortal terror (of the young man after his liver and lights) or when driven by adult torment (to lie about his first visit to Satis House); the fact is that his desire to preserve himself forced him from the path of virtue. During the impressionable period of his early youth, when his conscience is taking its lasting form, Pip is much in the position of the outcasts mentioned earlier, for whom to exist is to do wrong. Upon visiting Newgate with Wemmick, he feels himself soiled not only in his genteel finery but in his soul, and meeting Estella immediately after, he cannot recall where he has seen her gesture of hand and her expression of face before; only when he has learned to replace Estella with Provis as the object of his love can Pip bear the knowledge that the cherished image of his dream life is as much a shoot from the dungheap as his own expectations.

The change in Pip's objects of love is the most obvious unveiling of a new moral world. Like his sister when she wishes to be forgiven, Pip repudiates conventional mores in pursuit of a more liberal sense of right. Estella always inspired him to cast off his best friend and deny his common sense, but with her marriage to Drummle and with the loss of Pip's financial expectations, Pip opens his heart to Provis, whom he has despised in his heart from earliest memory. He learns indifference to worldly and materialistic change when Provis calmly draws the analogy of his life with the river on which they hope to escape, and the death struggle in the depths of that river, coming so soon after Pip's struggle with fire at Satis House and the review of his past life when confronted with the vengeful Orlick, seems an al-[121/122]legory similar to Mrs. Joe's awakening to love through the shock of Orlick's attack, for Pip rises from his baptism in the river, and from his fever afterwards, utterly dead to the demands of the world and resolved to use the world as best he may to insure a proper moral economy throughout the rest of his life.

Such an enlightened and expanded version of individual conscience is radical in its effect on society. Pip has been as objectively divorced from society by his symbolic death and rebirth as Mrs. Joe was by her aphasia, which was moral as well as actual. We know Dickens' opinion of Parliament, the New Poor Law, and industrialism, but we know too that he was far from advocating a Red revolt. He was as much committed to the status quo as Plugson of Undershot. Like Tennyson, who was concerned in the *Idylls* with betrayal by what is false within, Dickens believed that economic and social reform could come by deliberate moral choice.

Consequently, the structure of the whole novel is calculated to illustrate social decay by the allegory of individual conscience. If conscience develops from spontaneous emotional response to experience, and if the emotions are basically good, then any suffering caused by the individual conscience must indicate evil in the social matrices that cast the susceptible moral nature into the forms of experience. That evil comes from the ignorance and complacency of all who compose the ranks among whom the individual wishes to rise. It becomes the duty of all men to examine their presuppositions.

For this reason, *Great Expectations*, the only other novel besides *David Copperfield* which Dickens narrates in the first person, is the record of one man's moral regeneration through an increasingly broadened point of view. A happy ending can be dispensed with because Pip, knowing that he has adjusted himself to expectations of a greater value than is found in the marketplace, does not even wish for the putative happiness of marriage and prosperity. Dickens means to imply that any man can be happy in any social order that will permit the operation of moral imperatives, and *Great Expectations* is his non-dogmatic religious assertion of a serious optimism which is all the more convincing for having brought social injustice home to the reader as his own original sin.   [end on 122]

PROBLEMS: John Lindberg

1. "The novel as a whole treats of social injustice," says John Lindberg [p. 118]. Make a case for or against social injustice as its theme.

2. Do you agree that Mrs. Joe, more than any other person, has shaped the conscience of Pip? What of Joe, Miss Havisham, Jaggers, Wemmick, or Herbert Pocket? What have other critics said of the characters who shaped Pip's conscience?

3. Explain in detail what Lindberg means by applying the words "maddening hypocrisy" to Mrs. Joe.

4. How and why does Lindberg apply the word "hysterical" to Mrs. Joe? Can that word be applied to more persons in the book than just Mrs. Joe? What importance has hysteria in the world of *Great Expectations?*

5. Lindberg says his analysis of Mrs. Joe's motives is highly interpretive. Do you agree with it?

6. Discuss in detail the validity of Lindberg's assertion that the underworld of *Great Expectations* is the bad conscience of society. Do other critics disagree with Lindberg on this?

7. Lindberg says that Magwitch returns to England out of love. Comment.

8. To what extent are Mrs. Joe and Pumblechook justified in their claims to having helped Pip to his station in life?

9. Using Lindberg and other critics, define Pip's "moral depravity."

10. In what ways is Pip like his sister? In what ways are they different?

11. What is the allegory of individual conscience that Lindberg finds in *Great Expectations?* Is it a "pure" allegory?

12. Lindberg says the happy ending is not necessary. Do you agree with his reasoning?

13. Lindberg says, "*Great Expectations* is his [Dickens's] non-dogmatic religious assertion of a serious optimism . . ." [p. 122]. Explain this statement.

The Moving I:
A Study of the Point of View
in *Great Expectations**

by ROBERT B. PARTLOW, JR.

ARTICLES LIKE Norman Friedman's (1955 *PMLA*) are reminders that
critical discussions and analyses of point of view in fiction have, in the
last half century, become steadily more subtle and penetrative. Henry
James, James Joyce, Joseph Warren Beach, Percy Lubbock, E. M.
Forster, and Mark Schorer, to mention only the most significant, have
made clear the strategic importance of the author's choice of a center
(his focus, his [122/123] position in relation to events) and his choices of
narrator and listener (his mode of transmission). Professor Friedman
asks the questions that must be answered about such choices and outlines the range of possible modes of transmission from editorial omniscience through neutral omniscience, "I" as witness, "I" as protagonist,
multiple selective omniscience and selective omniscience, to the dramatic
mode and the camera method. Within the limits of a short article, he
marks out the major categories and hints at some of the possible variations, combinations, and overlappings. He also provides us with the
critical terminology needed for a close study of a specific novel, *Great
Expectations* for example.

Assuming—perhaps gratuitously—that the characters, story line, and
theme had been established in mind and that Dickens had chosen to

* From *College English*, XXIII, 2 (November 1961), pp. 122–126, 131. Reprinted with
permission of the National Council of Teachers of English.

write autobiographically, in the "I" as protagonist mode, what specific problems would necessarily have cropped up at once? Certainly these, at the least: (1) What is to be the position of the narrator in time: contemporary throughout with the events of the story proper, contemporary only with the later sections of the story, posterior to the story events, or shifting? To what extent are the characters and events of the story to be presented as history? Is the narrator to be seated in front of a panorama or is he to take his place in events as they are happening? (2) If the historical or panoramic method is chosen, is the narrator to act as an interpreter or merely as a cameraman or recorder? What degree of omniscience, if any, is to be shown? (3) What will be the relationship between narrator and author? (4) What audience is to be selected? (5) Which of all the possible means of presentation (including dialogue, interior monologue, pictured action, description of people and events, and external comment) shall be used? What is to be the relative proportion and balance among these means? The answers to these and similar questions, whether made with full awareness or not, will determine the structure and, to some extent, the tone of the novel.

In *Great Expectations*, the narrator is neither Pip nor Mr. Pip, but Mr. Pirrip, a moderately successful, middle-aged businessman, a *petit bourgeois* who has risen in life by his own exertions and a fine bit of luck. Now home from his work overseas, he is telling his life story many years after all the events have occurred. Unlike the Pip of all except the last two chapters, he is a mature man, sober, industrious, saddened, aware of his own limitations, and possessed of a certain calm wisdom— the wisdom of a Cinderella who learned the shoe did not fit and the fairy godmother was psychotic and criminal. He also has a keen sense of the ludicrous and the grotesque which cannot be ascribed to himself when younger. As we read the story, it becomes more and more evident that he cannot entirely grasp what Pip was or why the young fellow acted as he did. The narrator, in fact, feels a kind of alienation from Pip. The boy and the young man did, after all, act according to motives and feelings which the older man sees not directly, but through a film of memory. In Chapter 6, for example, the narrator remarks about young Pip:

My state of mind regarding the pilfering from which I had been so unexpectedly exonerated, did not impel me to frank disclosure; but I hope it had some dregs of good at the bottom of it. I do not recall that I felt any tenderness of conscience to Mrs. Joe, when the fear of being found out was lifted off me. But I loved Joe—perhaps for no better reason in those early days than because the dear fellow let me love him—and, as to him, my inner self was not so easily composed. . . . The fear of losing Joe's confidence, and of thenceforth sitting in the chimney-corner at night staring drearily at my for ever lost companion and friend, tied my tongue. I morbidly [123/124] represented to myself that if Joe knew it, I never afterwards could see him at the fireside feeling his fair whisker, without thinking that he was meditating on it. . . . In a word, I was too cowardly to do what I knew to be right, as I had been too cowardly to avoid doing what I knew to be wrong. I had had no intercourse with the world at that time, and I imitated none of its many inhabitants who act in this manner. Quite an untaught genius, I made the discovery of the line of action for myself.

This passage, which is a typical one, suggests that the narrator does not feel identified with Pip. Sympathetic, yes, and amused—but these are feelings associated with others, not one's self. Even more, the narrator judges Pip's fear from an adult position, with a sophistication impossible for a seven-year-old boy, directs his gaze forward a dozen years later to Pip's subsequent experiences, and comments sardonically on customary human behavior. Even more, the diction and turn of phrase are those of a skillful writer, not those of an untaught blacksmith's boy. But all this is exactly in keeping with the position and character of the narrator and is part of Dickens' admirable control of his technique in this novel. The choice of point of view almost obviates the interior monologue, except at a remove; neither are we taken very deeply into Pip's mind. In this and other passages the narrator is neither Pip nor an omniscient author; he is an older man trying, not always with complete success, to recall the exact dimensions of an emotion formerly felt and the real motives for an action far back in time. Occasionally he reminds the reader, especially in the early chapters, that the view is down a long corridor only fitfully lighted. In Chapter 12, for instance, while he is discussing the boy's relations with the other characters, he stops to say:

I reposed complete confidence in no one but Biddy; but, I told poor Biddy everything. Why it came natural for me to do so, and why Biddy had a deep concern in everything I told her, I did not know then, though I think I know now.

And in Chapter 38 there are three passages which remind the reader of the gap between the present telling and past events:

It is impossible to turn this leaf of my life without putting Bentley Drummle's name upon it; or, I would, very gladly.... I tell this lightly, but it was no light thing to me. For, I cannot adequately express what pain it gave me to think that Estella should show any favour to a contemptible, clumsy, sulky booby, so very far below the average.... And now that I have given the one chapter to the theme that so filled my heart, as so often made it ache and ache again, I pass on, unhindered, to the event that had impended over me longer yet.

The scrupulous attention to tenses and tense sequences in these and other chapters is also noteworthy. All events in the main story line are placed in one of the past tenses; in all except the dramatic scenes present and future tenses are reserved for the narrator's use. Once the reader has recognized the point of view being used, this practice is not obtrusive or distracting; it provides, indeed, an economical means of keeping the narrator's observations and emotions distinct from those of Pip.

Dickens was not—perhaps could not be—equally scrupulous in his use of the pronoun *I*. As a result the reader does not always know at once if it means "I-the-narrator, as I am now" or "I-as-Pip, as I was." In this novel the two are so different that separate pronouns might well have been used, perhaps in the manner that the French distinguish between *tu* and *vous*. If the reader is very attentive, he will get this effect anyway: there is often such a great difference between the two *I*'s that the latter, the "I-as-I-was," becomes virtually "he." Thus we may say that the point of [124/125] view seems to combine the first person protagonist method with third person selective omniscient. Perhaps an image would make the point clearer. Consider a man showing sound moving pictures of his early life and explaining them for the benefit of his guests. He watches the action with them, and comments lovingly or sadly or ironically about events and people; occasionally he refers to something that has not yet appeared in the time sequence of the film;

he speeds up the dull parts and slows down the moving or humorous parts, mentioning, as he does so, that the characters were not playing roles and certainly took themselves seriously, not as actors working to evoke tears or laughter; he feels himself an especially knowledgeable member of the present audience and so looks at himself as he was, in the film, from a distance, as half a stranger.

But not always. Dickens was too competent a novelist merely to tell a story and too confirmed a dramatist not to let the sound-film speak for itself at least part of the time. Almost every chapter, therefore, combines the distant and close views, the narrative and the dramatic modes of presentation, telling and showing—all very smoothly. Take as example Chapter 4, that delightful account of the Christmas dinner at Joe Gargery's. Paragraph 1 is narrative, an adult commentary upon the action going on in the moving picture; notice the un-Pippian "reaping" in the last sentence. In the next three paragraphs the presentation is dramatic: Mrs. Joe is allowed to speak for herself. Paragraphs 5 through 16 are a complex mixture of modes of presentation: they set the scene for the dinner, describe Joe and Wopsle both externally and in terms of Pip's reactions, photograph certain actions, and include comments by the narrator from his vantage point outside of and superior to the action. Paragraphs 17 through 40 are very largely dramatic and immediate, with only brief intrusions by the narrator. Paragraphs 41 through 55 combine the dramatic and narrative modes, but the narrative is unlike that used earlier in the chapter in that the narrator identifies himself with Pip for the moment, so closely indeed that we see events through the boy's eyes; we get, not a statement or a recapitulation, but the almost direct expression of the boy's emotions, even though the diction and the wit are the narrator's.

Thus, though it is true that the narrator occupies a fixed position in time, in the now, and has to look back at earlier events, we get the impression that the point of view shifts. This impression derives partly from the frequent use of dramatic scenes, which are necessarily immediate, and even more importantly from what is often called psychological distance. As the term suggests, the narrator sometimes feels very close to the events that happened and to Pip's feelings at the time, so close that they no longer have to be called up from the memory but are immediately given. When, for example, the narrator tells of the death of Magwitch in Chapter 56, he is not merely looking at Pip through the blur of time; he is not remembering or recounting the young man's experience so much as he is reliving it. At such times the narrator and Pip seem to merge. It is almost as if, to revert to the image of the host showing pictures to guests, the narrator occasionally forgets his audience and his present position in society, drops down into the depths of his mind, and there repeats the original experience in something like its original intensity. At other times, especially when Pip is acting the fool, the narrator reassumes his role as polished adult. Of this type is the ironic passage in Chapter 30 during which Pip's newly-budded self-esteem is sadly wounded by Trabb's boy. The whole episode is observed from a great pyshological distance by a judge who is at once amused, scornful, and a little disgusted. Although the point of view [125/126] is apparently Pip's (we seem to be looking through his eyes and we are told about his reactions), neither reader nor narrator is close to him; Pip, like a gaudy and rather pathetic butterfly, is being held up to inspection. At other times, however, the narrator gives the curious impression both of being with Pip, or of reliving the experience, and of being withdrawn, or of being superior to it. In Chapter 8, to cite only one example, narrator and reader are *with* Pip in Satis House playing cards with Estella under the watchful eyes of Miss Havisham, but at least part of our minds is outside the actions and the interplay of emotions, in some god-like, detached position above and away from the scene.

We get this effect because of the psychological distance between Mr. Pirrip and Pip, signalized by the technical devices already noted (the handling of tenses, the ambiguity in the use of the pronoun *I*, and the interweaving of the different means of transmitting information), and also because the narrator does not hesitate to break the illusion of immediacy and contemporaneity, as when he interrupts the first conversation of Pip and Estella to remark: "I think it will be conceded by my most disputatious reader that she could hardly have directed an unfortunate boy to do anything in the wide world more difficult to be done under the circumstances." In other chapters the narrator forgets exactly what happened or cannot remember precisely how Pip felt at a given moment, as in the beginning of Chapter 43, just after Pip has heard Magwitch's life story. "Why," asks the narrator,

Why should I pause to ask how much of my shrinking from Provis might be traced to Estella? Why should I loiter on my road, to compare the state of mind in which I had tried to rid myself of the stain of the prison before meeting her at the coach-office, with the state of mind in which I now reflected on the abyss between Estella in her pride and beauty, and the returned transport whom I now harboured? The road would be none the smoother for it, the end would be none the better for it; he would not be helped, nor I extenuated.

The psychological distance is even more obvious in those scenes in which the tone is not that which the reader might expect of Pip or Mr. Pip, but that of the adult narrator. The Christmas dinner in Chapter 4 was actually a long torture of mind and body for the boy, but is presented as immensely amusing. Pip's pain and anger are mentioned, but they are not realized. Even when mentioned, they are reduced in size and their significance is modified because the narrator, from his adult vantage point, no longer feels the direct force of the cruelty and violence, though he does understand the comic nature of the event and the characters as none of the real actors ever could. In such a paragraph as the following, there is a sizeable psychological difference between the "I-as-I-was" and the "I-as-I-am-now":

Among this good company I should have felt myself, even if I hadn't robbed the pantry, in a false position. Not because I was squeezed in at an acute angle of the table-cloth, with the table in my chest, and the Pumblechookian elbow in my eye, nor because I was not allowed to speak (I didn't want to speak), nor because I was regaled with the scaly tips of the drumsticks of the fowls, and with those obscure corners of the pork of which the pig, when living, had had the least reason to be vain. No; I should not have minded that if they would only have left me alone. But they wouldn't leave me alone. They seemed to think the opportunity lost, if they failed to point the conversation at me, every now and then, and stick the point into me. I might have been an unfortunate little bull in a Spanish arena, I got so smartingly touched up by these moral goads.

Apparently, then, the position of the narrator in psychological time shifts. Usually he remains at some distance from [126/127] himself-as-Pip, looks *at* Pip rather than out from him, and does not, because he cannot, probe deeply into the mind of the boy. Occasionally, however, and with marked emotion, he comes very close to his past self, even to the point of identification. The normal relation is a kind of dissociation. All in all, Dickens handled his point of view with admirable skill in *Great Expectations*.   [end on 131]

PROBLEMS: Robert B. Partlow, Jr.

1. Do you agree with Partlow's opinion of the passage he quotes [pp. 123-124]? Point to evidence in the passage that "the narrator does not feel identified with Pip." Find other passages which support this statement. If you disagree with it, look for evidence to refute it.

2. What do you think of the degree of success with which the narrator seems to reconstruct his childhood? Find passages which support your answer, and cite corroborating opinion among the critics.

3. Partlow says that upon occasion "the narrator forgets exactly what happened or cannot remember precisely how Pip felt at a given moment..." [p. 126]. Do you agree? Can you supply instances? What do you think of the instance Partlow supplies? Of what importance to the novel is this point?

4. What does Partlow say about the development of Pip?

5. What is Partlow saying about point of view in *Great Expectations*?

6. How does the narrator of *Great Expectations* make his shifting point of view believable? What reflection does your answer cast upon Dickens's artistry?

Suggestions for Discussion
and Research

THE FOLLOWING TOPICS propose possible areas of study in *Great Expectations*. You may decide to select a topic exactly as it appears here; more probably the topics presented will serve to guide you toward a related idea closer to your particular interest and ability.

I. *Themes of the Novel*

One way of realizing the achievement of *Great Expectations* is to become acquainted with the number of human problems which Dickens was able to explore in it. Consider several of the following suggestions carefully before you select one area for particular research.

1. Victorian England as seen by Dickens in *Great Expectations*
2. The theme of incommunication in Pip's world
3. *Great Expectations* as a study of the ethic of work
4. The themes of love, romance, and marriage in *Great Expectations*
5. A study of mental derangement in *Great Expectations*
6. Expectations and degeneration; disappointment and regeneration
7. *Great Expectations* as religious utterance
8. The power of sympathy as portrayed in *Great Expectations*
9. Appearance versus reality
10. Law and order in Dickens's England
11. Country versus city in *Great Expectations*
12. *Great Expectations* and the theme of forgiveness
13. *Great Expectations*: another chapter in "The Book of Snobs"
14. Dickens's attitude toward death as shown in *Great Expectations*
15. *Great Expectations* as an attack on the ideal of leisure for the upper class

16. The world of Wemmick and Jaggers: business and the law
17. The problems of family life as reflected in *Great Expectations*
18. The theme of decay in *Great Expectations*
19. Opposing themes of darkness and light
20. *Great Expectations* and the theme of guilt by association
21. Dickens's study of human isolation
22. The theme of oppression in *Great Expectations*
23. Parenthood and authority as a theme in *Great Expectations*
24. The theme of time
25. The violent world of *Great Expectations*

II. *Type of Novel*

It is often difficult to classify a complex novel. Consider some of the complex elements of *Great Expectations*, and decide whether your understanding of it is better for placing it in a specific category, or for refusing to see it as any particular type of novel. Can you make a case for *Great Expectations* as one of the following?

1. Tragedy
2. Novel of manners
3. Melodrama
4. Comedy
5. Dramatic novel
6. An optimistic (or pessimistic) novel
7. Allegory, parable, fantasy, or fairy tale
8. Novel of social purpose

III. *Characterization*

Dickens is one of the greatest creators of character to write in any language. The following topics suggest a few approaches to the study of his characterizations.

1. Dickens's method of creating character
2. The use of tag names and character "signatures"
3. Character development in *Great Expectations*
4. The importance of Mrs. Joe

5. The role of Orlick
6. The personality and psychology of Pumblechook
7. Jaggers's motives
8. The psychology of Estella
9. The role of Biddy
10. The attractions of Estella (for Pip, and for the reader)
11. Pip as the villain
12. Shame and motivation in *Great Expectations*
13. Why Pip wrote his story
14. The creation of grotesque characters
15. Dickens's use of caricature
16. The education of Estella
17. The motivation of Magwitch
18. The role of Trabb's boy
19. What Bentley Drummle represents
20. What Pip learns
21. The guilt and goodness of Abel Magwitch
22. Who are the Pockets?
23. Pip as hero
24. Pip's path through his great expectations
25. What Compeyson represents
26. Miss Havisham's dementia
27. *Alter egos* in *Great Expectations*
28. Pip's oedipus complex
29. Love as motivation in *Great Expectations*
30. Revenge as motivation in *Great Expectations*

IV. *Elements of the Novel*

Dickens's craftsmanship in respect to the elements of fiction other than characterization has caused considerable controversy; your attempts to evaluate the arguments will strengthen your command of the novel. Consider some of the following:

1. The foreshadowing of future events in *Great Expectations*
2. The structure of *Great Expectations*
3. Dickens's ability to handle dialogue

4. Symbols in *Great Expectations*
5. Wemmick as a person and as a symbolic representation
6. Symbols of the criminal world in Dickens
7. The two endings of *Great Expectations*
8. Digressions in *Great Expectations*
9. A defense of (or attack upon) Dickens's use of coincidence
10. Dickens's use of the first-person point of view
11. Dickens as creator of scenes
12. Scenes of reconciliation in *Great Expectations*
13. The limitations of *Great Expectations*
14. The atmosphere of *Great Expectations*
15. Sentimentality: weakness or asset in *Great Expectations?*
16. The use of irony in *Great Expectations*
17. The role of the author in *Great Expectations*
18. A critical study of the opening passage of *Great Expectations*
19. Anticlimax in *Great Expectations*
20. Dickens's use of pathos
21. Comic parody of the main action in *Great Expectations*
22. Charles Dickens: a poetic novelist
23. Dickens's use of imagery
24. Prison images in *Great Expectations*
25. Dickens's style
26. Exaggeration as a hallmark of Dickens's style
27. The humor of *Great Expectations*
28. Changes of pace in *Great Expectations*
29. How Dickens ends his chapters
30. The use of conflict in *Great Expectations*

V. *Other Topics*

The following will guide you back to one or more of the above areas; they are listed here so that the researcher may work out his own approach.

1. *Pride and Prejudice* as an alternate title for *Great Expectations*
2. Why the Finches of the Grove appear in *Great Expectations*
3. A study of *Great Expectations* in terms of its title

4. Mythic elements in *Great Expectations*
5. Hallucinations in *Great Expectations*
6. Miss Havisham and the attempt to stop time
7. Definition of "portable property"
8. Occupations and their influence on personality in *Great Expectations*
9. *Great Expectations* as autobiography
10. Father images in *Great Expectations*

Suggestions for Library Study

1. Use historical writing to support or attack Dickens's picture of Victorian England in *Great Expectations*.
2. For what reasons would you use *Great Expectations* as the title of another of Dickens's novels?
3. Discuss the autobiographical elements of *Great Expectations*.
4. Consider *Great Expectations* as its author's penance.
5. Report on Ellen Ternan as an historical precedent for Estella.
6. Evaluate *Great Expectations*; can it be called Dickens's best novel?
7. Write a report on how *Great Expectations* was written.
8. Present a factual picture of Dickens's London.
9. Prepare an historical summary of the criticism of *Great Expectations*.
10. Summarize the immediate public reaction to *Great Expectations*.
11. To what extent may we read *Great Expectations* as a fable for our own times?
12. *Great Expectations* has been called Dickens's most representative novel. Discuss this in the light of at least two other kinds of novels he has written.
13. Write a study of Dickens's waifs—for example, David Copperfield, Oliver Twist, and Pip.
14. Trace through Dickens's novels his developing answer to one of society's problems.
15. In what ways might *Great Expectations* be called "Paradise Lost"?
16. Write a paper with this title: "*Great Expectations: David Copperfield Redone.*"
17. In the light of nineteenth-century law, explore the legal problem of Pip's inheritance.
18. Consider the theme of madness in Dickens's novels.
19. Study *Great Expectations* in the light of Luke 8:5–8.
20. Compare or contrast Estella with the revengeful women in Rudyard

Kipling's *The Light That Failed*, W. Somerset Maugham's *Of Human Bondage*, and Samuel Butler's *The Way of all Flesh*.

21. Using *Great Expectations*, *Oliver Twist*, *A Christmas Carol*, *Hard Times*, and *Bleak House*, describe Dickens's attack upon Victorian commercialism.

22. After reading *Nicholas Nickleby*, *Hard Times*, and *Great Expectations*, write a paper entitled "Dickens and Education."

23. Critics have said that water is used symbolically in Dickens's novels. Read *Oliver Twist*, *Our Mutual Friend*, and *Great Expectations*, and support this statement in an extended essay.

24. Suffocation, according to some critics, is a strong motif in several of Dickens's works. Document this assertion. (Note especially drowning, and smothering by cloth, smoke, dust, and fog.)

25. Read *Sketches by Boz*; what techniques do you find here which Dickens has developed in later fiction?

26. Explain Dickens's political or social philosophy.

27. Compare Dickens to his great contemporary rival, Thackeray; what are the fundamental likenesses and differences?

28. John H. Hagan, Jr., calls *Bleak House*, *Little Dorrit*, and *Our Mutual Friend* "the great social 'trilogy' of Dickens's later years," and indicates that *Great Expectations* could very well make it a "tetralogy." Read these novels and Edgar Johnson's biography of Dickens. Make a study of these four novels as "a great social tetralogy."

29. Compare William Faulkner's Miss Emily Grierson (in "A Rose for Emily") and Dickens's Miss Havisham.

30. Study Dickens's increasing use of symbolism in his works.

Selected Reading List

A., J. "Great Expectations." *The Ladies' Companion and Monthly Magazine*, XX (1861), pp. 218–220.

Becker, May Lamberton. "Introduction." *Great Expectations*. New York, Dodd, Mead, 1942.

Butt, John. "Dickens's Plan for the Conclusion of *Great Expectations*." *The Dickensian*, XLV (1949), pp. 78–80.

Chesterton, G. K. *Charles Dickens, A Critical Study*. New York, Dodd, Mead, 1906, pp. 253–256.

Davis, Earle. "Introduction." *Great Expectations*. New York, Rinehart, 1948.

Dickens, Charles [the Younger]. "Introduction." *Great Expectations* and *Hard Times*. London and New York, Macmillan, 1904, pp. ix–xvii.

Edminson, Mary. "The Date of the Action in *Great Expectations*." *Nineteenth-Century Fiction*, XIII (June 1958), pp. 22–35.

Ford, George H. *Dickens and His Readers*. Princeton, Princeton University Press, 1955.

Friedman, Norman. "Versions of Form in Fiction—*Great Expectations* and *The Great Gatsby*." *Accent*, XIV (Autumn 1954), pp. 246–264.

"*Great Expectations*." *The Athenaeum* (July 13, 1861), pp. 43–45.

"Great Expectations." *Eclectic Review*, CXIV (October 1861), pp. 458–477.

"*Great Expectations*." *The Rambler* (January 1862), pp. 274–276.

Hagan, John H., Jr. "Structural Patterns in Dickens's *Great Expectations*." *Journal of English Literary History*, XXI (March 1954), pp. 54–66.

Hill, T. W. "Notes on *Great Expectations*." *The Dickensian*, LIII (May 1957), pp. 119–126; LIII (September 1957), 184–186; LIV (January 1958), pp. 53–60; LIV (May 1958), pp. 123–125; LIV (September 1958), p. 185; LV (January 1959), pp. 57–59; LVI (May 1960), pp. 121–126.

House, Humphry. *All in Due Time*. London, Rupert Hart-Davis, 1955, pp. 201–220.

Jackson, T. A. *Charles Dickens, The Progress of a Radical*. New York, International Publishers, 1938, pp. 192–200.

Lindsay, Jack. *Charles Dickens, A Biographical and Critical Study*. New York, Philosophical Library, 1950, pp. 369–374.

Livensparger, Clark Cory. "Introduction." *Great Expectations*. Cleveland, Fine Editions, 1952.

Monod, Sylvère. "*Great Expectations* a Hundred Years After." *The Dickensian*, LVI, 3 (September 1960), pp. 133–140.

"Mr. Dickens's Last Novel." *The Dublin University Magazine*, LVIII (December 1861), pp. 685–693.

Nisbet, Ada. *Dickens and Ellen Ternan*. Berkeley, University of California Press, 1952.

Oxenham, John. "Introduction." *Great Expectations*. London, Waverley Book Company, n.d., pp. v–viii.

Philip, Alex. J. "With Pip in Kent" (Literary Pilgrimages—Dickens's Country, no. 1). *The United Methodist Magazine* (March 1909), pp. 118–120.

Reed, James. "The Fulfilment of Pip's Expectations." *The Dickensian*, LV, 1 (January 1959), pp. 12–18.

"Sensation Novels." *Blackwood's Magazine*, LV (May 1862), pp. 564–584.

Shaw, George Bernard, "Introduction." *Great Expectations*. London, Limited Editions Club, 1937.

Waugh, Arthur. "Introduction." *Great Expectations*. London, Chapman and Hall; New York, Charles Scribner's Sons, 1899, pp. v–xi.

Whipple, Edwin Percy. *Charles Dickens, The Man and His Work*. Boston and New York, Houghton Mifflin, 1912. 2 vols., vol. 2, pp. 201–231.

Documenting Your Research Paper

*Footnotes and Bibliography**

THE READER of your research paper expects to find in it both your work and an accounting of the sources from which you have drawn your information. This accounting is your documentation. It is also your thanks, or at least your acknowledgment, to any people whose writings or other works have furnished you the information that you have organized into your paper.

Whether as thanks or as report of sources, your documentation must be explicit and specific. It must tell your reader where you found your information so that he can, if he wishes, appraise your sources, perhaps go to them himself and see whether you have conveyed their facts faithfully or reasoned soundly from them.

All of your sources are listed together in a bibliography at the end of your paper; this is *general* documentation. Any source you cite is named at the point where you cite it, usually in a footnote; this is *specific* documentation.

Most of your sources will be books or magazine articles, aside from the selections in this book.

DOCUMENTATION REFERRING TO A BOOK

A bibliography entry for a book will be organized thus:

May, Rollo. *Man's Search for Himself.* New York, 1953.

Period	Period	Comma Period
Name of the author, surname first for alphabetizing.	Title of book, in italic type or underscored to indicate that it is a publication.	City and year of publication. The name of the publisher may appear between the city and the date.

First line begins at margin; if there is a second line, indent it 5 spaces.

---

* Prepared by the general editor of Chandler Publishing Company.

The footnote for a citation from this book would be organized thus:

[1] Rollo May, *Man's Search for Himself* (New York, 1953), pp. 223–224.

	Comma	Paren- thesis	Paren- thesis Comma Comma
Index (number or asterisk).	Name of author, in normal order, as footnotes are not alphabetized.	Title of book, in italic type or underscored to indicate that it is a publication.	City and year of publication.

Period   Numbers of pages that contain the information documented. Some people prefer to omit the abbreviation "pp."

First line of footnote indented as paragraph; second line at margin.

The order of the items in this information, the use of the index mark (raised number or asterisk), the punctuation, the parentheses, and the use of italic or underscores are customs that spare a writer the labor of writing many words and his reader some quantity of reading. The footnote would otherwise have to be something like:

This information comes from pages 223–224 of a book by Rollo May, entitled *Man's Search for Himself,* published in New York in 1953.

If you name the publisher of a book, the forms for bibliography and footnote are:

May, Rollo. *Man's Search for Himself.* New York: W. W. Norton & Company, 1953.

[1] Rollo May, *Man's Search for Himself* (New York: W. W. Norton & Company, 1953), pp. 223–224.

DOCUMENTATION REFERRING TO A PLAY

Any citation of a play almost necessarily refers to it as published in a book. Accordingly you cite a play as you would a book. To specify the location of a passage, the page number may be sufficient. But it may be more useful to give act, scene, and if possible line numbers. Hence:

Shakespeare, William. *The Tragedy of Coriolanus,* ed. William Allan Neilson. New York, 1906.

[1] William Shakespeare. *The Tragedy of Coriolanus,* ed. William Allan Neilson (New York, 1906), Act IV, Sc. vii, lines 2–3.

DOCUMENTATION REFERRING TO A MAGAZINE ARTICLE

If your source is a magazine article, your bibliography entry might read:

Kirstein, Lincoln. "The Future of American Opera," *Atlantic* 199:3 (March, 1957), pp. 50–55.

Comma Period		Comma	
Name of author, surname first.	Title of article, in quotation marks to indicate that it is not a separate publication.	Name of magazine, in italic type or underscored to indicate that it is a publication.	Volume and number.

Comma	Period
Issue, in parentheses.	Page numbers of the entire article.

First line begins at margin; second and subsequent lines indented 5 spaces.

Your footnote to this magazine article as your source might read:

[1] Lincoln Kirstein, "The Future of American Opera," *Atlantic* 199:3 (March, 1957), p. 54.

	Comma		Comma	
Index (number or asterisk).	Name of author, in normal order.	Title of article in quotation marks.	Name of magazine, italic or underscored.	Volume and number.

Comma Period	
Issue, in parentheses.	Page number to which the footnote refers.

First line of footnote indented as paragraph; second line at margin.

As is documentation from books, documentation from magazines is made briefer and less laborious by the customs of word order and punctuation.

DOCUMENTATION REFERRING TO A NEWSPAPER ARTICLE

Citations from newspapers cannot be so precise as citations from books or magazines, since many newspapers have several editions in a day and the same article may appear on different pages in different editions; even more troublesome, it may be rewritten, reheaded, or dropped in later editions, and it may not appear in the early editions of a given date.

A bibliography entry concerning a newspaper might therefore appear thus:

"State to Up Vet Home Loan Rate." *San Francisco Chronicle,* Sept. 17, 1959. Dated Sacramento, Sept. 16.

The corresponding footnote might be:

[1] "State to Up Vet Home Loan Rate," *San Francisco Chronicle,* Sept. 17, 1959; dated Sacramento, Sept. 16.

If the writer of this newspaper article were named, his name would precede the title of the article in both the bibliography entry and the footnote. If the story were sent to the *Chronicle* by a news service, such as United Press International or Associated Press, this fact should appear in parentheses at the end of both bibliography and footnote, in full or abbreviated:

... Sept. 16 (United Press International).
... Sept. 16 (UPI).

THE ESSENTIAL IN DOCUMENTATION

Information comes to the writer from so many sources that specimen bibliography entries and footnotes for all possible needs would overflow any book. So it is necessary to keep in mind the basic reason for documenting: namely, to give the source of a statement so it can be appraised, and located, by the reader. These are basic, though some other details may be put into the documentation.

If your bibliography entries and footnotes answer the following questions, they will be satisfactory:

1. *Who?* Who is the author who made the statement? What individual, collaborating group, or institution is the author? Or is the statement published in a work that does not identify the author?
2. *In what publication?* What book, magazine article, newspaper story, speech, broadcast program, or other? At exactly what point in this work? (Can a reader find your citation, from what the documentation tells him?)
3. *When and whence?* In what city and in what year was the book published? On what date was the periodical published?

The next sections contain numerous models for footnotes and bibliography entries, but all are guided by these three principles. Since almost every research project will require documentation referring to some source not covered by a model, you need to perceive the principles as they are demonstrated in the models.

EXAMPLES OF BIBLIOGRAPHY ENTRIES

The entries in a bibliography are ordinarily arranged in alphabetical order, as these examples are. To help in comparing them with corresponding footnotes, the footnote examples (pages 218-221) are numbered in series and the explanatory remark that follows each bibliography entry gives the number of the footnote.

Baker, Charles T. "Patients' Perceptions of Psychologists." Unpublished master's thesis, Ohio State University, 1953. [An unpublished doctor's dissertation or other research paper would be treated in this same way. See footnote 18.]

Boddy, Francis M., et al. *Applied Economic Analysis.* New York, 1948. [This book has six authors. If only one author card is carried in a library catalogue for it, the card will be in the name of the senior author, here given. See footnote 3 and pages 226–227 of this book.]

Bowman, Isaiah. *The New World.* 4th ed., Yonkers and Chicago, 1928. [An often revised book in political geography; marked differences between editions make it important to specify the edition used, as here. See footnote 6.]

Brahms, Johannes. *Concerto No. 2 in B Flat Major for Piano.* Alexander Uninsky, piano; Willem van Oterloo conducting The Hague Philharmonic Orchestra. Epic LC-3303, 1958. [For some purposes it might be unnecessary to identify the musicians presented on a phonograph record, but the information usually is significant. The record number and the "publisher" appear on the record label. See footnote 23.]

Doe, John. "Indexing of Dissertations." Paper read at methodology seminar, —— University, October 19, 1962. In —— University Library. [If this paper were not in a library and you were citing from your notes, you would write instead, "Notes of reading," or something of the sort. See footnote 19.]

Dumas, Alexandre, fils. Letter to Joseph Méry, Oct. 18, 1844. Unpublished. Collection of Simone André-Maurois. [Letters of famous men often are microfilmed for study, even if not published. If you use a microfilm letter, mention it; as, "Microfilm in —— Library." See footnote 20.]

"The Good ex-President," *Time* 74:14 (Oct. 5, 1959), p. 34. [A magazine article published without the author's name. It is therefore alphabetized according to its title, ignoring "The." See footnote 14.]

Gunther, John. "Inside Space." *John Gunther's High Road,* American Broadcasting Company (WABC-TV), Oct. 17, 1959. [A broadcast program in a series. The same form could be used for either radio or television. The station call letters and date might be enough in addition to the program name and the name of its "author." If no author, alphabetize on the program name. See footnote 26.]

Joyce, James. *Finnegan's Wake.* Folkways Records, FDF934, 1956. Tape. [It might be unnecessary to write "Tape," but may be useful. See footnote 25.]

Keats, John. *The Complete Poetical Works and Letters of John Keats,* [ed. Horace E. Scudder]. Cambridge, Mass., 1899. [Scudder's name does not appear in this book, but he is known to be the editor, hence the information is supplied but enclosed in brackets; if the fact appeared on the title page no brackets would be needed. Note that "Mass." is specified to avoid giving the impression that the book was published in Cambridge, England. See footnote 5.]

Kelly, Alfred H., and Winfred A. Harbison. *The American Constitution.* New York, 1948. [A book by two authors; observe that the second author's name is in normal order. Incidentally, this is the first edition of a book that was later published in a second edition; unless another edition is specified, the edition of a book is assumed to be the first. See footnote 2. See also the entry for Isaiah Bowman's book above.]

Kelly, George A. *The Psychology of Personal Constructs.* 2 vols. New York, 1955. [If your references were to only one of these volumes, you would write "2 vols., vol 1. New York, 1955." See footnote 7.]

Kirstein, Lincoln. "The Future of American Opera," *Atlantic* 199:3 (March, 1957), pp. 50–55. [Discussed earlier in detail. See footnote 13 and page 213 in this book.]

"Kite." *Encyclopedia Americana,* 1955 ed. [Encyclopedia article by an unnamed author. The names of editors and the like for a well-known reference book are not ordinarily needed. Neither is the page number in a book whose contents are alphabetically arranged. See footnote 12.]

Learned, Philip. Lecture given in English 346. Edwardian Criticism, —— University, May 17, 1962. Tape recording. [If there were no tape recording, an equivalent statement should appear: "Notes taken by John Doe, student," or the like. Observe that the course title is not italicized or enclosed in quotation marks. See footnote 21.]

Macaulay, Thomas Babington. "Bunyan, John." *Encyclopaedia Britannica,* 11th ed. [Macaulay signed this article simply "M"; the full name was gotten from the list at the end of the last volume. Observe the order of Bunyan's names; he is listed under Bunyan, not John. Observe that there are no page numbers or volume number, since neither is needed for locating an article in an alphabetically organized reference book. See also "Kite," above in this list. See footnote 11.]

May, Rollo. *Man's Search for Himself.* New York, 1953. [Discussed earlier in detail. See footnote 1 and pages 211–212 of this book.]

Ohneschatten, Dermann, Director, —— State Hospital. Interview, May 27, 1964. Tape recorded. [The subject of the interview could be mentioned, if important. See footnote 22.]

Poore, Charles. Review of Henry B. Kranz, ed., *Abraham Lincoln: A New Portrait. New York Times,* Oct. 17, 1959. [See footnote 16, footnote 17, and "Review . . ." below.]

Quintanilla, Luis. "Basic Tenets of Latin American International Policy." In Philip W. Buck and Martin B. Travis, Jr., eds., *Control of Foreign Relations in Modern Nations.* New York, 1957. [See footnote 8.]

Review, unsigned, of Henry B. Kranz, ed., *Abraham Lincoln: A New Portrait. Reviews of the Quarter,* vol. 21, no. 4 (Nov., 1959), p. 37. [To alphabetize the entry for this review at K for Kranz would suggest that Kranz wrote the review or that the entry was for the book rather than for the review. There is much variety of opinion about how to handle this kind of entry. If your reader-instructor has a strong opinion, follow his preference. See footnote 17.]

Shakespeare, William. *The Tragedy of Coriolanus,* ed. William Allan Neilson. New York, 1906. [See page 212 of this book, and see footnote 9.]

"State to Up Vet Home Loan Rate," *San Francisco Chronicle,* Sept. 17, 1959. Dated Sacramento, Sept. 18. [Discussed on pages 213–214 of this book. See footnote 15.]

Swedish Modern Jazz. Arne Domnerus and his group. RCA Camden, CAL-417, 1958. Record. ["Record" is unnecessary unless needed to distinguish the described item from a tape recording or other work of similar name. The record is a collection of works performed by one orchestra. If the name of one work or its composer were the important item, this information would be given first, followed by "In *Swedish Modern Jazz.* . . ." See footnote 24.]

Sypher, Wiley, ed. *Enlightened England.* New York, 1947. [An anthology. Any book identified by the name of its editor rather than an author would be presented similarly. See footnote 4.]

Two Thousand Years of Season's Greetings. New York: Photogravure and Color Company, 1951. [This is the kind of irregular publication sometimes called a "bulletin." Since it may be hard to locate, you help the reader by giving the name of the publisher. Since no author name is given, alphabetize it by the title. See footnote 10.]

We Discover the Dictionary. Coronet Films, 16V4906, 1949. Film. [The author's name, if one were given, would precede the title in this entry, and would govern the alphabetical position of the entry. "Film" may be unnecessary. See footnote 27.]

EXAMPLES OF FOOTNOTES

These specimen footnotes are numbered to help in referring to them for comparison with the corresponding specimen bibliography entries in the section preceding this.

[1] Rollo May, *Man's Search for Himself* (New York, 1953), pp. 223–224. [Book, single author. Discussed on pages 211–212 of this book.]

[2] Alfred H. Kelly and Winfred A. Harbison, *The American Constitution* (New York, 1948), p. 64. [Book, two authors.]

[3] Francis H. Boddy *et al., Applied Economic Analysis* (New York, 1948), p. 346. [Book with many authors, in this instance six. Unless courtesy or other special reason calls for them, the names of the junior authors are replaced by *et al.* See pages 226–227 of this book.]

[4] Wiley Sypher, ed., *Enlightened England* (New York, 1947), p. 451. [Book, single editor. This is an anthology, containing works of numerous writers, who need not be named in this kind of entry. To cite the work of one author included in such a collection, follow the model of footnote 8 below.]

[5] John Keats, *The Complete Poetical Works and Letters of John Keats* [ed. Horace E. Scudder] (Cambridge, Mass., 1899), p. 232. [Book by a single author in a version edited by another person. Observe the brackets enclosing the editor's name; these are present because Scudder is not named on the title page of the book but is known to be the editor; if the title page bore his name there would be no brackets; compare footnote 9, below. Note the "Mass." to prevent confusion with Cambridge, England, another publishing center.]

[6] Isaiah Bowman, *The New World,* 4th ed. (Yonkers and Chicago, 1928), p. 704. [Book, edition specified. Unless an edition is specified, it is assumed that the first edition is being cited.]

[7] George A. Kelly, *The Psychology of Personal Constructs* (New

York, 1955), vol. 1, p. 133. [Book, more than one volume. The citation here is to a page in one volume, and the number of volumes need not be stated; that information is in the bibliography entry. If your paper were to have no bibliography, this kind of footnote should read: ". . . 1955), 2 vols., vol. 1, p. 133."]

8 Luis Quintanilla, "Basic Tenets of Latin American International Policy," in Philip W. Buck and Martin B. Travis, Jr., eds., *Control of Foreign Relations in Modern Nations* (New York, 1957), p. 188. [Work of one author in an edited collection of works by several authors.]

9 William Shakespeare, *The Tragedy of Coriolanus,* ed. William Allan Neilson (New York, 1906), Act IV, Sc. vii, lines 2–3. [Play, in book form. If the printed version had no line numbers, a page number would be given. Discussed in the text of this book, page 212.]

10 *Two Thousand Years of Season's Greetings* (New York: Photogravure and Color Company, 1951), p. 5. [Irregular publication, that is, one not published in the usual course of any publishing enterprise— the named publisher is an engraver-printer and this cited work is an advertising piece. The name of the publisher is therefore given even in a footnote plan which does not include names of publishers of standard books. If it had a named author, his name would be at the beginning, as usual.]

11 Thomas Babington Macaulay in *Encyclopaedia Britannica,* 11th ed., *s.v.* "Bunyan, John." [Signed article in a reference book alphabetically organized. The abbreviation "*s.v.*" means "*sub verbo*" or "*sub voce,*" English "under the word" or "under the heading." The word "Bunyan" is as accurate a guide as a page number could be, and may be better since encyclopedias are sometimes repaged to make room for new entries inserted late in the life of a numbered edition. Macaulay's article on Bunyan fills two pages; if it were a very long article, and the citation to a single sentence or other brief passage, the reader might be helped by being given a volume and page number: ". . . 'Bunyan, John,' vol. 4, p. 805." Observe the spelling *Encyclopaedia.*]

12 "Kite," *Encyclopedia Americana,* 1955 ed. [Unsigned article in a reference book alphabetically organized. See footnote 11 concerning the omission of page number. Observe the spelling *Encyclopedia* in the title of this work.]

13 Lincoln Kirstein, "The Future of American Opera," *Atlantic* 199:3 (March, 1957), p. 54. [Magazine article. Discussed at length in this book, page 213.]

14 "The Good ex-President," *Time* 74:14 (Oct. 5, 1959), p. 34. [Magazine article, unsigned.]

[15] "State to Up Vet Home Loan Rate," *San Francisco Chronicle,* Sept. 17, 1959; dated Sacramento, Sept. 16. [News article in a newspaper. Discussed in this book, pages 213–214.]

[16] Charles Poore, review of Henry B. Kranz, ed., *Abraham Lincoln: A New Portrait, New York Times,* Oct. 17, 1959. [Signed book review. Such reviews often have titles, either individual or departmental; it is usually unnecessary and confusing to give such titles.]

[17] Unsigned review of Henry B. Kranz, ed., *Abraham Lincoln: A New Portrait, Reviews of the Quarter* 21:4 (Nov. 1959), p. 37. [Unsigned review of a book, in a periodical—here an imaginary periodical. The bibliography entry corresponding to this footnote is alphabetized at Review.]

[18] Charles T. Baker, "Patients' Perceptions of Psychologists" (unpublished master's thesis, Ohio State University, 1953), p. 31. [Unpublished work, such as thesis or dissertation.]

[19] John Doe, "Indexing of Dissertations" (paper read at methodology seminar, —— University, October 16, 1962; in —— University Library). [Paper read but not published. See the specimen bibliography entry at Doe.]

[20] Alexandre Dumas fils, letter to Joseph Méry, Oct. 18, 1844, unpublished, in the collection of Simone André-Maurois. [Unpublished letter.]

[21] Philip Learned, lecture given in English 346, Edwardian Criticism, —— University, May 17, 1962, from a tape recording. [Unpublished lecture. If the lecture were cited from memory, or from the writer's notes, or from notes of another listener, that fact should be given instead of the reference to a tape recording.]

[22] Dermann Ohneschatten, Director, —— State Hospital, interview, May 27, 1964, from a tape recording. [Unpublished interview. No interviewer being named, the assumption is that the interview was with the writer. If the citation were not from a recording, that fact should be given instead.]

[23] Johannes Brahms, *Concerto No. 2 in B Flat Major for Piano,* Alexander Uninsky, piano; Willem Oterloo conducting The Hague Philharmonic Orchestra (Epic LC-3303, 1958), record. [Phonograph record. The word "record" may be unnecessary, or may distinguish between a disk and a tape recording of the same work and performance.]

[24] *Swedish Modern Jazz,* Arne Domnerus and his group (RCA Camden CAL-417, 1958), record. [Phonograph record, title without com-

poser's name. This record has several works by various composers and is thus comparable to a book of the type cited in footnote 8 above.]

[25] James Joyce, *Finnegan's Wake* (Folkways Records, FDF 934, 1956), tape recording. [Recorded book. To locate a cited passage more exactly, one might add "at 22 min." or the like. The tape does not contain the entire book. When a recorded work has several tapes, the one concerned may be specified, as "tape 3 at 17 min."]

[26] John Gunther, "Inside Space," *John Gunther's High Road*, American Broadcasting Company (WABC-TV, New York), October 17, 1959. [Television or radio broadcast; this footnote is for a television program. The network being named, the station call letters and city are extra information; but the latter would suffice if there were no network or the network were not known.]

[27] *We Discover the Dictionary* (Coronet Films, 16V4906, 1949), film. [Film. If the text at the citation does not make it clear that a film is meant, the word "film" is needed in the footnote, since many companies that distribute films also distribute sound tapes, disk records, and books having the same titles. Films usually are the work of writing-producing teams and are published without any "author" name; if an author is named, his name belongs first in the footnote.]

HOW TO FIND DOCUMENTATION DATA

Where do you get information for documentation?

Most books published in the United States and many published in other countries carry this information in the preliminary pages of the book itself. The title page normally has the name of the author (or authors), the title of the book, the name of the editor instead of or in addition to the name of the author, the name of the publisher, the volume number and number of volumes if the book has more than one, the edition number if later than the first, the city of publication, and sometimes the date. But the date may appear only in the copyright notice on the back of the title page, and there may be several copyright dates owing to renewals and revisions (if there are, use the latest). If the title-page date is other than the copyright date, give both dates (as "New York, 1938; title page dated 1949"). You and your reader, seeing this discrepancy, may reasonably wonder whether the title-page date is an effort to suggest that the book is more recent than it really is.

Often you have documentation information on a book even before you see the book itself, for library cards usually contain all of it, and

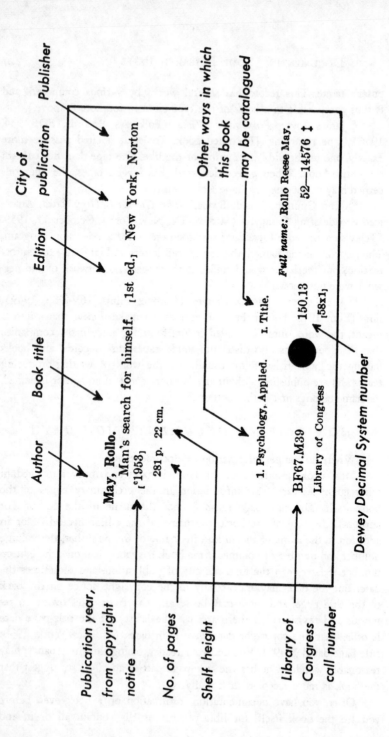

Publication year, from copyright notice

No. of pages

Shelf height

Library of Congress call number

Author

Book title

Edition

City of publication

Publisher

Other ways in which this book may be catalogued

May, Rollo.
Man's search for himself. [1st ed.] New York, Norton
[ʿ1953]
281 p. 22 cm.

Full name: Rollo Reese May.

1. Psychology, Applied. ɪ. Title.

BF67.M39   150.13
Library of Congress   [58x1]

52—14576 ‡

Dewey Decimal System number

more, especially those cards prepared by the Library of Congress and distributed to libraries throughout the country. (See page 222.)

Magazines usually provide the bibliographical information in a note somewhere in the early pages, less often on the cover or on a page near the end of the issue. Finding it may take some hunting, since practice is not uniform. In most magazines it will be on the page with the table of contents. Also, as with books, a researcher often gets the information from a library card for the article before he has to search it out from the publication itself. He may also get it from the entry for the article in *The Readers' Guide to Periodical Literature.*

The title page of an unpublished dissertation or thesis will give you all the information you need for documentation, as will the file copy of a paper read at a scholarly meeting but not published. For letters, personal communications, lectures, interviews, and the like, you must formulate the documenting statement from information you get at first hand.

The label of a phonograph record gives you the name of the song, speech, collection, or other work recorded, the names of the composer and of the performing musician or his analogue, the name of the maker, distributor, or publisher of the record, his identifying number or code letters, the date of issue, and sometimes other information. You may have to get some facts from the album cover or record envelope, or from the distributor's list.

Documentation data for tape recordings and films will almost necessarily come from the label. Films usually carry it on the title frames at the beginning.

Radio and television programs contain almost too frequent mention of the program name, its principal personality, the call letters of the broadcasting station, and the name of the broadcasting system. You may thus get this information from the program itself. You may also be able to get it from the program listing in a newspaper or periodical. Sometimes you may get the script of a program from the sponsor or the broadcasting company; if so, the first page or two of the script will contain many of the documentation data.

RECORDING DOCUMENTATION DATA

You begin documenting your research paper before you begin writing it, even before you begin taking your research notes. If you were to collect material, write your paper, then try to work back to find where you got your material in order to document it, you would find the effort hopeless. When you decide to investigate a book or magazine article or other source, therefore, you should prepare a bibliography card immediately, recording all the documenting information you will need if you refer to the source—this before you take your first note! Then, when you write a note card, it should have a record of its source. The record need not be complete to identify it with your bibliography card—a short "slug" something like "May *Man's Search*" is enough. Thus your bibliography card would read:

> May *Man's Search*   M 150.13
>
> May, Rollo. *Man's Search*
> *for Himself*. New York,
> 1.9 5 3.

Then a note card might look like this:

> May *Man's Search*   224
> "... Courage is the capacity
> to meet the anxiety which arises
> as one achieves freedom. ..."

With the note card and the bibliography card, you are prepared to put accurate documentation into your finished research paper.

CITATIONS AFTER THE FIRST—BOOKS

When a writer must cite numerous statements from the same source at intervals throughout his paper, repeating long footnotes would become tedious for him and for his reader. When the first footnote has given full information, later footnotes may be shortened in many ways, providing the shortening does not make them confusing.

A second citation from the May book might come immediately after the first one, with no other footnote intervening. For such immediately succeeding footnotes, scholars have long used this style of shortening:

2 *Ibid.*, p. 231.

This means "From page 231 of the same source given in the immediately preceding footnote." The abbreviation *Ibid.* for *ibidem* (literally, "in the same") is typical of the many abbreviations and Latin expressions that we have inherited and continued to use since early scholars established them. Because they are in some sense part of an omnilingual scholarly vocabulary, many instructors require their students to learn them and use them. But some people think of them as Latin and, if they or their readers do not know Latin, feel that the use of Latin expressions is pretentious or even dishonest. Such people would prefer to use some equivalent English-language form like

2 May, p. 231.

—or even, if May's name is mentioned in the text, nothing more than

2 P. 231.

The writer of a research paper does well to learn what preference his instructor has in matters of this sort, and to follow it.

If some citation from other source material were to intervene between the first and second citations from the May work, then the *ibid.* would be wrong, for "in the same" would point to the most recently cited work. The old scholarly usage would be

3 May, *op. cit.*, p. 231.

This means, "From page 231 of the work by May which has already been cited." "*Opere citato*" is the unabbreviated Latin. Those who misgive Latin expressions might prefer to write any of four other forms:

    [3] May, p. 231.
    [3] May, *Man's Search*, p. 231.
    [3] *Man's Search*, p. 231.
    [8] P. 231.

The first-given form would serve if only one of May's books were being used as a source. If two or more were being used, it would be necessary to mention the title and to mention the author's name also, as in the second-given form, unless May's name were mentioned in the text. If the text mentioned May, but not the book title, the third-given form would be sufficient documentation. The last-given and briefest form would be correct and sufficient if the text language made clear what book and author were being considered.

    When these English shortened forms are to be used, it is a frequent and helpful practice to tell the reader so in the first full footnote. Thus, after citing the source in full, you would add, perhaps: "This will here (in)-after be cited as May," or ". . . as May, *Man's Search*."

CITATIONS AFTER THE FIRST— MAGAZINE ARTICLES

    The short expression *op. cit.* is not used when the source cited is a magazine article or other work not independent and complete in itself, such as an article in a symposium, an encyclopedia entry, or a newspaper story. For such sources, instead of *op. cit.* the footnote Latin is *loc. cit.* for *locus citatus,* Englished as "the place cited" or "the passage cited." Thus several alternative entries for the later footnote to a magazine article:

    [3] Kirstein, *loc cit.*
    [3] Kirstein, p. 55.
    [3] Kirstein, "Future," p. 55.
    [3] "Future," p. 55.
    [8] P. 55.

These five forms of short documentation correspond in function to the similar five forms for books. But note that *loc. cit.* cannot be followed by a page number; such is the convention. The other forms may therefore be preferable as more specific.

CITING WORKS BY NUMEROUS AUTHORS

    A Latin expression that often appears in documentation is the abbreviation combination *et al.* for *et alii,* which means "and others." Writers who are not alert in their Latin often punctuate this expression improperly; those who choose to use it need to remember that *et* is a word and that *al.* is an abbreviation.

The proper use of this expression is to save writing or repeating the names of two or more co-authors of a cited source. Thus a first and later footnote might be:

¹ Francis M. Boddy, Frank E. Childs, Wendell R. Smith, O. H. Brownlee, Alvin E. Coons, and Virgil Salera, *Applied Economic Analysis,* New York, 1948, p. 363.

³ Boddy *et al., op. cit.,* p. 370.

Instead of *et al.,* those who object to Latin would use "and others":

³ Boddy and others, p. 370.

If the names of the junior authors are not important for the citation, even the first footnote may have them packaged into *et al.* or "and others":

¹ Francis M. Boddy *et al., Applied Economic Analysis,* New York, 1948.

It is not courteous to use *et al.* in substitution for the name of a single author.

DOCUMENTATION WITHOUT FOOTNOTES

In some people's view the footnote is the most useful and explicit form of specific documentation, the least likely to be misconstrued, and the minimum civil acknowledgment that a writer can make to his source. With all these merits, footnotes are disliked by other people as obtrusive, overformal, distracting, and an extreme nuisance for the typist. Their preference is to put some or all of the specific documentation into the text itself.

In-text documentation for books, magazine articles, and other sources requires the same information that is given in footnotes. A writer citing a statement from a book might therefore write:

... A definition of Rollo May (*Man's Search for Himself,* New York, 1953, p. 224) describes courage as ". . . the capacity to meet the anxiety which arises as one achieves freedom." Seen as such, courage is demanded ...

The parenthetical documentation would be worded to accord with the text language. If it were to follow the quoted passage rather than precede it:

"The capacity to meet the anxiety which arises as one achieves free-dom" (Rollo May, *Man's Search for Himself,* New York, 1953, p. 224) is a definition of courage as it is demanded from all of us. . . .

A writer uses footnote or in-text documentation as he and his readers prefer. If his readers are instructors who grade his research papers, their preference may well overrule the writer's. The general documentation is needed, in the usual bibliography form, to support either style of specific documentation.

Some writers attempt to have the best features of both kinds of documentation by using a footnote for the first mention of a source, then using brief parenthetical notes for later references. This practice might give:

. . . May found that "the greatest block to a person's development of courage is his having to take on a way of life which is not rooted in his own powers" (*Man's Search,* p. 231). . . .

Or it might give:

. . . May (p. 231) found that . . .

Either of these two parenthetical documentations might be replaced by the more traditional "*op. cit.,* p. 231" or if proper by "*Ibid.,* p. 231."

BRIEF DOCUMENTATION

It is often unnecessary to give a complete footnote for every citation from a source, yet necessary to document the citation. It seems redundant, when a text has mentioned an author's name or his book's title, or both, to repeat them in a footnote. The footnote then need contain only those facts not given in the text; but all the documenting facts must be given in one place or the other. For examples:

. . . Rollo May, in his *Man's Search for Himself,*[1] defines courage . . .
[1] New York, 1953, p. 224.

. . . Rollo May[1] defines courage as . . .

[1] *Man's Search for Himself* (New York, 1953), p. 224.

Specific documentation can be kept brief by using the general documentation, the bibliography, after notifying the reader that footnotes or in-text references identify the names of sources given in full in the bibliography. Thus a writer might refer to Rollo May's book thus, even on first mention:

> . . . Courage is "the capacity to meet the anxiety which arises as one achieves freedom" (May, p. 224). Seen as such, . . .

The reader is then expected to understand that he will find the source given in full in the bibliography, thus:

> May, Rollo. *Man's Search for Himself.* New York, 1953.

If several books by May were in the bibliography, the brief documentation would have to be explicit enough to prevent confusion. To this end, "May, *Man's Search*" would be used rather than "May" alone.

Sometimes the entries in the bibliography are numbered. If in such a bibliography the May book were to be numbered 221, then the citing note might read "221, p. 224."

DIVERSE PRACTICE IN DOCUMENTATION

Custom and agreement have not established uniform practice as to correct documentation. Readers' needs differ; scholars in different fields have different kinds of source material to identify and describe; and editors, teachers, and research directors have strong preferences which they can enforce on their contributors, students, and staff. The student writer who goes beyond this discussion in exploring documentation can find some additional and different recommendations in any of four books, especially:

ELINOR YAGGY, *How to Write Your Term Paper.* Chandler Publishing Co., 604 Mission Street, San Francisco 5, California. Contains a thorough discussion of documentation forms, with numerous examples. Primarily for undergraduate writers.

BLANCHE ELLSWORTH, *English Simplified.* Chandler Publishing Co., 604 Mission Street, San Francisco 5, California. An appendix on Writing the Research Paper contains directions for preparing a bibliography and for using footnotes, with a chart of model footnotes and corresponding bibliography entries in parallel columns. Primarily for undergraduate writers.

KATE L. TURABIAN, *A Manual for Writers of Term Papers, Theses, and Dissertations.* The University of Chicago Press, Chicago 37, Illinois. Has chapters on footnotes and bibliography, with numerous examples. Primarily for graduates and advanced undergraduate writers.

WILLIAM RILEY PARKER, compiler, *The MLA Style Sheet.* The Modern
Language Association of America, 6 Washington Square North, New
York 3, New York. Primarily for writers of material to be published
in Modern Language Association periodicals. This has a supplement
dealing with the preparation of masters' theses and doctors' dissertations. Widely accepted and authoritative, especially for papers on
literary subjects.

THE DOCUMENTATION OF MATERIAL IN THIS COLLECTION

This collection, being a book of special character compiled for the
convenience of students writing research papers, differs from general
books and periodicals that might be found in a library. Footnotes and
bibliographical entries describing sources in this collection must identify
both the source and the collection.

There would be some question of propriety, or even of honesty, if a
writer were to name an original source in a documentary citation without
making it clear that he examined the material in a collection—whether
this collection or another. A reader has the right to know whether a
writer is working from original or secondary sources: whether for instance
he has seen George Washington's actual diary or has seen only an edited
version of the diary in print. For edited versions, even carefully and
scrupulously edited versions, may depart from originals.